Palgrave Studies in the History of Social Movements

Series Editors
Stefan Berger
Institute for Social Movements
Ruhr University Bochum
Bochum, Germany

Holger Nehring
Contemporary European History
University of Stirling
Stirling, UK

Around the world, social movements have become legitimate, yet contested, actors in local, national and global politics and civil society, yet we still know relatively little about their longer histories and the trajectories of their development. This series seeks to promote innovative historical research on the history of social movements in the modern period since around 1750. We bring together conceptually-informed studies that analyse labour movements, new social movements and other forms of protest from early modernity to the present. We conceive of 'social movements' in the broadest possible sense, encompassing social formations that lie between formal organisations and mere protest events. We also offer a home for studies that systematically explore the political, social, economic and cultural conditions in which social movements can emerge. We are especially interested in transnational and global perspectives on the history of social movements, and in studies that engage critically and creatively with political, social and sociological theories in order to make historically grounded arguments about social movements. This new series seeks to offer innovative historical work on social movements, while also helping to historicise the concept of 'social movement'. It hopes to revitalise the conversation between historians and historical sociologists in analysing what Charles Tilly has called the 'dynamics of contention'.

More information about this series at
http://www.palgrave.com/gp/series/14580

Prudence Flowers

The Right-to-Life Movement, the Reagan Administration, and the Politics of Abortion

palgrave
macmillan

Prudence Flowers
College of Humanities, Arts,
   and Social Sciences
Flinders University
Adelaide, SA, Australia

Palgrave Studies in the History of Social Movements
ISBN 978-3-030-01706-4   ISBN 978-3-030-01707-1 (eBook)
https://doi.org/10.1007/978-3-030-01707-1

Library of Congress Control Number: 2018956585

© The Editor(s) (if applicable) and The Author(s), under exclusive license to Springer Nature Switzerland AG 2019
This work is subject to copyright. All rights are solely and exclusively licensed by the Publisher, whether the whole or part of the material is concerned, specifically the rights of translation, reprinting, reuse of illustrations, recitation, broadcasting, reproduction on microfilms or in any other physical way, and transmission or information storage and retrieval, electronic adaptation, computer software, or by similar or dissimilar methodology now known or hereafter developed.
The use of general descriptive names, registered names, trademarks, service marks, etc. in this publication does not imply, even in the absence of a specific statement, that such names are exempt from the relevant protective laws and regulations and therefore free for general use.
The publisher, the authors and the editors are safe to assume that the advice and information in this book are believed to be true and accurate at the date of publication. Neither the publisher nor the authors or the editors give a warranty, express or implied, with respect to the material contained herein or for any errors or omissions that may have been made. The publisher remains neutral with regard to jurisdictional claims in published maps and institutional affiliations.

Cover illustration: Mono Circles © John Rawsterne/patternhead.com

This Palgrave Pivot imprint is published by the registered company Springer Nature Switzerland AG
The registered company address is: Gewerbestrasse 11, 6330 Cham, Switzerland

Series Editors' Preface

Around the world, social movements have become legitimate, yet contested, actors in local, national, and global politics and civil society, yet we still know relatively little about their longer histories and the trajectories of their development. Our series reacts to what can be described as a recent boom in the history of social movements. We can observe a development from the crisis of labor history in the 1980s to the boom in research on social movements in the 2000s. The rise of historical interests in the development of civil society and the role of strong civil societies as well as nongovernmental organizations in stabilizing democratically constituted polities has strengthened the interest in social movements as a constituent element of civil societies.

In different parts of the world, social movements continue to have a strong influence on contemporary politics. In Latin America, trade unions, labor parties, and various left-of-center civil society organizations have succeeded in supporting left-of-center governments. In Europe, peace movements, ecological movements, and alliances intent on campaigning against poverty and racial discrimination and discrimination on the basis of gender and sexual orientation have been able to set important political agendas for decades. In other parts of the world, including Africa, India, and South East Asia, social movements have played a significant role in various forms of community building and community politics. The contemporary political relevance of social movements has undoubtedly contributed to a growing historical interest in the topic.

Contemporary historians are not only beginning to historicize these relatively recent political developments; they are also trying to relate them to a longer history of social movements, including traditional labor organizations, such as working-class parties and trade unions. In the longue durée, we recognize that social movements are by no means a recent phenomenon and are not even an exclusively modern phenomenon, although we realize that the onset of modernity emanating from Europe and North America across the wider world from the eighteenth century onwards marks an important departure point for the development of civil societies and social movements.

In the nineteenth and twentieth centuries, the dominance of national history over all other forms of history writing led to a thorough nationalization of the historical sciences. Hence social movements have been examined traditionally within the framework of the nation-state. Only during the last two decades have historians begun to question the validity of such methodological nationalism and to explore the development of social movements in comparative, connective, and transnational perspective taking into account processes of transfer, reception, and adaptation. Whilst our book series does not preclude work that is still being carried out within national frameworks (for, clearly, there is a place for such studies, given the historical importance of the nation-state in history), it hopes to encourage comparative and transnational histories on social movements.

At the same time as historians have begun to research the history of those movements, a range of social theorists, from Jürgen Habermas to Pierre Bourdieu and from Slavoj Žižek to Alain Badiou as well as Ernesto Laclau and Chantal Mouffe to Miguel Abensour, to name but a few, have attempted to provide philosophical-cum-theoretical frameworks in which to place and contextualize the development of social movements. History has arguably been the most empirical of all the social and human sciences, but it will be necessary for historians to explore further to what extent these social theories can be helpful in guiding and framing the empirical work of the historian in making sense of the historical development of social movements. Hence the current series is also hoping to make a contribution to the ongoing dialogue between social theory and the history of social movements.

This series seeks to promote innovative historical research on the history of social movements in the modern period since around 1750. We bring together conceptually informed studies that analyze labor movements, new social movements, and other forms of protest from early modernity to the present. With this series, we seek to revive, within the context of historiographical developments since the 1970s, a conversation between historians on the one hand and sociologists, anthropologists, and political scientists on the other.

Unlike most of the concepts and theories developed by social scientists, we do not see social movements as directly linked, a priori, to processes of social and cultural change and therefore do not adhere to a view that distinguishes between old (labor) and new (middle-class) social movements. Instead, we want to establish the concept "social movement" as a heuristic device that allows historians of the nineteenth and twentieth centuries to investigate social and political protests in novel settings. Our aim is to historicize notions of social and political activism in order to highlight different notions of political and social protest on both left and right.

Hence, we conceive of "social movements" in the broadest possible sense, encompassing social formations that lie between formal organizations and mere protest events. But we also include processes of social and cultural change more generally in our understanding of social movements: this goes back to nineteenth-century understandings of "social movement" as processes of social and cultural change more generally. We also offer a home for studies that systematically explore the political, social, economic, and cultural conditions in which social movements can emerge. We are especially interested in transnational and global perspectives on the history of social movements, and in studies that engage critically and creatively with political, social, and sociological theories in order to make historically grounded arguments about social movements. In short, this series seeks to offer innovative historical work on social movements, while also helping to historicize the concept of "social movement." It also hopes to revitalize the conversation between historians and historical sociologists in analyzing what Charles Tilly has called the "dynamics of contention."

The Right-to-Life Movement, the Reagan Administration, and the Politics of Abortion is an important study of one of the most important global social movements of the last decades, the Right-to-Life Movement. It is difficult to classify on a left-right spectrum, as it is essentially concerned with ethical and moral issues that evade a straightforward left-right division. Nevertheless, it has been drawn into such divisions, as women's liberation has been associated so much with the right of women to have an abortion and a left-of-center political agenda. Hence the "pro-lifers" were often associated, in the United States and elsewhere, with the political right, influenced by powerful Christian and other religious beliefs. Prudence's book assesses the pro-life movement during the Reagan years in the United States by tracing its movement from high hopes at the beginning of the Reagan presidency to almost complete disillusionment and internal strife at the end of Reagan's terms of office.

Based on an impressive amount of primary research in eight major libraries and archives across the United States, Prudence Flowers seeks to answer a variety of different questions, ranging from the question how divided the right-to-life movement in the United States was via the question to what extent it can be classified as a moral crusade to the question of how successful it has been in the United States in reorienting the debate surrounding abortion.

She delivers a lucid contextualizing history of the US movement to end abortion before discussing in detail the opposition of pro-lifers to the appointment of Sandra Day O'Connor to the Supreme Court. Subsequently, she highlights the divisions among pro-lifers using the example of the Helms/Hatch struggle over legislation to ban abortion in the United States. In both cases, the movement failed, among much internal infighting, to generate political decisions that would foster their agenda. Defeat led to a reorientation of strategies and policy goals would eventually result in what many class as the most important success of the pro-life movement in the 1980s, the 1984 Mexico City policy that led to a defunding of organizations advocating population control.

Yet the Reagan legacy was often more rhetoric than reality, as shown by the impact of some of the key alleged pro-life decisions made by Reagan in 1987. New regulations for domestic family planning grants, the President's Pro-Life Bill, and the nomination of archconservative Robert Bork to the Supreme Court all were more symbolic than real victories for the pro-life movement. While the Reagan years are hailed by the pro-life movement until this very day as somehow golden years for the movement, Flowers can show clearly that those years were incredibly divisive for the movement. The 1980s were a decade of symbolic victories and practical defeats for the movement. Reagan was the first in a succession of Republican presidents that talked the talk but did not necessarily walk the walk of the pro-lifers who in turn had to adopt very pragmatic and piece-meal strategies to ensure their final goal. Unfortunately, the book also provides ample evidence that these strategies have led to important successes, especially at state level during the 2010s, when, ironically, a Democratic president ruled in the White House.

Bochum, Germany   Stefan Berger
Stirling, UK   Holger Nehring

ACKNOWLEDGEMENTS

This book is the outcome of a large research project, and I am indebted to a great number of people, communities, and organizations that have made this piece of work possible.

This book is based upon extensive archival work, drawing from materials at the Gerald Ford Presidential Library, the Ronald Reagan Presidential Library, the Southern Baptist Historical Library and Archive, the University of Notre Dame Archives, the John Hay Library at Brown University, the Andover-Harvard Theological Library, the Schlesinger Library at the Radcliffe Institute, and the Library of Congress. In each institution, archivists and librarians were a huge resource and were incredibly helpful, which was especially useful as I had to travel from afar to access primary materials. Closer to home, I would also like to thank the Liaison Librarians at Flinders University, who acquired microfilm copies of several of the major right-to-life publications.

Research and travel funding was assisted by a Lillian Ernestine Lobb Scholarship, the University of Melbourne's PORES and TRIPS programs, a Gerald R. Ford Presidential Library Research Travel Grant, and a Flinders University Establishment Grant.

In developing this book, I have been lucky to be shaped by rigorous thinkers who have deepened my approach to historical practice. This research began under the guidance of Katherine Ellinghaus and David Goodman at the University of Melbourne, both of whom are models for academic integrity and passion. Jennine Carmichael, Sianan Healy, and Timothy W. Jones were research comrades in arms, undertaking inspiring projects of their own with style and panache. My ideas were also sharpened by the broader insights provided by members of the Australian and New Zealand American Studies Association, a community of scholars who study the United States from afar. An earlier version of this research benefited greatly from the insights of Leslie Reagan and Robert Self. Sharon Block provided feedback on the section on Sandra Day O'Connor, which was further shaped by the insights and guidance of the editors and anonymous reviewers at the *Journal of Contemporary History*.

At Flinders University, the collegiality of the History Discipline has provided an inspiring environment in which to work and conduct research. A broader interdisciplinary community of scholars has also read or commented on elements of this book. Thanks go to Barbara Baird, Joanne Baker, Johanna Conterio, Don DeBats, Matthew Fitzpatrick, Carol Fort, Jane Haggis, Catherine Kevin, Rob Manwaring, Susanne Schech, Cassandra Star, and Christine Winter. Special acknowledgment goes to Melanie Oppenheimer, whose mentoring and guidance in the last two years has been invaluable both personally and professionally.

The near finished manuscript was chosen by the College of Humanities, Arts and Social Sciences at Flinders University for a first book workshop, and received special funding. I would like to thank Claire Smith and Phyllis Tharenou for their support and encouragement. Christine Winter, with initiative and drive, accompanied me and the manuscript through the workshop and preparatory period. I also thank Michelle Arrow, Barbara Baird, Kylie Cardell, Don DeBats, David Goodman, Catherine Kevin, and Christine for their intellectual generosity and their astute comments on the manuscript.

Molly Beck at Palgrave Macmillan has been an enthusiastic editor, helping usher the book into the world in an extremely efficient way. My thanks also to the anonymous reviewer, whose kind and thoughtful feedback helped strengthen the project as a whole.

My research and writing would have been impossible without being reminded that life does not begin and end with a book. Yolanda, Suzi, Kathleen, Lauren, and Hayley have been an enjoyable source of distraction (and Hayley also provided thoughtful feedback on a key chapter). Jo-Anne has been a source of wise counsel. My family, Dulcie, Peter, Regina, and Jennifer, have provided me with love and laughter. My mother, Barbara, has been inspiring and motivating, an outside-the-box thinker and a cheerleader for my intellectual endeavors. She has been quick to read and comment on my work, even while undertaking her own massive writing project.

Lastly, I owe an immense debt of gratitude to Daniel, a friend and a true partner. We have markedly different ways of understanding the world and more times than I can count, he has asked challenging and important questions as I puzzled through this project. He has also been a devoted father to our wonderful and hilarious son Theo, who came along and reoriented our lives for the better.

Contents

1 **Introduction**   1
   Chapters   4
   A United Movement?   5
   A Moral Crusade?   6
   A Politically Successful Movement?   8

2 **A Brief History of the National Movement to End Abortion**   15
   An Institutional History   16
   Ronald Reagan and Abortion Politics   25
   Partisan Shifts   28
   The Pro-life Movement in the Reagan Years   32
   Perception and Reality   33

3 **"A Prolife Disaster": The Sandra Day O'Connor Nomination**   41
   A Series of Promises   42
   Choosing a Nominee   44
   Sandra Day O'Connor: Pro-abortion, Pro-ERA, Anti-family?   45
   Divisions Among Conservatives   48
   Opposing the Nomination   52
   The Senate Votes   54
   Insights   56

4 "A Movement in Disarray": The Hatch/Helms Fight 63
Abortion and the Legislative Branch 65
The Human Life Bill and the Human Life Federalism Amendment 67
The Movement Divides 70
The Catholic Church 71
"Name-Calling, Backbiting, Threats, and Scurrilous Behind-the-Scenes Intrigue" 73
Republican Priorities 75
Abortion in the Senate 79
Aftermath 81

5 "Voodoo Demographics": The Right-to-Life Movement Confronts the Population Establishment 89
Pro-lifers and Population Aid 90
The One-Child Policy 93
An Expedient New Policy 96
The Mexico City Conference and the 1984 Election 99
Defunding the Population Establishment 102
Monitoring AID 103
Exporting the Abortion War 106

6 Cultivating Reagan's Abortion Legacy: His Last Years in Office 113
In the Doldrums 115
The President's Pro-life Bill 118
Rewriting Title X 121
The Nomination of Robert Bork 125
A Pro-life Legacy 130

7 The Lessons of the Reagan Years 137

Index 153

Abbreviations

ACCL	American Citizens Concerned for Life
AHCDL	Ad Hoc Committee in Defense of Life
AID	Agency for International Development
ALL	American Life League/American Life Lobby
AUL	Americans United for Life
CAC	Christian Action Committee
CC	Conservative Caucus
CV	Christian Voice
CWA	Concerned Women for America
EF	Eagle Forum
FotF	Focus on the Family
HHS	Department of Health and Human Services
HLI	Human Life International
IPPF	International Planned Parenthood Federation
IWYC	International Women's Year Conference
LAPAC	Life Amendment Political Action Committee
LC	Library Court
MCCL	Minnesota Citizens Concerned for Life
MM	Moral Majority
NAE	National Association of Evangelicals
NCCB	National Conference of Catholic Bishops
NCHLA	National Committee for a Human Life Amendment
NOW	National Organization for Women
NPFC	National Pro-Family Coalition
NPLPAC	National Pro-Life Political Action Committee
NRLC	National Right to Life Committee

NRLPAC   National Right to Life Political Action Committee
NWPC   National Women's Political Caucus
OR   Operation Rescue
PF   Pathfinder Fund
PP   Planned Parenthood Federation of America
PLAL   Pro-Life Action League
PPLF   Pennsylvania Pro-Life Federation
RR   Religious Roundtable
SBC   Southern Baptist Convention
UN   United Nations
UNFPA   United Nations Fund for Population Activities
USCC   United States Catholic Conference
USCL   United States Coalition for Life

CHAPTER 1

Introduction

Abstract This book offers a political, ideological, and social history of the national right-to-life movement under President Ronald Reagan. It explores anti-abortion activism and engagement with the legislative, judicial, and executive branches, and offers what is frequently a narrative of disappointment and factionalism. It is driven by a desire to understand why most of the movement against abortion stayed loyal to the Republican Party in the 1980s and beyond. This chapter outlines the empirical basis for the analysis, the core concerns and historiographical interventions, and summarizes the rest of the chapters. It ends by exploring questions of unity, morality, and success, three themes that link the specific case studies and raise insights into activism, social movement formation, religion, and politics.

Keywords History · Abortion · Social movements · Religion · Politics · Ronald Reagan

In 1987, near the end of the conservative presidency of Republican Ronald Reagan, Nellie Gray and Paul Brown, two prominent figures in the national pro-life movement, publicly excoriated Reagan for his lack of leadership on abortion.[1] Gray, the founder and president of March for Life (MfL), had spent years railing against the use of local funds to provide abortions for low-income women in Washington, DC.

© The Author(s) 2019
P. Flowers, *The Right-to-Life Movement, the Reagan Administration, and the Politics of Abortion*, Palgrave Studies in the History of Social Movements, https://doi.org/10.1007/978-3-030-01707-1_1

On 22 January 1987, when Reagan spoke via telephone to the 10,000 pro-lifers attending the snowy MfL rally in the nation's capital, he again assured Gray that he shared her concerns. After another round of failed lobbying, she chastised the President in a letter circulated to pro-lifers nationwide:

> Mr. Reagan, it is frustrating that your wrong actions for abortion continue to provoke to the point where I, a grassroots prolife volunteer, must remind you once more of your duty to stop contributing to killing preborn children in America.[2]

Paul Brown, speaking for American Life League (ALL), was more scathing in his summary of the problem with the Reagan administration. Displeased by new Supreme Court nominee Anthony Kennedy's unclear stance on *Roe v. Wade* and the constitutionality of abortion, Brown told the media, "Our problem is we don't trust the White House in any way, shape or form."[3] Although Brown and Gray were angry about specific issues, these outbursts were representative of the broader frustrations of the anti-abortion movement during the Reagan years. Right-to-lifers spent much of this period publicly and privately expressing their disenchantment with the President, his advisors, and Republicans in Congress.

This situation was in stark contrast to their high hopes at the beginning of the 1980s, when anti-abortion activists believed they were a significant political force. Reagan was a high-profile and vocal political ally, and the resurgence of conservatives within the Republican Party seemed to guarantee success in the battle to end legal abortion. Most pro-lifers expected Reagan's powerful rhetoric on abortion would be accompanied with equally decisive action. Just a few months into Reagan's presidency, anti-abortionists were forced to reconsider this relationship, and they spent the remainder of the Reagan years confronting the limits of their influence and grappling uncomfortably with questions of compromise, pragmatism, and coalition building. Right-to-lifers worked to obscure the extent of their discontent during the 1980s, producing hagiographic statements after Reagan's death lauding him as a "pro-life hero."[4] My research suggests such myth-making began during his presidency—a strategic choice made by some national leaders who wished to preserve their authority within the movement and at a federal level.

This book offers a political, ideological, and social history of the national American pro-life movement during the Reagan years, which,

I argue, is a history of disappointment and factionalism. My research is driven by a desire to understand why most of the movement against abortion stayed loyal to the Republican Party in the 1980s. This premise might run counter to how some understand the period. Certainly, Reagan's public persona and the rhetoric of right-to-life leaders frame the decade as a time of great power and influence for opponents of abortion. However, in the anti-abortion materials from this period, the unhappiness and dissatisfaction are a palpable and near-constant theme. I am interested in how this disjunction between external perceptions of power and internal feelings of impotence impacted pro-life political activity. Right-to-life experiences in the crucial eight years from 1981 to 1989 reshaped the priorities, strategies, and rhetoric of the movement. The turbulence of these years limited the types of ideas and approaches possible at a national level, while making much of the right-to-life movement beholden to partisan imperatives. Although sharp polarization over abortion began in the late 1970s, politicians and activists in the 1980s were the ones who solidified the place of the abortion wars in contemporary politics.

In writing this history, I have aspired to a degree of neutrality, attempting to eschew the binary way the abortion debate is often framed. To this end, I have relied heavily on the tools of the historian, foregrounding analysis based upon empirical evidence. Research in the archival papers of pro-life individuals and groups, as well as presidential papers, has allowed insights that go beyond the public face of both.[5] Newsletters, magazines, pamphlets, institutional minutes, memorandum, speeches, autobiographies, and private letters illuminate the complex dynamics among opponents of abortion and between the movement and the administration. I hope readers will approach this book willing to take seriously the hopes and disappointments it analyzes.

Early scholarship on the US pro-life movement assumed that antiabortionists were inherently socially and religiously conservative. A subset of this work positioned the movement as a product of the backlash against second-wave feminism.[6] Over the past decade, this narrative has been increasingly contested. Sociologist Ziad Munson has illuminated the diverse motivations, behaviors, and beliefs of contemporary pro life activists. Gender historian Karissa Haugeberg has revealed the place of grassroots women in the movement, challenging assumptions about gender and social conservatism and the place of harassment and violence in pro-life activism. Religious historian Daniel Williams and legal historian Mary Ziegler have offered nuanced insights into the early years of the movement and share two interrelated conclusions: the right-to-life cause initially had a distinctively liberal and progressive element, but for strategic rather than ideological reasons, the national movement moved to the right in the late 1970s.[7] Williams' and Ziegler's research has deepened understanding of abortion politics in the United States, but they are focused primarily on events before Reagan's presidency.[8] Examining the period of conservative dominance reveals that this new political alliance required sacrifice from pro-lifers almost from the moment polling places closed on 4 November 1980. I view polarization and partisanship as an ongoing process, seeking to understand the consolidation and maturation of the movement against abortion. In so doing, I shine a light upon the competition and diversity within the contemporary Right.

Chapters

The case studies in this book center on the judicial, legislative, and executive branches, teasing out how national anti-abortion leaders and groups engaged with federal politics during the 1980s. Chapter 2 is contextual, offering a history of movement formation, partisan realignments, and abortion politics, as well as exploring the relationship between pro-lifers and Reagan. Chapter 3 charts right-to-life protests over the nomination of Sandra Day O'Connor to the Supreme Court, arguing that within the first six months of Reagan's presidency there were significant fissures between the movement and the administration. Anti-abortionists were deeply troubled by the realization that access did not translate into influence and shocked that abortion was not a litmus test for Reagan. Analyzing the passionate reaction to O'Connor, the chapter charts the fragility of the coalition that opposed her. Chapter 4 explores pro-life efforts to use the legislative branch to ban abortion. In 1981, faced with two imperfect Congressional approaches, right-to-lifers exploded with bitter internal fighting over movement resources and authority, reflecting complex schisms along religious, ideological, and strategic lines. As the movement feuded, the Reagan administration and Congressional Republicans tried to remain aloof. Chapters 3 and 4 are explorations of pro-life failure, demonstrating that the place of abortion opponents in the new conservatism was far more uncertain than we have remembered. However, rather than being a simple declension narrative, these early and deeply negative experiences were instrumental in pushing the national movement in new directions.

Chapters 5 and 6 explore how this early disillusionment shaped movement goals and attitudes toward lobbying and political action. Chapter 5 focuses on an unequivocal victory for the movement and Reagan's most important anti-abortion action, the 1984 Mexico City Policy. Placing the policy in a broad context, the chapter looks at the work right-to-lifers undertook in their quest to defund international population non-governmental organizations (NGOs). Tellingly, key movement groups no longer trusted the White House to prosecute its own agenda. Chapter 6 looks at the events of 1987, the year Reagan was suddenly willing to take on the mantle of right-to-life leadership. Within six months, he demanded new regulations for domestic family planning grants, pushed for passage of the President's Pro-Life Bill, and nominated arch conservative Robert Bork to the Supreme Court. Although this pleased anti-abortionists and they lavished praise on the President, they were generally modest in their ambitions and judicious in how they expended energy. Despite the strong rhetoric from the White House, most of these initiatives functioned as gesture politics, and both the administration and the movement manipulated them for legacy building purposes.

Abortion is often treated as an inherently polarizing subject. Following James Davison Hunter's "culture wars" thesis, legal abortion is seen as a core issue about which morally traditional and progressive Americans do battle because of their diametrically opposed values.[9] I seek to disrupt this notion, viewing the culture wars of the 1980s as a product of the choices made and the strategies adopted. These case studies provide insights into moments that were important in the development of federal abortion politics, but they also speak to some of the broader challenges faced by conservative social movements during this period. The rest of this Introduction will outline three core questions that link the case studies and raise insights into activism, group identity, religion, and politics. As contemporary commentators talk of the revival of the culture wars, historicizing and problematizing this period reveal the way social movements and partisan politics can exacerbate controversy and division.

A United Movement?

Analyzing the national right-to-life movement's engagement with the Reagan administration necessitates studying the impact of these years on opponents of abortion. Sometimes, right-to-lifers were unified in their response to the White House, but just as frequently, they were at odds.

Allies divided over questions of authority and claims to grassroots energy in a contest about the future of the movement and its function within civil society. These fault lines were partly triggered by the diverse reasons individuals engaged in right-to-life activism: some were motivated by strict theological concerns, while some viewed abortion through the lens of a morally conservative, progressive social justice, or humanistic and constitutional agenda. These competing motivations caused significant problems when anti-abortionists were faced with the possibility of translating some or all of their goals into policy. There was no one unified pro-life movement. In addition to internal tensions between anti-abortionists, they were reacting to political disillusionment and struggling to make sense of what the Reagan Revolution meant in practice. Pro-lifers attacked each other over perceived pragmatism and expediency, yet also routinely despaired about political naivety and misdirected resources. Whatever the cause, the public sniping had a damaging effect. Although the national right-to-life movement now seems like an enduring and powerful force within American politics and society, these tensions remain.

A Moral Crusade?

From the late 1960s onwards, anti-abortionists struggled with the perception that they were motivated by sectarian dogma rather than universal values.[10] Mainstream groups strove to ensure that the public face of the movement was ecumenical and that they drew from medical, legal, scientific, and ethical arguments. The initial challenge to this approach came from the interventions of the Catholic bishops in abortion politics; in the late 1970s, this was compounded by the emergence of the conservative fundamentalist and evangelical Christians known as the Religious Right. The merging of the spiritual and the secular in the anti-abortion cause posed marked difficulties.

The Religious Right injected an explicitly devout, often apocalyptic, tone into national politics and the abortion debate. They presented legal abortion as the great moral crisis of the age, symptomatic of the social and spiritual decay triggered by secular humanism, second-wave feminism, and the gay rights movement. The rhetoric of family values was a powerful tool in mainstreaming conservative gender and sexual politics. Recent studies by historians of religion such as Daniel Williams and Neil Young have challenged prevailing assumptions about the origins of the Religious Right. Williams demonstrates that the connection between conservative evangelicals and fundamentalists and the Republican Party predated the rise of Reagan and the self-proclaimed New Right.[11] Young focuses on the theological and ecumenical claims of the Religious Right, but concludes that there was little consensus among conservative Protestant, Mormon, and Catholic leaders.[12] Williams and Young deepen understanding of the religious and political changes of the late twentieth century, but there is still much to uncover about the Religious Right's place in civil society.

Religious Right leaders and groups claimed deep common cause with the pro-life movement. For one faction of anti-abortionists, this was a welcome development. Even right-to-lifers who did not share the spiritual or ideological concerns of conservative evangelicals and fundamentalists were excited by the reach and energy of televangelists and the electric church. However, this alliance meant framing opposition to abortion as a morally traditional cause rather than one that could appeal to all Americans. Throughout the 1980s, the right-to-life movement diverged over the types of arguments it deployed and the uses of theological and spiritual claims. There was also competition over resources. A core problem for pro-lifers was offering one coherent message to the White House; the multi-issue agenda of the Religious Right complicated this situation further. Thus, movement strategies and priorities, rather than religious beliefs, frequently split pro-lifers. It is striking that at the end of the Reagan years, opponents of abortion still operated in separate, occasionally overlapping circles, often paying little attention to each other.

Beyond doctrine, a broader issue was politics itself. Even before *Roe*, the right-to-life movement routinely presented itself as engaged in a moral crusade akin to the abolitionists of the nineteenth century. Reagan heavily emphasized this parallel in his article (later book) "Abortion and the Conscience of the Nation."[13] However, this narrative could lend itself to viewing any compromise as ceding the moral high ground. This ambivalence was particularly pronounced in the 1980s because it was the first time the movement had any sense of national power and influence. While some groups operated easily within this milieu, others expected an almost impossible level of ideological purity from their politician allies and attacked pro-lifers who were willing to make concessions. For some, lobbying and deal-making were fundamental distortions of their true agenda, negating their moral claims.

A Politically Successful Movement?

In the 45 years since *Roe*, pro-lifers in the United States have succeeded in stigmatizing abortion, polarizing discourse, and limiting access. Analyzing right-to-life discontent during the Reagan years is not intended to suggest that his presidency had no impact on reproductive rights. Globally, the Mexico City Policy significantly affects the provision of population and family planning services. Nationally, abortion and family planning providers experienced intrusive government audits, regular threats to federal funding, and new types of prohibitive regulations. From 1985, Attorney General Edwin Meese III called on the Supreme Court to overturn *Roe*. Reproductive rights groups spent the decade engaged in costly lawsuits against the administration. At the local level, there was a dramatic escalation in harassment, death threats, kidnappings, bombings, and arson directed at abortion clinics and providers. Confrontational protest techniques such as "side-walk counseling" and "rescues" became increasingly popular. Reagan's emotive rhetoric and consistent claim that legal abortion was "a great moral evil and assault on the sacredness of life" helped polarize politics and culture.[14] Reagan's presidency, and the precedent he set for the Republican Party, have had immense consequences on the place of legal abortion in the United States.

However, when one looks closely at the goals of right-to-lifers at the start of the 1980s, movement leaders exercised limited influence. At the start of Reagan's first term, pro-lifers wanted to see a right-to-life amendment added to the US Constitution and opponents of Roe appointed to the Supreme Court. By the end of Reagan's presidency, right-to-lifers still embraced the judicial strategy, but tended to pursue more marginal legislative and political goals, frequently making the President's goals and rhetoric their own. Even groups that adapted their lobbying priorities and techniques still struggled to achieve victory at a federal level, but this was generally kept from the grassroots, as was the fact that the Republican Party was unreliable. In 1981, right-to-lifers had outsized expectations about the power of the presidency and their new level of federal authority. These hopes remained an undercurrent that shaped all their interactions with the White House. Rather than turn their back on the President, many pro-lifers rewrote their own narratives, fashioning him into the ally they had hoped for.

As a result of Reagan's general inaction on abortion, there was consistent tension over symbolism versus tangible achievement. Reagan's symbolism was deeply important. It emboldened anti-abortionists, reassuring them of the rightness of their cause and making them feel heard and respected, bestowing legitimacy upon their ideas and arguments. But pro-life leaders expected more. As Gray told the *Washington Post* in 1982, Reagan's "words were beautiful, but the words have to be backed up with action."[15] Five years later, Gray angrily reminded the President that every year he told "our preborn brothers and sisters" to "wait, while you focus on some favorite political agenda items."[16] Contemporary historians have concluded that Reagan practiced a "pragmatic conservatism" that belied his hard-right reputation.[17] This book does not dispute the sincerity of Reagan's personal beliefs, but suggests his pro-life interventions were frequently pieces of theater triggered by electoral concerns, which came only after much prodding by White House advisors and movement leaders. He expended very little political capital. Reagan's pro-life actions were infused with gesture and performance, but by the end of his presidency, some movement leaders celebrated because he had done something rather than nothing. Perhaps the very nature of Reagan's neo-liberal, deregulatory politics meant that symbolism had to hold more weight. There is a marked tension between how social and economic conservatives understand the role of the government; Reagan's solution was to use the rhetoric of the morally interventionist state without offering the resources to enact this vision.

Indeed, the Reagan years are illustrative of a seeming paradox: some social and political movements derive strength from failure. Right-to-lifers understood themselves as an inherently oppositionary movement and were particularly effective when they functioned as political outsiders. After Reagan's victory, many right-to-lifers struggled with their sudden status as political insiders. What makes this particularly interesting is that anti-abortionists are motivated by the overwhelming belief that they are working to save lives. Defeat means more victims of abortion and yet, in the 1980s, some moments of failure were politically rejuvenating, helping to fuel activism and reenergize the base. Failure could demonstrate the significance of their challenge to the social and political order.

This book approaches the 1980s from the perspective of national right-to-life groups, seeking to understand why they were so frequently frustrated by events in Washington, DC and how this shaped the development of the movement. It analyzes the period when abortion politics entered the mainstream. As we bear witness to seemingly unprecedented political and cultural change in the contemporary United States, it is timely to return to the Reagan era to explore lessons from the origin of modern American conservatism. Reagan helped oversee the marriage between social and economic conservatives; he taught Republicans that abortion was a politically advantageous issue and provided a model of how to maintain pro-life loyalty without actually delivering on their core goals. His actions have become templates for Republican successors. President Donald Trump has clearly been a keen student; the question now is whether he will move beyond Reagan's cautious pro-life symbolism.

Notes

1. Although both sides of the abortion debate challenge the terminology used by their opponents, in this book I follow the self-identification of the movements, referring to opponents of legal abortion as "pro-life," "right-to-life," and "anti-abortion" and supporters of legal abortion as "pro-choice" and advocating for "reproductive rights."
2. Nellie Gray to Ronald Reagan, 18 September 1987, Box 144, Folder 10, March for Life 1983–1989, Christian Life Commission Resource Files (hereafter CLC), Southern Baptist Historical Library and Archive. On 30 September 1988, after four years of agitation from right-to-lifers and their political allies, the FY1989 District of Columbia spending measure prohibited local as well as federal abortion funding.
3. Brown quoted in "Abortion Foes Are Split on Whether to Support Kennedy for Supreme Court," *Baltimore Sun*, 16 November 1987.
4. Steven Ertelt, "Ronald Reagan: A Pro-life Hero, Champion on Abortion," *Life News*, 5 June 2004.
5. This book uses material from the American Citizens Concerned for Life Files, the George Hunston Williams Files, the Paul Marx Papers, the William A. Rusher Papers, the Christian Life Commission Resource Files, the Southern Baptists for Life Files, the Hall–Hoag Collection of Dissenting and Extremist Printed Propaganda, the United States Coalition for Life Archive, the Pro-Life Newsletter Collection, and staff files from the Ronald Reagan Presidential Library. It is also informed by movement publications, particularly *National Right to Life News* (*NRL News*), *A.L.L. About Issues*, and *Moral Majority Report*.
6. For works that view the movement as inherently conservative, see Dallas Blanchard, *The Anti-abortion Movement and the Rise of the Religious Right: From Polite to Fiery Protest* (New York: Twayne, 1994); Michele McKeegan, *Abortion Politics: Mutiny in the Ranks of the Right* (New York: Free Press, 1992); and Connie Paige, *The Right to Lifers: Who They Are,*

How They Operate, Where They Get Their Money (New York: Summit Books, 1983). For work that focuses on right-to-lifers and conservative gender politics, see Kristin Luker, *Abortion and the Politics of Motherhood* (Berkeley: University of California Press, 1984); Rosalind Petchesky, *Abortion and Woman's Choice: The States, Sexuality, and Reproductive Freedom* (Boston: Northeastern University Press, 1984); and Rickie Solinger, *Pregnancy and Power: A Short History of Reproductive Politics in America* (New York: New York University Press, 2005). Robert Self's recent work on breadwinner liberalism and breadwinner conservativism also shares this perspective, see Robert Self, *All in the Family: The Realignment of American Democracy Since the 1960s* (New York: Hill and Wang, 2012).
7. Ziad Munson, *The Making of Pro-life Activists: How Social Movement Mobilization Works* (Chicago: University of Chicago Press, 2009); Karissa Haugeberg, *Women Against Abortion: Inside the Largest Moral Reform Movement of the Twentieth Century* (Urbana: University of Illinois Press, 2017); Daniel Williams, *Defenders of the Unborn: The Pro-life Movement Before Roe v. Wade* (New York: Oxford University Press, 2016); Mary Ziegler, *After Roe: The Lost History of the Abortion Debate* (Cambridge: Harvard University Press, 2015).
8. Williams summarizes 1980–2013 in an epilogue. Ziegler's study reaches to 1983, but the majority of her book is focused on pro-life and pro-choice legal developments and strategies in the 1970s. This periodization also occurs in recent work on family values discourse and social conservativism. See Seth Dowland, *Family Values and the Rise of the Christian Right* (Philadelphia: University of Pennsylvania Press, 2015); Self, *All in the Family*; and Stacie Taranto, *Kitchen Table Politics: Conservative Women and Family Values in New York* (Philadelphia: University of Pennsylvania Press, 2017).
9. See James Davison Hunter, *Culture Wars: The Struggle to Control the Family, Art, Education, Law, and Politics in America* (New York: Basic Books, 1991). Subsequent scholarship by political scientists rejects the idea that the American public is deeply divided on issues of morality. See Morris Fiorina, *Culture War? The Myth of a Polarized America?* (New York: Pearson Longman, 2005); and Irene Thomson, *Culture Wars and Enduring American Dilemmas* (Ann Arbor: University of Michigan Press, 2010). Nonetheless, the concept remains embedded in the popular and journalistic imagination.
10. Williams, *Defenders of the Unborn*; Michael Cuneo, "Life Battles: The Rise of Catholic Militancy Within the American Pro-life Movement," in Mary Weaver and R. Scott Appleby (eds.), *Being Right: Conservative Catholics in America* (Bloomington: Indiana University Press, 1995), 270–99.

11. For an insider's account of the New Right's rise and goals, see Richard Viguerie, *The New Right: We're Ready to Lead* (Falls Church: Viguerie Company, 1981). For histories of the New Right and conservative realignment, see Donald Critchlow, *The Conservative Ascendancy: How the GOP Right Made Political History* (Cambridge: Harvard University Press, 2007); and Lee Edwards, *The Conservative Revolution: The Movement that Remade America* (New York: Free Press, 1999). For work that places the rise of the New Right in a broader political and social context, see Amy Ansell, *New Right, New Racism: Race and Reaction in the United States and Britain* (New York: New York University Press, 1997); Joseph Lowndes, *From the New Deal to the New Right: Race and the Southern Origins of Modern Conservatism* (New Haven: Yale University Press, 2008); Lisa McGir, *Suburban Warriors: The Origins of the New American Right* (Princeton: Princeton University Press, 2002); Self, *All in the Family*; and Whitney Strub, *Perversion for Profit: The Politics of Pornography and the Rise of the New Right* (New York: Columbia University Press, 2010).
12. Daniel Williams, *God's Own Party: The Making of the Christian Right* (New York: Oxford University Press, 2010); Neil Young, *We Gather Together: The Religious Right and the Problem of Interfaith Politics* (New York: Oxford University Press, 2016). For other scholarship on the Religious Right, see Randall Balmer, *Thy Kingdom Come: How the Religious Right Distorts Faith and Threatens America* (New York: Basic Books, 2007); Sara Diamond, *Spiritual Warfare: The Politics of the Christian Right* (Boston: South End Press, 1989); Kenneth Heineman, *God is a Conservative: Religion, Politics, and Morality in Contemporary America* (New York: New York University Press, 1998); Michael Lienesch, *Redeeming America: Piety and Politics in the New Christian Right* (Chapel Hill: University of North Carolina Press, 1993); William Martin, *With God On Our Side: The Rise of the Religious Right in America*, Revised edition (New York: Broadway Books, 2005); and Clyde Wilcox, *Onward Christian Soldiers? The Religious Right in American Politics* (Colorado: Westview Press, 1996). For work historicizing family values rhetoric, see Dowland, *Family Values and the Rise of the Christian Right*; J. Brooks Flippen, *Jimmy Carter, the Politics of Family, and the Rise of the Religious Right* (Athens: University of Georgia Press, 2011); Gil Frank, "Save our Children: The Sexual Politics of Child Protection in the United States, 1965–1990," Ph.D. Thesis, Brown University, 2009; Self, *All in the Family*; and Taranto, *Kitchen Table Politics*.
13. Reagan discussed *Dred Scott v. Sanford* (1857), English abolitionist William Wilberforce, the 14th Amendment, and Abraham Lincoln. Ronald Reagan, *Abortion and the Conscience of the Nation* (Nashville: Thomas Nelson Publishers, 1984), 19, 27–9, 36–7.

14. For accounts of the reproductive rights movement and abortion providers in the 1980s, see Johanna Schoen, *Abortion After Roe* (Chapel Hill: University of North Carolina Press, 2015); Suzanna Staggenborg, *The Pro-choice Movement: Organization and Activism in the Abortion Conflict* (Oxford: Oxford University Press, 1991); and Ziegler, *After Roe*. For discussion of pro-life violence and harassment in the 1980s, see Patricia Baird-Windle and Eleanor Bader, *Targets of Hatred: Anti-abortion Terrorism* (Palgrave: St Martin's Press, 2001); Alesha Doan, *Opposition and Intimidation: The Abortion Wars and Strategies of Political Harassment* (Ann Arbor: University of Michigan Press, 2007); Faye Ginsburg, "Rescuing the Nation: Operation Rescue and the Rise of Anti-abortion Militance," in Rickie Solinger (ed.), *Abortion Wars: A Half Century of Struggle, 1950–2000* (Berkeley: University of California Press, 1998), 227–50; Jennifer Jefferis, *Armed for Life: The Army of God and Anti-abortion Terror in the United States* (Santa Barbara: Praeger, 2011); Carol Mason, *Killing for Life: The Apocalyptic Narrative of Pro-life Politics* (Ithaca: Cornell University Press, 2002); and James Risen and Judy Thomas, *Wrath of Angels: The American Abortion War* (New York: Basic Books, 1997). For quote, see Ronald Reagan to Jesse Helms, 5 April 1982, Box 1, Abortion (3), Roger Jepsen Files (hereafter RJ), Ronald Reagan Presidential Library.
15. Judith Valente, "25,000 Foes of Abortion March Here," *Washington Post*, 23 January 1982.
16. Nellie Gray to Ronald Reagan, 18 September 1987, Box 144, Folder 10, March for Life 1983–1989, CLC.
17. See W. Elliot Brownlee and Hugh Graham (eds.), *The Reagan Presidency: Pragmatic Conservatism and Its Legacies* (Lawrence: University Press of Kansas, 2003); Kyle Longley, Jeremy Mayer, Michael Schaller, and Joan Sloan (eds.), *Deconstructing Reagan: Conservative Mythology and America's Fortieth President* (Armonk: M.E. Sharpe, 2007); Richard Conley (ed.), *Reassessing the Reagan Presidency* (Lanham: Rowman & Littlefield, 2003); Paul Kengor and Peter Schweizer (eds.), *The Reagan Presidency: Assessing the Man and His Legacy* (Lanham: University Press of America, 2005); and Doug Rossinow, *The Reagan Era: A History of the 1980s* (New York: Columbia University Press, 2015).

CHAPTER 2

A Brief History of the National Movement to End Abortion

Abstract This chapter is a group biography of sorts, noting the origins and orientations of the most significant organization and leaders that opposed abortion in the 1970s and 1980s. It charts the complex web of groups that emerged after the Supreme Court legalized abortion, and summarizes some of their divergent views on ideology, politics, religion, and activism. It then locates the anti-abortion movement in the broader national political context, charting the evolution of abortion politics for Republicans and Democrats. It explores the relationship between Ronald Reagan and opponents of abortion before and after the 1980 election, outlining his strong pro-life rhetoric and the elevation of the movement as a national political force. The chapter concludes by outlining the tension that surrounded much of Reagan's anti-abortion symbolism, as the movement confronted the gap between words and deeds.

Keywords Right-to-life movement · Conservatism · Catholic Church · Religious Right · Political polarization · Ronald Reagan

The national pro-life movement emerged as a political force relatively rapidly. This chapter is a group biography of sorts, noting the origins and orientations of the most significant right-to-life organizations and leaders during the 1970s and 1980s. The movement against abortion must be understood as a complex web of organizations with different histories

© The Author(s) 2019
P. Flowers, *The Right-to-Life Movement, the Reagan Administration, and the Politics of Abortion*, Palgrave Studies in the History of Social Movements, https://doi.org/10.1007/978-3-030-01707-1_2

and perspectives. Groups were often in competition with one another, and some had contradictory attitudes toward alliances, compromise, lobbying, and movement building. Similarly, when it came to abortion, both the Democrats and the Republicans were in flux. Many treat the union between pro-lifers, the New Right, the Religious Right, and the Republican Party as essentially settled ground after Ronald Reagan's victory in 1980. In contrast, I argue that this relationship remained fraught and subject to contestation until the end of Reagan's presidency.

An Institutional History

On 22 January 1973, the Supreme Court handed down its decisions in *Roe v. Wade* and *Doe v. Bolton*, legalizing all first-trimester and many second-trimester abortions and overturning the law in all but four states. In its 7–2 verdict, the Supreme Court drew upon the right to privacy first outlined in 1965 in *Griswold v. Connecticut*. It rejected the argument that the fetus was protected by the US Constitution, ruling that the "word 'person,' as used in the Fourteenth Amendment, does not include the unborn."[1] The legalization of abortion was a seismic event in contemporary US history. Second-wave feminists and supporters of abortion law repeal heralded the court's decision as a major victory. For opponents of abortion, 22 January became a day for mourning and mass protest. In the late 1960s, the anti-abortion movement emerged in parallel with the abortion reform and repeal movements, but most pro-life activism occurred at the local and state levels and was reactive.[2] Anti-abortionists thought "the American public would stand up and scream bloody murder … which is what abortion is" about *Roe*.[3] Instead, the national abortion rate almost doubled between 1973 and 1981.[4] Thus the right-to-life movement grew rapidly at a national level as pro-lifers desperately sought to end legal abortion. Some national groups focused on politics and lobbying, others specialized in litigation, some pushed for sex education or welfare reform, and others focused on pregnancy counseling and adoption. All shared the goal of overturning *Roe*, either via a new Supreme Court ruling or an amendment to the constitution that banned abortion.

By the early 1980s, the national movement opposing legal abortion consisted of an array of groups with a veritable alphabet soup of acronyms. Aside from their shared abhorrence of abortion, there was no one common profile among leaders. They ranged in age from their thirties to their sixties, most were in their fifties. Many were Catholic but there were also influential Protestant voices. They came from an array of backgrounds, including doctors, lawyers, priests, and homemakers. After *Roe*, the movement worked hard to address the perception that it was anti-woman. Between 1973 and 1981, three of the five presidents of the National Right to Life Committee (NRLC) were Protestant women: Marjory Mecklenburg, Dr. Mildred Jefferson, and Dr. Carolyn Gerster. Women were also leaders and high-profile figures in several other nationally important groups. This was not just about optics; by 1974 women made up over 80% of the grassroots pro-life movement.[5] Most of the leaders who were not clergy had children, although some prominent women such as Jefferson and Nellie Gray of MfL did not. While the movement's leadership was relatively balanced in terms of gender and exhibited some religious diversity, it was racially homogeneous.

The oldest and most significant pro-life organization was the NRLC, which was founded by the National Conference of Catholic Bishops (NCCB) in 1967. Shortly after *Roe*, it voted to end this relationship with the Catholic hierarchy. By 1980, it was an umbrella organization for 1800 chapters and affiliates at the local and state levels, claiming to represent 10–13 million members.[6] The NRLC defined its scope as the "life issues" of abortion, euthanasia, and infanticide. It produced a twice-monthly publication, *National Right to Life News* (*NRL News*). Politicians often treated the NRLC as "the movement," and its leaders had the most consistent and high levels of access in the Reagan White House. It was an ecumenical group, and most of its presidents in the 1970s were Protestant. However, in the 1980s, Catholics reemerged as the most prominent figures within the organization. Jean Doyle served as president from 1983 to 1984, while Douglas Johnson was legislative director from 1981 onwards—an increasingly influential role after the NRLC focused on lobbying. The most powerful right-to-lifer in the NRLC—perhaps "the most famous Pro-life Spokesman in the world"— was Dr. John "Jack" Willke, a former obstetrician. In 1971, Willke and his wife, Barbara, a nurse, co-authored the *Handbook on Abortion*, which was the right-to-life reference text for many years. He was president of the NRLC from 1980–1983 to 1984–1991. Willke believed the movement needed to be strictly single-issue and that political compromise was a necessity, for an "all-or-nothing approach will gain us nothing, and the entire [abortion] holocaust will continue."[7]

Like the NRLC, Americans United for Life (AUL) was established before *Roe* and articulated a pragmatic and ecumenical vision of abortion politics. AUL had a similar pedigree to the NRLC in terms of age and significance, but from its founding in 1971 it was a professional rather than a membership organization, with a small board and no interest in engaging the grassroots. Dennis Horan, who was chairman of AUL from 1975 to 1988, was a prominent Catholic lawyer who, in the immediate aftermath of *Roe*, served as a legal advisor to both the US Catholic Conference (USCC) and the NRLC. Under Horan's leadership, AUL focused narrowly on litigation, and it has played a role in most significant abortion cases since *Roe*. The NRLC and AUL both embraced a moderate, incrementalist pro-life strategy, aiming to gradually erode abortion rights and avoid moments of legislative or judicial failure.

After the *Roe* decision, several new national groups were established. The Ad Hoc Committee in Defense of Life (AHCDL) was founded in 1973 by Catholic journalist Jim McFadden, who also established the *Human Life Review* in 1974. By the 1980s, AHCDL's primary influence stemmed from its monthly newsletter, *Lifeletter*, aimed at political insiders and those interested in Beltway abortion gossip. American Citizens Concerned for Life (ACCL) was established in 1974 by Mecklenburg, a liberal Methodist and former home economics teacher. ACCL folded in 1982—a particularly significant collapse given it was a progressively inclined pro-life organization interested in increasing access to contraception and fostering public and government support for pregnant women and single mothers. Also in 1974, Gray, a liberal Democrat lawyer in the Labor Department, organized the first MfL on the anniversary of *Roe*, which became *the* annual mass demonstration for the pro-life movement. While the organization did not engage directly with federal politics, Gray, a convert to Catholicism, used her platform for lobbying. She rejected all types of political compromise and believed elected officials who did not act against abortion would one day "be held accountable just as the Nuremberg trials found individuals personally responsible for crimes committed against humanity."[8]

At the end of the 1970s and the beginning of the 1980s, a wave of new groups formed that shared a morally conservative interpretation of contemporary American society. The National Pro-Life Political Action Committee (NPLPAC) and Life Amendment Political Action Committee (LAPAC) were founded in 1977. Both groups capitalized on campaign finance reform after Watergate to raise money to defeat pro-choice politicians, and both used provocative tactics. The NRLC founded the National Right to Life Political Action Committee

(NRLPAC) in 1979, copying their model, although not the controversial methods. NPLPAC was founded by Father Charles Fiore and LAPAC by Paul Brown, both conservative Catholics.[9] LAPAC and NPLPAC initially experienced striking success, but by the mid-1980s both groups had significant debt and were politically irrelevant. Human Life International (HLI), founded in 1981 by Father Paul Marx, was global in scope. Marx saw himself as a "missionary" working to address the lack of "pro-life consciousness" in poor and developing countries.[10] HLI taught natural family planning methods, trained pro-life leaders outside the United States, and was interested in population control and family planning issues. It shared this concern with the small US Coalition for Life (USCL), founded in 1972. USCL was established and run by Randy Engel, a Catholic researcher who edited *The Vietnam Journal* in the 1960s before she became an anti-abortion activist. Engel and Marx were unusual in that they were always internationalist in their approach.

Of all the groups started in this moment, the most significant was ALL, established in 1979.[11] ALL was the so-called "marine corps" of the pro-life movement, and was founded and run by Judie Brown, a Catholic homemaker. She was married to Paul Brown of LAPAC, whom she met while they were both regional office managers for Kmart. Although Judie stopped working after she married, she almost simultaneously became involved in the Washington state anti-abortion movement in 1970. She served as executive director of the NRLC from 1976 to 1979, when she quit, ostensibly over political strategy. ALL viewed pro-life compromise as an "abomination" that was "a denial of the very reason for our existence as [a] movement."[12] In the late 1970s, Judie was courted by New Right conservatives and provided with financial and strategic assistance to establish ALL. The Browns viewed the legalization of abortion as symptomatic of deeper social and cultural decay and found an easy home in the interlocking pro-family, New Right, and Religious Right circles that operated in Washington, DC. By the early 1980s, ALL had over 4000 affiliates across the nation and boasted approximately 56,000 readers of its magazine, *A.L.L. About Issues*. To many, Judie Brown was the new face of the right-to-life movement. In Reagan's first term, she was part of the inner circle of pro-lifers with high levels of White House access, but in 1985 the Browns fell out of favor with Reagan's advisors after refusing to stick to issues in the "briefing book." They viewed this as proof of their autonomy and commitment to the cause, later commenting about the NRLC, "They're invited into the White House. Big deal."[13] ALL, along with LAPAC, HLI, and Pro-Life Action League (PLAL), spent much of the decade undermining the NRLC's authority. These groups were absolutist in orientation, furiously rejecting the incrementalism of ACCL, AUL, and the NRLC. They sought an absolute ban on abortion, often with no exceptions, and believed that anything less damaged the moral and political claims of the movement.

Throughout the 1970s and 1980s, the influence of the Catholic hierarchy within the pro-life movement was a controversial undercurrent. Sociologist Michael Cuneo argues that, "without Catholics the movement might never have gotten started."[14] The NCCB founded the NRLC, and before *Roe* at least 75% of grassroots activists were Catholic. After the NRLC became independent, the NCCB established the National Committee for a Human Life Amendment (NCHLA) in 1974. Other pro-life groups frequently dismissed and ignored NCHLA, viewing it as a mouthpiece for the hierarchy. Both the NCCB and the USCC selectively intervened in abortion politics, which angered both pro-life and pro-choice advocates. USCL, LAPAC, NPLPAC, ALL, PLAL, and HLI were all explicitly conservative Catholic anti-abortion groups. They had an adversarial relationship with the hierarchy, vociferously condemning the bishops for their tepid response to the spiritual crisis of legal abortion.

Individual Protestants were always active within the pro-life movement and some, such as Mecklenburg, Jefferson, Gerster, and George Hunston Williams, were leaders in AUL and the NRLC. However, in the 1970s, right-to-life Protestants did not have a strong institutional presence and were not acting as part of established religious traditions. Before *Roe*, many mainline and evangelical Protestant churches endorsed abortion law reform, as did more conservative bodies such as the National Association of Evangelicals (NAE) and the Southern Baptist Convention (SBC). Several major Protestant denominations supported abortion on demand. After 1973, many Protestants still reflexively viewed opposition to abortion as a Catholic issue. The first explicitly Protestant right-to-life group was Christian Action Council (CAC), founded in 1975 by Dr. C. Everett Koop, a pediatric surgeon and prominent evangelical, and Harold O.J. Brown, an evangelical theologian and editor of *Christianity Today*. CAC pushed evangelicals to realize that protection of fetal life was not sectarian. Denominational groups, such as Presbyterians Pro-Life and Lutherans for Life, both founded in 1976, and Southern Baptists for Life (SBL), founded in 1984, were generally small and focused on prayer, volunteer efforts, and church policy, rarely undertaking federal lobbying. This was partly because of uncertainty around whether political speech from the pulpit jeopardized the tax-exempt status of religious organizations.[15] The spiritual and ideological transformation of the right-to-life cause in the late 1970s occurred primarily because of two interrelated developments: the efforts of the self-proclaimed New Right and the awakening of the Religious Right.

In the 1970s, the New Right—led by Howard Phillips, Richard Viguerie, Terry Dolan, and Paul Weyrich—worked to revitalize conservatism and push the Republican Party to the right. Although New Right think tanks and Political Action Committees exerted a great deal of influence, they operated as outsiders and did not have formal partisan connections. Political historian Donald Critchlow argues this allowed them "to press with impunity an agenda that interjected new issues and policies into the political arena."[16] The New Right's chief innovation lay in mobilizing conservative evangelical and fundamentalist Christians—the "greatest tract of virgin timber on the political landscape."[17] The New Right spent much of the 1970s criticizing second-wave feminism and gay liberation, using the rhetoric of family values to condemn the social, sexual, and gender shifts of the post-World War II period. Focusing on issues such as the Equal Rights Amendment (ERA), sex education, school textbooks, pornography, and above all, abortion, they offered a broad indictment of the liberal state. What made the New Right "new" was its elevation of the so-called social issues to a point of near equality with staple conservative concerns such as small government, fiscal restraint, strong defense, and anti-communism. The language of moral decline was instrumental in drawing previously apolitical conservative evangelical and fundamentalist Christians into worldly affairs, and the Religious Right quickly became a striking new element in federal politics.

The influx of Protestants into the anti-abortion movement occurred primarily through multi-issue Religious Right groups, which had agendas that covered an array of spiritual, social, economic, and foreign policy concerns. Although prominent conservative Protestants did not begin to speak out against abortion until the end of the 1970s, they frequently claimed that *Roe* was the "stick of dynamite" that forced them to reengage with secular politics. They were inspired by evangelical philosopher and theologian Francis Schaeffer, particularly his 1979 book and five-part film series *Whatever Happened to the Human Race?* co-authored with Koop. Schaeffer argued that legal abortion was an atrocity akin to the Holocaust and that the forces of secular humanism were working against the Christian basis of society. Schaeffer called on conservative fundamentalists to put aside their long-standing hostility to Catholics, Mormons, Jews, and mainline Protestants and create a mass movement based on common political goals rather than theological agreement. Cooperation proved difficult in practice, but the Religious Right played an important role in transforming the public perception of abortion politics in the late 1970s.

Religious Right groups relied on a morally traditionalist framework, presenting their actions as literally "saving" the nation. The most high-profile Religious Right group was Moral Majority (MM), started by the Southern Baptist televangelist Reverend Jerry Falwell in 1979. MM described itself as "pro-life, pro-family, pro-moral, and pro-American."[18] It functioned as a spiritual organization and political lobbying group, and within its first year claimed to have worked with over 72,000 fundamentalist preachers, providing them with the tools to get people "out of the pew and into the precinct." Other organizations, such as Focus on the Family (FotF), founded in 1977, Christian Voice (CV), founded in 1978, Religious Roundtable (RR) and Concerned Women for America (CWA), both founded in 1979, and the National Pro-Family Coalition (NPFC), founded in 1980, also became involved in abortion politics. Of these organizations, only FF and CWA survived into the 1990s, although new Religious Right groups quickly emerged. The size and influence of the Religious Right are difficult to ascertain. In the 1980s, approximately one-third of Americans identified as "born again," although this did not automatically mean they were ideologically conservative. Exit polls indicated that 12–15% of Reagan's vote came from born-again Christians. In the 1990s, when exit poll questions changed, over 20% of voters self-identified as part of the Religious Right.[19]

In the 1980s, evangelicals and fundamentalists were significant in the growing militancy of anti-abortionists. Since the 1970s, a fringe element of Catholic pro-lifers endorsed sit-ins (which they came to call "rescues") and direct action protest techniques, physically blocking access to abortion providers. Activists such as John Cavanaugh O'Keefe, who later worked for HLI, insisted that the 1960s civil rights movement should be a model for the right-to-life cause. In 1980, the former Benedictine monk Joseph Scheidler established PLAL, which embraced aggressive and combative clinic protests. In 1985, a group of right-to-lifers formed the Pro-Life Action Network to help train the grassroots in direct action. These piecemeal efforts became a mass phenomenon because of Randall Terry, a 27-year-old evangelical who founded Operation Rescue (OR) in 1986. Terry's "clinic rescues" attracted broad grassroots support, as did the challenge he posed to the movement, "If you think abortion is murder, act like it!"

OR mainstreamed the idea of nonviolent civil disobedience for opponents of abortion, and at the end of the 1980s, tens of thousands of activists were arrested for clinic blockades. Although Conservative Catholics such as Marx and Judie Brown strongly supported this confrontational style of right-to-life witness, the Catholic hierarchy generally disavowed combative tactics. Moderate groups such as the NRLC refused to even comment on OR because it endorsed breaking the law. In contrast, Terry was lauded by Religious Right leaders such as Pat Robertson of the Christian Broadcasting Network, Dr. James Dobson of FotF, and Falwell. The Religious Right viewed the founding of OR as the start of a "new era" for pro-lifers, arguing that these types of clinic blockades were "the only way to bring an end to the biological holocaust in this country."[20] OR's popularity stemmed from Terry's ability to persuade evangelicals and fundamentalists to put their bodies on the line, but it also reflected broader grassroots dissatisfaction about the movement's failure to achieve meaningful change working within the system. Despite OR's rapid rise, it was plagued by financial problems, lawsuits, and infighting and formally dissolved in 1990, although similarly named subgroups operated on the fringes of the movement.[21]

Conservative pro-life groups had obvious points of ideological agreement with Religious Right groups, but even moderates such as the NRLC embraced organizations such as MM in the late 1970s. Historian Mary Ziegler suggests this association was triggered by concerns about movement building and operational strength. The Religious Right seemed to offer a level of political influence that had so far eluded the anti-abortion movement, made pressing by the fact that the NRLC was deeply in debt. However, the relationship between these factions was fraught. Because of the Religious Right's broad agenda, moderate anti-abortionists were apprehensive when they acted on behalf of the cause. Conservative Catholic pro-lifers were suspicious of the Religious Right for doctrinal reasons, believing all Protestant groups were wrong when it came to sexual morality. Privately, Marx warned Judie Brown that ecumenical collaboration should be pursued only if pro-life organizations could avoid being "enmeshed or identified" with the Religious Right. Such relationships needed to be undertaken with "the greatest care, always knowing to what extent they are not really Catholics and so not really Christian." By the early 1980s, Paul Brown dismissively told reporters that Falwell "couldn't spell abortion five years ago."[22]

Although the movement became more religiously diverse in the 1970s and 1980s, almost all its leaders were white. This was despite strong pro-life efforts to reach out to African Americans.[23] Right-to-lifers relied heavily on arguments made in the 1960s by black nationalists, who framed abortion and contraception as tools intended to decimate the race. Even before *Roe*, pro-lifers discussed abortion in the context of black genocide and drew explicit parallels between the legal non-personhood of slaves in the mid-nineteenth century and the contemporary status of fetuses.[24] After *Roe*, right-to-lifers emphasized the disproportionally high rates of abortion among African Americans, presenting the black fetus as an especially vulnerable subject. Groups such as ALL also targeted abortion providers, insisting that Planned Parenthood Federation of America (PP) was forever tainted by the eugenic views of its founder, Margaret Sanger.[25]

While much of this engagement originated from white anti-abortionists, there were a handful of nationally prominent African American pro-lifers, including Reverend Jesse Jackson, Kay James, Erma Craven, and Jefferson. Jackson and Craven were liberals and Democrats; Jefferson and James were conservative Republicans. While they had different political and ideological reasons for opposing abortion, all shared the view that abortion must be understood in a racialized context. This put Jefferson and James at odds with the modern black conservative intellectual tradition, which downplays race as a structural issue in contemporary society.[26] These two black women were the most influential African Americans in the national pro-life movement. Jefferson was NRLC president from 1975 to 1978, and James was the NRLC's Director of Public Affairs from 1985 to 1989. In 1986, James oversaw the creation of a new NRLC subgroup, Black Americans for Life (BAL), which engaged in outreach with African American churches and organizations. BAL also served as a visible rebuttal to media depictions of "pro-life activists as rightwing zealots waging an unholy crusade against women and minorities."[27]

On the surface, these overtures toward African Americans should have been successful. In the 1970s, blacks were less likely than whites to support liberalized access to abortion, although they were also less likely to completely oppose abortion.[28] Pro-lifers also used language and examples that originated within the African American community. However, as the anti-abortion movement became increasingly aligned with conservatism, the potential for significant black engagement diminished. The modern conservatism of the 1970s and 1980s presented itself as "color blind," but the Right's priority was attracting white Southern Democratic voters and perfecting Republican President Richard Nixon's "Southern strategy." Historian Doug Rossinow describes Reagan as "the most successful white backlash politician in American history." Certainly, rightwing attacks on affirmative action and busing, pathologization of the black family, and deployment of racially loaded tropes such as "welfare queen" meant African Americans were leery of the conservative resurgence. In 1980, only 14% of African Americans voted for Reagan; in 1984 that number dropped to 9%.[29] Despite the spiritual and social traditionalism of large parts of the black church, the Religious Right was also overwhelmingly white. In 1980, MM boasted a national membership of over 400,000, but "only a couple of hundred" were black preachers. Weyrich, a New Right strategist instrumental in founding MM, told the *New York Times*, "This is not a minority movement." Indeed, religious historian Randall Balmer has argued that the origins of evangelical and fundamentalist political mobilization lay not with *Roe*, as they frequently claimed, but with an Internal Revenue Service attempt to compel private religious schools to racially integrate or lose their tax-exempt status.[30] By and large, African Americans were not part of the Reagan Revolution.

RONALD REAGAN AND ABORTION POLITICS

The political ascendance of the right-to-life movement was closely connected to the presidential ambitions of Reagan, a former B-movie actor and Governor of California. Reagan emerged as a rightwing darling during conservative Republican Barry Goldwater's failed bid for the presidency in 1964, and he was championed by the New Right throughout the 1970s. Reagan was an unlikely pro-life hero. As Governor, he signed the 1967 *Therapeutic Abortion Act*, which resulted in a dramatic surge in legal abortions, increasing from 5018 in 1968 to more than 100,000 in 1972. At the end of 1975, as he prepared to challenge the incumbent Republican President Gerald Ford, he branded this past action a mistake and reached out to the right-to-life movement. Reagan explained that he had struggled with the decision to sign the bill and had done so upon the advice of his aides and at the urging of Republican legislators. No one expected the massive increase in abortions. Reagan emphasized that he believed abortion was the taking of a human life and that he was now opposed to all abortion except to save the life of the mother.[31] His identification with the cause, coupled with the influence of the New Right and Religious Right in the late 1970s, gradually pushed much of the Republican Party toward at least a publicly pro-life stance.

Although he did not win the Republican nomination in 1976, Reagan's bid had significant consequences for national abortion politics. The 1976 Republican Party Platform was shaped by a fierce power struggle between Ford and Reagan supporters. It included an anti-abortion plank as a concession to win support from Reagan delegates and to try to attract Catholic and pro-life Democratic voters. Leading Republican women urged the party not to take a position on *Roe*, but ultimately sacrificed abortion to preserve party support for the ERA, which Reagan also opposed. The abortion plank, brokered by Senator Bob Dole (R-KS) and drafted by Senator Jesse Helms (R-NC), put the party on record in supporting "the efforts of those who seek enactment of a constitutional amendment to restore protection of the right to life for unborn children." In contrast, after strong lobbying from groups including the National Women's Political Caucus (NWPC) and the National Organization for Women (NOW), the 1976 Democratic Party Platform described pro-life efforts to amend the constitution as "undesirable."[32]

Despite this, abortion was not yet a starkly partisan issue. Both Ford and Democratic candidate Jimmy Carter described themselves as personally opposed to abortion, but neither shared the movement's policy goals and right-to-lifers did not flock to one party over the other. Indeed, some anti-abortionists believed they would be best served by the Democrats. In 1976, Ellen McCormack began her bid for the presidency in the Democratic primaries before running as the Right to Life Party candidate. Pro-lifers had high-ranking Democratic allies in both the House and the Senate. Between 1973 and 1984, Democrats sponsored most Congressional anti-abortion legislation. Significant right-to-life measures such as the Church Amendment, the Helms Amendment, and the Hyde Amendment passed in Democratic-majority Congresses. From the mid-nineteenth century, the Democrats had reliably attracted the Catholic vote, and well into the 1980s, ordinary Democrats were more likely to be pro-life than ordinary Republicans. Within the right-to-life movement, there was a strong liberal element that framed opposition to abortion through a social justice lens.³³ In the 1970s, national groups generally believed a bipartisan solution was required to end abortion. However, this vision of the pro-life movement as a broad church did not endure in the 1980 campaign.

Initially, right-to-lifers worked against candidates, targeting Democratic contenders such as Carter and Senator Edward Kennedy (D-MA) as well as Republicans such as George H.W. Bush, Senator Howard Baker (R-TN), and Representative John Anderson (R-IL). Reagan made explicit overtures to the movement and its leaders. In January 1980, he met twice with Gerster seeking the NRLC's endorsement. In February, he wrote to Gray, expressing his hope "that future Marches for Life will be addressed by a President of the United States who shares the historic respect for life embodied in the Hippocratic Oath." That same month he telegrammed NPLPAC promising to pick a "pro-life running mate." In June, in a letter read at the NRLC's annual convention, Reagan assured attendees that "never before has the cause you espouse been more important to the future of our country."³⁴ Thus major right-to-life groups such as the NRLC, MfL, LAPAC, ALL, NPLPAC, and AHCDL went on record supporting him. The Religious Right strongly backed Reagan, although his Presbyterianism had few parallels with the faith of evangelical and fundamentalist Americans. The 1980 Republican platform had a stronger anti-abortion plank and, after 40 years of endorsing the ERA, the party dropped its support for the amendment. Political scientist Lisa Young suggests that from this point on, the Republican Party defined "itself in opposition to the women's movement and feminist issues."³⁵ At the Republican National Convention, Reagan announced Bush as his pick for Vice President, angering conservatives and pro-life supporters. Bush was a moderate Republican with a long record of political support for family planning and population control and he had consistently opposed the Human Life Amendment. However, pro-lifers and the Religious Right were placated by assurances that Bush would abide by the Republican platform.

Not all anti-abortionists embraced Reagan and their new conservative allies. Right to Life Party candidate McCormack ran negative newspaper ads highlighting Reagan's track record as Governor of California and condemning his promise to support Republican Congressional candidates who were not pro-life. ACCL, uncomfortable with the recent ideological drift of the movement, asked in one mailing whether right-to-lifers were "bothered by over 1 million abortions a year but turned off by hard-line, single issue pro-life politics?" In an October editorial, it pointed out that in LAPAC's infamous hit lists, "prominent liberals appear most often in the pro-abortion column [while] pro-abortion conservatives are conspicuously absent." In the liberal Catholic magazine *America*, Monsignor George Higgins warned that anti-abortionists should "scrutinize more closely this apparent attempt to transform prolife sentiment into a rightwing political movement." Such critiques were not popular within the movement. As McCormack's campaign manager noted, the consensus seemed to be, "Reagan isn't perfect, but he's electable." Reagan's resounding victory in November 1980 was interpreted as a victory for the right-to-life cause, as was the victory of 11 Senators. Willke, the new NRLC president, described the results as "Fantasy Island come true."[36]

Partisan Shifts

Opposition to abortion was a prominent element of Reagan's political identity, but pro-life groups were only a small component of a much larger electoral strategy. In 1969, Kevin Phillips, a Nixon advisor, argued that demographic and electoral shifts meant that the New Deal coalition, first pieced together by Democratic President Franklin D. Roosevelt in the 1930s, was vulnerable. This strategy was instrumental in Nixon's landslide 1972 victory, and Reagan and his advisors aimed to capture the same disaffected Democratic voters and embed them within a new, permanent Republican majority. In addition to the Southern strategy, Reagan had a Northern strategy that involved courting blue-collar workers, Catholics, and "ethnics," claiming that Democrats no longer represented ordinary Americans but were beholden to liberals, minorities, and special-interest groups. These overtures were successful, and "Reagan Democrats" made up more than one-quarter of his base in the 1980 and 1984 elections.[37]

Once Reagan was in office, his advisors generally talked about abortion in terms of voting blocs. In 1982, Office of Policy Development staffer Gary Bauer reminded his superiors that "even when we are on the 'wrong' side of some of these issues from a public opinion standpoint, they still may be politically positive." His supporting example was the role of abortion in attracting urban Catholic voters in 1980. Conservative Christians, along with the New Right, were also viewed as factions that were mollified by action on abortion. Pro-lifers were not treated as a distinct voting bloc, presumably because only a small percentage of the population believed abortion should be illegal in all circumstances. Indeed, during the legislative fight over abortion in the early 1980s, Lee Atwater, Deputy Assistant to the President for Political Affairs, quoted polls suggesting that 22% of the population was "intensely pro-life," versus 39% of voters who were equivalently pro-choice.[38] And of course, opposition to abortion did not automatically lead to activism and engagement with the right-to-life movement.

At the start of the 1980s, Republican politicians were divided on the social issues. Throughout the 1960s and 1970s, many moderate Republicans supported birth control and legal abortion. In the early 1980s, this element of the party remained powerful, particularly in the Senate. Senate Majority Leader Howard Baker (R-TN) was pro-choice, as was Senator Bob Packwood (R-OR), Senator Arlen Specter (R-PE), Senator Lowell Weicker (R-CT), Senator John Chafee (R-RI), and Senator Barry Goldwater (R-AZ). As political scientists Barbara Craig and David O'Brien point out, "Throughout the 1970s and 1980s, the [abortion] battles in the Senate were fought with Republicans as the admirals on both sides." Reagan's electoral victory in 1980 formalized the union between economic and social conservatives, but the tensions between these political worldviews did not vanish overnight. In 1982, Packwood successfully filibustered a significant pro-life bill. In 1983, almost one-third of Senate Republicans voted against a right-to-life constitutional amendment that was already a compromise measure rather than an outright ban . In 1984, Weicker led a group of Republican moderates who unsuccessfully tried to mute New Right and Religious Right influence in the Republican Party Platform, warning that they were becoming "God's Own Party." However, over the course of the Reagan years, voting patterns on abortion became much more partisan. By the end of the 1980s approximately 80% of Senate Republicans cast consistently anti-abortion votes.[39]

Simultaneously, the Democratic leadership was becoming more pro-choice. In the 1976 campaign, Carter, like Ford, stressed that he personally opposed abortion. During Carter's presidency, feminists in the White House and the bureaucracy were sharply critical of his policies and statements. In 1980, NOW denounced Reagan for his "medieval" views but refused to endorse Carter. It was the growing influence of the women's movement, both as a faction within the party and as delegates at the Democratic National Conventions, which pushed Democrats to make stronger statements on abortion. The 1980 Democratic Party Platform acknowledged the divisions that existed within American society over abortion, but affirmed the party's support for *Roe* and officially opposed attempts to overturn it. It also endorsed government funding of Medicaid abortions for low-income women, going against the position of Carter, the candidate.[40]

In the 1984 campaign, the Democrats explicitly presented themselves as the party of choice. Political scientist Lisa Young suggests that this was part of a "gender gap" strategy intended to capitalize on Reagan's problem attracting women voters. The Democrats insisted that Reagan and the Republicans were hostile to women's rights, and Young credits this approach, and the choice of Vice Presidential candidate, to the influence of feminist organizations. The Democratic Party Platform dropped its prior acknowledgement of the social division over *Roe*, instead pledging its firm commitment to "reproductive freedom." Walter Mondale, the Democratic presidential nominee, clashed with Reagan over abortion in presidential debates. Mondale also selected Representative Geraldine Ferraro (D-NY) as his running mate, the first time a woman was on the presidential ticket of a major political party. Ferraro, who identified as both Catholic and pro-choice, became a lightning rod for pro-life hostility and anti-abortion protests dogged her campaign stops. An ALL alert claimed that Ferraro had a record that "any down-the-line, radical feminist, pro-abortion advocate could be proud" of. Several prominent members of the Catholic hierarchy publicly criticized Ferraro for misrepresenting church teaching, dismissing her views on abortion and her faith as "absurd" and "not a rational position." Right-to-life Democrats were angered by their party's stance on abortion. Rita Radich, a prominent figure in the NLRC, complained they were "being pushed out of our party," while Sandra Faucher, director of NRLPAC, accused the party hierarchy of treating pro-lifers with "total bias and total discrimination."[41]

Supporters and opponents of legal abortion framed the 1984 election as a contest over the future of the Supreme Court. The Democratic Party Platform explicitly warned that five Justices were over the age of 75 and that the "fundamental right of a woman to reproductive freedom … could easily disappear during a second Reagan term." In the early 1980s, pro-life efforts to amend the US Constitution imploded, and the judicial strategy was suddenly of heightened significance to the national movement. Thus from the start of the campaign, anti-abortionists viewed Reagan as the only acceptable candidate. The NRLC described the choice as "very clear-cut," arguing that if Reagan were defeated "it would be a substantial setback" for the cause. In *Action Line*, the CAC insisted that the 1984 election was the "most significant" since *Roe*. It suggested that pro-lifers needed to think more like their pro-choice opponents; the focus should not be on what Reagan did or did not do in his first term but on "what he is likely to do" if reelected. A group photograph of the sitting justices was captioned, "Who will name their successors?"[42]

By the end of the 1980s, approximately 80% of Senate Democrats cast consistently pro-choice votes and anti-abortionists dubbed the Democrats "the party of death." In 1988, every major Democratic presidential contender embraced the right to choose, even if, like Senator Al Gore (D-TN), Representative Dick Gephardt (D-MO), or Reverend Jesse Jackson, they had once condemned *Roe*. Anti-abortionists were particularly appalled by Michael Dukakis, the eventual Democratic nominee, describing him as the "most pro-abortion candidate to ever run for the U.S. presidency." Faucher declared that in 1988, "millions of pro-life Democrats have been abandoned by their party again." Despite their frequent disappointment with both the Reagan White House and Republicans in Congress, the evolution of the Democrats on abortion over the 1980s seemed to leave pro-life voters with no meaningful electoral choice.[43]

Although the parties became ever more polarized on abortion, this did not determine how most people voted. Throughout the 1980s, the views of rank-and-file Democrats and Republicans did not map easily on to their respective party platforms or candidates. In 1980 and 1984, abortion had a negligible impact in the presidential and Congressional elections. Exit polls indicated that economic matters were paramount. In the 1988 and 1992 elections, abortion had an effect, in that it pushed pro-choice voters away from the Republican Party. Republican voters were still more pro-choice than Democratic voters until the late 1980s and early 1990s. Even at the Republican National Conventions, only 40% of delegates in 1988 and 33% in 1992 supported a constitutional amendment banning abortion, which had been a party goal for over a decade.[44] Despite Reagan's uncompromising rhetoric, he was not leading a party that was clearly opposed to abortion.

The Pro-life Movement in the Reagan Years

National right-to-life organizations knew it would not be possible to overturn *Roe* with the stroke of a pen, but after the 1980 election they expected the next four to eight years would bring significant gains in the battle against abortion. They assumed Reagan would champion the interests of the movement and capitalize on the opportunities afforded by the first Republican majority in the Senate since 1954. Their confidence and optimism were bolstered on 22 January 1981. Richard Schweiker, the new head of the Department of Health and Human Services (HHS), addressed the MfL rally, assuring the audience of between 50,000 and 65,000 right-to-lifers that they had "a pro-life friend" in the bureaucracy. This was the first time a member of Cabinet had addressed the most important annual right-to-life event.[45] After the rally, Reagan met several national anti-abortion leaders—the first citizens group in the White House. Reagan promised that "the prospects are good for fulfilling the pledges contained in our Republican platform."[46]

When it came to symbolism and rhetoric, Reagan's eight years in office were a triumph for pro-lifers. He marked the movement's major events, regularly addressing the annual MfL rally and the NRLC convention. He used the bully pulpit of the presidency to condemn abortion and champion the rights of the unborn and mentioned abortion in his State of the Union address in 1984, 1985, 1986, and 1988.[47] In 1983, he published a pro-life article in *Human Life Review*, which ultimately became the book *Abortion and the Conscience of the Nation*. Right-to-lifers boasted that he was the first sitting President to publish a book. In his speeches and writing, Reagan brought pro-life arguments into the mainstream. The White House even hosted a special screening of the controversial pro-life documentary *The Silent Scream*. Reagan also used his office to shape the national calendar, declaring 22 January 1984 National Sanctity of Human Life Day. He reissued this proclamation annually for the rest of his presidency.[48]

Reagan elevated the movement as a political force. Right-to-lifers and social conservatives such as Mecklenburg of ACCL, Gary Crum of ALL, and Jo Ann Gasper, editor of *The Right Woman*, were placed in charge of family planning and population programs within HHS. Opponents of abortion peppered the ranks of the bureaucracy, including high-level appointments such as Schweiker as head of HHS and Koop as Surgeon General. Pro-lifers had loyal advocates in the Office of Public Liaison and the Office of Policy Development.[49] Right-to-life leaders were also granted significant access to the White House. Not all groups experienced the consistently high levels of contact enjoyed by the NRLC, but the meetings after the January rally ensured that most prominent groups had at least annual personal encounters with Reagan and his advisors. These gatherings were also a key opportunity for pro-lifers to obtain the ultimate form of symbolic capital, photographs with the President.

However, even at the level of symbolism, there were problems. Although the MfL's annual rally began on the Ellipse, close enough to the White House that Reagan once appeared on the balcony and waved to the marchers, he never physically attended.[50] In his first term, the marchers heard statements from the President read by someone else. From 1985 to 1988, he spoke to them "live" via a combination of telephone call and loudspeaker hookup. Similarly, although he sent messages, he never attended the annual NRLC convention or any external abortion rallies. By the White House's own reckoning, Reagan's "first major Presidential address on the prolife issue" did not occur until July 1987. Right-to-lifers encountered the President only within the confines of the Oval Office, generally at gatherings that lasted approximately 30 minutes. Most of their interactions were with his advisors. Increasingly, the meetings that followed the MfL became a site not for pro-lifers to shape policy but for the White House to manage movement frustration. As Elizabeth Dole, Director of the White House Office of Public Liaison, warned Edwin Meese III, Counselor to the President, after a "spirited" January 1983 gathering, "The absence of such a meeting would have created an explosive situation in this important segment of the President's coalition."[51] While right-to-lifers were repeatedly assured of Reagan's unyielding commitment to the cause, meetings, speeches, access, and photographs often functioned *as* the show of support. When one looks beyond symbolic and rhetorical displays, the Reagan years were divisive for the movement and his Presidency was marked by frequent disappointments.

PERCEPTION AND REALITY

Even this short history demonstrates that the motivation and values of activists and politicians were not static. Being mindful of the differences between single-issue pro-life organizations, as well as the place of the Catholic Church and multi-issue Religious Right groups in the abortion struggle, allows for greater understanding of why certain policies and approaches provoked so much disunity and why intra-movement dynamics were so complex. Challenging the idea that Reagan was a "pro-life hero" and that Republicans were the "party of life" complicates our understanding of the partisan realignments of this decade. Analyzing the anti-abortion movement as an element of civil society allows us to view polarization and the culture war as a process. Above all, this book is a study of the gap between perception and reality in the abortion politics of the 1980s.

Notes

1. *Roe v. Wade*, 410 US 113 (1973). For more on privacy rights and reproduction, see Leigh Ann Wheeler, *How Sex Became a Civil Liberty* (Oxford: Oxford University Press, 2013), 121–52.
2. For a discussion of the abortion law reform and repeal movements, see Donald Critchlow, *Intended Consequences: Birth Control, Abortion, and the Federal Government in Modern America* (New York: Oxford University Press, 1999); Carole Joffe, *Doctors of Conscience: The Struggle to Provide Abortion Before and After Roe v. Wade* (Boston: Beacon Press, 1995); and Leslie Reagan, *When Abortion Was a Crime: Women, Medicine, and the Law in the United States 1867–1973* (Berkeley: University of California Press, 1997). For further discussion of the pro-life movement before *Roe*, see Linda Greenhouse and Reva Siegel, "Before (and After) *Roe v. Wade*: New Questions About Backlash," *Yale Law Journal*, Volume 120 (2011): 2028–87; Robert Karrer, "The National Right to Life Committee: Its Founding, Its History, and the Emergence of the Pro-life Movement Prior to Roe v. Wade," *Catholic Historical Review*, Volume 97, Number 3 (July 2011): 527–57; and Williams, *Defenders of the Unborn*.
3. Luker, *Abortion and the Politics of Motherhood*, 126.
4. Guttmacher Institute, "Induced Abortion in the United States," Factsheet (January 2018), https://www.guttmacher.org/fact-sheet/induced-abortion-united-states.
5. Luker, *Abortion and the Politics of Motherhood*, 138, see also 192–7. For more on female pro-lifers, see Haugenberg, *Women Against Abortion*; and Taranto, *Kitchen Table Politics*.
6. These membership numbers had a dubious basis. See Judie Brown quoted in Paige, *The Right to Lifers*, 86; Jack Willke and Carolyn Gerster, quoted in Andrew Merton, *Enemies of Choice: The Right to Life Movement and Its Threat to Abortion* (Boston: Beacon Press, 1982), 201–2.
7. Jack Willke to Paul Marx, 25 May 1990, Box 5, Folder 12, Willke, Dr. Jack, Paul Marx Papers (hereafter PM), University of Notre Dame Archives.

8. Gray quoted in Barbara Gamarekian, "Leader of 'March for Life' Sees Issue as Apocalyptic," *New York Times*, 13 March 1981.
9. LAPAC's other founders were Sean Morton Downey, Jr., and Robert Sassoe, but Brown was its public face.
10. Paul Marx to Mr. and Mrs. George Guettler, 24 July 1981, Box 3, Folder 9, OSB—Foundation of HLI—1981, PM.
11. American Life League and American Life Lobby were both founded in 1979. American Life Lobby folded in 1991.
12. "Hotlines," *A.L.L. About Issues*, February 1981, 2.
13. Brown quoted in "Abortion Foes Are Split on Whether to Support Kennedy for Supreme Court."
14. Cuneo, "Life Battles," 273–4; Karrer, "The National Right to Life Committee."
15. The NRLC was still addressing these concerns in 1988, a decade after the emergence of the Religious Right. James Bopp, "Guidelines for Political Action by Churches and Pastors," *NRL News*, 20 October 1988, 3, 4.
16. Critchlow, *The Conservative Ascendancy*, 131.
17. Martin, *With God on Our Side*, 191.
18. Risen and Thomas, *Wrath of Angels*, 129.
19. Wayne King, "G.O.P. Sees Signs of a Robertson Incursion," *New York Times*, 22 November 1987; Clyde Wilcox, Ted Jelen, and Rachel Goldberg, "Full Pews, Musical Pulpits: The Christian Right at the Turn of the Millennium," *Public Perspective* (May/June 2000), 37.
20. Howard Kurtz, "Operation Rescue Aggressively Antiabortion," *Washington Post*, 6 March 1989; Paul Smith, "A New Era for the Pro-life Movement," *Citizen Magazine*, October 1988, 1, 2, Box 5, Folder 4, Focus on the Family—Citizen, 1988–1991, Southern Baptists for Life Records (hereafter SBL), Southern Baptist Historical Library and Archive.
21. This account of the movement is a synthesis of the following: Judie Brown, *It Is I Who Have Chosen You* (Stafford: American Life League, 1997); Cuneo, "Life Battles"; Joe Gulotta, *Pro-life Christians: Heroes for the Pre-Born* (Rockford: Tan Books, 1992); Haugeberg, *Women Against Abortion*; Robert Karrer, "The Pro-life Movement and Its First Years Under *Roe*," *American Catholic Studies*, Volume 122, Number 4 (Winter 2011): 47–72; Robert Karrer, "The Pivotal Year of 1979 and the New Narrative: Evangelicals and Fundamentalists Join the Pro-life Movement," *Human Life Review*, Volume 40, Number 2 (2014): 87–103; McKeegan, *Abortion Politics*; Risen and Thomas, *Wrath of Angels*; Williams, *Defenders of the Unborn*; Young, *We Gather Together*; and Ziegler, *After Roe*.
22. Ziegler, *After Roe*, 202–3; Paul Marx to Judie Brown, 6 May 1982 and 19 July 1982, Box 3, Folder 30, Brown, Judie 1981–1987, PM; Paige, *The Right to Lifers*, 225.

23. The NRLC, which was the group most interested in diversification, did not begin working on Spanish-language translations of core materials until the late 1980s. Its Hispanic outreach began in earnest in the 1990s through the efforts of Raimundo Rojas.
24. Erma Craven, "Abortion, Poverty, and Black Genocide," in Thomas Hilgers and Dennis Horan (eds.), *Abortion and Social Justice* (New York: Sheed and Ward, 1972), 231–45; MCCL, "Abortion and Slavery," fliers, 1972, Box 54, Folder 3, OSB—Abortion—1961–1975, PM.
25. "Margaret Sanger: The Deception of CBS," *A.L.L. About Issues*, April 1980, 1.
26. Louis Prisock, "Uneasy Alliance: The Participation of African Americans in Conservative Social, Political, and Intellectual Movements," Ph.D. Thesis, University of Massachusetts Amherst, 2007, 130.
27. Clarence Pollard, "Black Americans for Life—A Major Presence at NRL '87," *NRL News*, 2 July 1987, 10.
28. Michael Combs and Susan Welch, "Blacks, Whites, and Attitudes Toward Abortion," *Public Opinion Quarterly*, Volume 46, Number 4 (1982): 510–20.
29. Rossinow, *The Reagan Era*, 8. Scholars such as Joseph Lowndes and Amy Ansell argue that race is crucial to understanding the shape of modern American conservatism. See Ansell, *New Right, New Racism*; and Lowndes, *From the New Deal to the New Right*. https://ropercenter.cornell.edu/polls/us-elections/how-groups-voted/how-groups-voted-1980/; https://ropercenter.cornell.edu/polls/us-elections/how-groups-voted/how-groups-voted-1984/.
30. Weyrich quoted in Dudley Clendinen, "Rev. Falwell Inspires Evangelical Vote," *New York Times*, 20 August 1980; Balmer, *Thy Kingdom Come*, 13–17.
31. Matthew Sitman, "The Conscience of a President," in *The Reagan Presidency*, 76.
32. Daniel Williams, "The GOP's Abortion Strategy: Why Pro-choice Republicans Became Pro-life in the 1970s," *Journal of Policy History*, Volume 23, Number 4 (October 2011): 513–39; "Republican Party Platform of 1976," 18 August 1976, http://www.presidency.ucsb.edu/ws/index.php?pid=25843; Andrew Flint and Joy Porter, "Jimmy Carter: The Re-Emergence of Faith-Based Politics and the Abortion Rights Issue," *Presidential Studies Quarterly*, Volume 35, Number 1 (March 2005), 38; "Democratic Party Platform 1976," 12 July 1976, http://www.presidency.ucsb.edu/ws/index.php?pid=29606.
33. For more on McCormack's campaign, see Stacie Taranto, "Ellen McCormack for President: Politics and an Improbable Path to Passing Anti-abortion Policy," *Journal of Policy History*, Volume 24, Number 2

2 A BRIEF HISTORY OF THE NATIONAL MOVEMENT TO END ABORTION 37

(2012): 263–87. For the political science on abortion and voting, see Greg Adams, "Abortion: Evidence of an Issue Evolution," *American Journal of Political Science*, Volume 41, Number 3 (1997): 718–37; and Edward Carmines and James Woods, "The Role of Party Activists in the Evolution of the Abortion Issue," *Political Behavior*, Volume 24, Number 4 (2002): 361–77. For discussion of pro-life progressivism, see Haugeberg, *Women Against Abortion*; Williams, *Defenders of the Unborn*; and Ziegler, *After Roe*.

34. "Is Reagan Scuttling Pro-lifers?" *Human Events*, 29 August 1981; Ronald Reagan to Nellie Gray, 7 February 1980, Box 1, Abortion (4), Dee Jepsen Files (hereafter DJ), Ronald Reagan Presidential Library; "Why It Probably Won't Be Baker," *Washington Post*, 9 May 1980; "Reagan Gets Backing of Right to Life Group for Stand on Abortion," *New York Times*, 28 June 1980; T.R. Reid, "Reagan Is Favored by Anti-abortionists," *Washington Post*, 12 April 1980.

35. "Republican Party Platform of 1980," 15 July 1980, http://www.presidency.ucsb.edu/ws/?pid=25844; Lisa Young, *Feminists and Party Politics* (Vancouver: UBC Press, 2000), 99.

36. Reid, "Reagan Is Favored by Anti-abortionists"; Frank Lynn, "Right to Life's Political Dilemma," *New York Times*, 20 July 1980; ACCL, "Are You Bothered by Over 1 Million Abortions a Year but Turned Off by Hard-Line, Single Issue Pro-life Politics?" mailing, Box 28, NCR, America, Commonwealth Prospect Mailing, June 1980, American Citizens Concerned for Life Files (hereafter ACCL), Gerald Ford Presidential Library; Editorial, *ACCL Update*, October 1980, Box 14, General Correspondence 1980 (5), ACCL; George G. Higgins, "The Prolife Movement and the New Right," *America*, 13 September 1980, Box 26, America, December 1980, ACCL; Willke quoted in Walter Isaacscon, "The Battle Over Abortion," *Time*, 6 April 1981.

37. Kevin Phillips, *The Emerging Republican Majority* (New Rochelle: Arlington House, 1969); Françoise Coste, "Ronald Reagan's Northern Strategy and a New American Partisan Identity: The Case of the Reagan Democrats," *Caliban: French Journal of English Studies*, Volume 31 (2012): 221–38; https://ropercenter.cornell.edu/polls/us-elections/how-groups-voted/how-groups-voted-1980/; https://ropercenter.cornell.edu/polls/us-elections/how-groups-voted/how-groups-voted-1984/.

38. Gary Bauer to Edwin Harper, 29 March 1982, WE 003, Box 3, #087082, White House Office of Records Management Subject Files (hereafter WHORM), Ronald Reagan Presidential Library; Lee Atwater to Edwin Harper, 2 September 1982, WE 003, Box 3, #087082, WHORM. Public opinion polling on abortion is notoriously difficult to quantify, as phrasing, number of questions, and order of questions have a significant

impact on responses. Gallup polling indicated a less dramatic split; from 1975 to 1988, between 16 and 22% of the population believed abortion should be completely illegal, and between 21 and 24% believed abortion should be completely legal, http://news.gallup.com/poll/1576/abortion.aspx.
39. Craig and O'Brien, *Abortion*, 117; Beth Spring, "Republicans, Religion, and Reelection," *Christianity Today*, 5 October 1984, 55; Adams, "Abortion," 724.
40. Karlyn Barker and Bill Peterson, "The Democrats in New York," *Washington Post*, 13 August 1980; Leslie Bennets, "NOW Rejects All 3 for President, Condemns Reagan as 'Medieval,'" *New York Times*, 6 October 1980; "1980 Democratic Party Platform," 11 August 1980, http://www.presidency.ucsb.edu/ws/index.php?pid=29607. For more on why feminists wielded such power in the Democratic Party in the 1970s and 1980s, see Jo Freeman, "The Political Culture of the Democratic and Republican Parties," *Political Science Quarterly*, Volume 101, Number 3 (1986): 327–56; and Young, *Feminists and Party Politics*.
41. Young, *Feminists and Party Politics*, 82; "1984 Democratic Party Platform," 16 July 1984, http://www.presidency.ucsb.edu/ws/index.php?pid=29608; ALL Alert, "Ferraro: A Catholic for Abortion," 18 July 1984, Box 8, United Nations, Population Aid, Abortion [Articles], John Svahn Files (hereafter JS), Ronald Reagan Presidential Library; Jane Perelz, "Ferraro Says Religion Won't Influence Policy," *New York Times*, 13 September 1984; Radich and Faucher quoted in Sandra Salmans, "Abortion Opponents See Reagan as 'Clear-Cut' Choice in Campaign," *New York Times*, 10 June 1984.
42. "1984 Democratic Party Platform"; Salmans, "Abortion Opponents See Reagan as 'Clear-Cut' Choice in Campaign"; "Antiabortionists Endorse Reagan," *Boston Globe*, 23 January 1984; "1984: Year of Decision," *Action Line*, 14 June 1984, 4, 1, 2, BMS 404/6, Folder 1, George Hunston Williams Papers (hereafter GHW), Andover-Harvard Theological Library.
43. Adams, "Abortion," 724; NRLPAC, "The Dukakis Record on Abortion," 1988 and NRLPAC, "Right-to-Life Leaders Predict Abortion Democrats' 'Achilles Heel' in '88," 21 July 1988, both in Box 2, Folder 6, Bush–Dukakis Election—Comparisons, 1988, SBL.
44. Donald Granberg and James Burlinson, "The Abortion Issue in the 1980 Elections," *Family Planning Perspectives*, Volume 15, Number 5 (Sep–Oct 1983): 231–8; Jerome Himmelstein and James McRae, "Social Conservatism, New Republicans, and the 1980 Election," *Public Opinion Quarterly*, Volume 48 (1984): 592–605; Donald Granberg, "The Abortion Issue in the 1984 Elections," *Family Planning Perspectives*,

Volume 19, Number 2 (Mar–Apr 1987): 59–62; Kevin Smith, "Abortion Attitudes and Vote Choice in the 1984 and 1988 Presidential Elections," *American Politics Quarterly*, Volume 22, Number 3 (July 1994): 354–69; Alan Abramowitz, "It's Abortion, Stupid: Policy Voting in the 1992 Presidential Election," *The Journal of Politics*, Volume 57, Number 1 (February 1995): 176–86; Adams, "Abortion," 728–33; Young, *Feminists and Party Politics*, 111.
45. Gamarekian, "Leader of 'March for Life' Sees Issue as Apocalyptic."
46. Gamarekian, "Leader of 'March for Life' Sees Issue as Apocalyptic"; Martin, *With God on Our Side*, 226; Ronald Reagan to Roger Jepsen, 23 January 1981, Box 1, Abortion (4), DJ.
47. Matthew Moen, "Ronald Reagan and the Social Issues: Rhetorical Support for the Christian Right," *The Social Science Journal*, Volume 27, Number 2 (1990): 202.
48. Ronald Reagan, "Proclamation 5147—National Sanctity of Human Life Day," 13 January 1984, https://www.reaganlibrary.archives.gov/archives/speeches/1984/11384c.htm.
49. Staff who were particularly proactive about pro-life issues were Morton Blackwell, Dee Jepsen and Elizabeth Dole (from the Office of Public Liaison) and Gary Bauer and Stephen Galebach (from the Office of Policy Development), as well as Carl Anderson, who worked in both offices.
50. Ronald Reagan, "23 January 1984," in Douglas Brinkley (ed.), *The Reagan Diaries* (New York: HarperCollins, 2007), 214.
51. Carl Anderson, "Meeting with Right to Life Leaders," 29 July 1987, Box 2, OA19224, Pro-life, Gary Bauer Files (hereafter GB), Ronald Reagan Presidential Library; Elizabeth Dole to Edwin Meese, 24 January 1983, Box 1, Abortion (9), DJ.

CHAPTER 3

"A Prolife Disaster": The Sandra Day O'Connor Nomination

Abstract In 1980, Ronald Reagan and the Republican Party Platform foregrounded the significance of Supreme Court nominations in promoting the "sanctity of human life" and "traditional family values." Opponents of abortion were thus confounded when, in the first six months of Reagan's presidency, he nominated Sandra Day O'Connor to the highest bench in the land. Right-to-lifers believed O'Connor was a supporter of abortion rights and feminist goals, and they were deeply troubled by the revelation that their access and symbolic capital did not translate into influence. The chapter demonstrates the fragility of the alliance between right-to-lifers, the New Right, and the Religious Right, as well as the fraught dynamics between the pro-life movement, the Reagan administration, and the Republican Party. The attempt to block O'Connor was doomed to failure, but it threw into stark relief which segments of the Reagan Revolution were willing to risk antagonizing the President in defense of their goals.

Keywords Abortion politics · Family values · Feminism · Conservatism · Supreme Court · Ronald Reagan

---

Jack Willke to Ronald Reagan, 1 July 1981, FG 051, #019837, WHORM.

© The Author(s) 2019
P. Flowers, *The Right-to-Life Movement, the Reagan Administration, and the Politics of Abortion*, Palgrave Studies in the History of Social Movements, https://doi.org/10.1007/978-3-030-01707-1_3

On 7 July 1981, President Ronald Reagan announced he was nominating Sandra Day O'Connor to the Supreme Court—the first woman selected in its 191-year history. Reagan praised O'Connor for "possessing ... unique qualities of temperament, fairness, intellectual capacity and devotion to the public good." The nomination won support from across the political spectrum and Reagan's opponents publicly praised it. Eleanor Smeal, president of NOW, dubbed the choice "a major victory for women's rights." Even House Speaker Representative Tip O'Neill (D-MA), who had been feuding with Reagan for months, offered backhanded praise, describing the choice as "the best thing [Reagan's] done since he was inaugurated."[1]

In contrast, the selection of O'Connor prompted vociferous condemnation from anti-abortion, socially conservative, New Right, and Religious Right groups. They described it as a betrayal of the right-to-life cause, Reagan's values, and the 1980 Republican Party Platform. This chapter explores the organized opposition to the O'Connor nomination, which elicited a strong, emotional reaction from segments of Reagan's base who struggled to understand his decision. Historians frequently treat the uproar over O'Connor as a side issue or ignore it completely, yet a case study of the nomination offers significant insights into the power and limits to power of social conservatives during a period when they were believed to be in the ascendance.[2]

A Series of Promises

In the 1970s, the most significant political goal of the right-to-life movement was ratification of a Human Life Amendment. However, this constitutional strategy operated in tandem with a judicial strategy to overturn *Roe*. Pro-lifers would have liked to see the seven justices who voted in favor of *Roe* acknowledge that they had incorrectly interpreted the constitution and were thus "responsible for the deaths of countless unborn persons." However, unless the sitting justices experienced an unlikely "quantum conversion," overturning *Roe* required the transformation of the court. The judicial strategy was initially a long-term goal pursued by moderate, incrementalist groups such as AUL and the NRLC. In 1975, when Justice William Douglas retired, the NRLC was "excited" by the first Supreme Court vacancy since 1973. However, it recommended that efforts to influence prominent Republicans or President Gerald Ford's administration "must of necessity be invisible," for if a right-to-life group was seen "to tout a particular candidate [it] would in effect be a kiss of death." Despite pro-life hopes of covertly wielding influence, Ford selected John Paul Stevens, a centrist without a clear position on *Roe*. During confirmation hearings, no Senator enquired about Stevens' stance on abortion, and he was quickly and unanimously confirmed.[3]

By 1981, the political climate had changed, as had the ambitions of anti-abortionists. In the 1980 election, right-to-life groups sought and received Republican support for their two major political goals, a constitutional amendment and a pro-life judiciary. In January, in private meetings with Dr. Carolyn Gerster, then president of the NRLC, Reagan pledged to "appoint pro-life jurists." In a more public commitment, the 1980 Republican Party Platform called for the appointment of judges "who respect traditional family values and the sanctity of human life." However, quite late in the campaign, Reagan made another promise about the courts that appealed to a different constituency. Throughout the election, he was dogged by the perception that because he rejected legal abortion and the ERA he opposed "full and equal opportunities for women." To counter this view, he vowed in October that "one of the first Supreme Court vacancies in my administration will be filled by the most qualified woman I can possibly find." He insisted that he still rejected "tokenism" and "false quotas" and that whoever he nominated would be expected to contribute to the "renewal of a community of values."[4]

The Reagan administration had almost three months warning that Associate Justice Potter Stewart was planning to retire. A list of candidates was compiled and care was taken to ensure that women made up at least half the names submitted for consideration. The advice from the White House was that nominating a woman would be "the right thing to do" while also being politically beneficial. Lyn Nofziger, Assistant to the President for Political Affairs, suggested that if Reagan did not seize this opportunity he would be perceived as breaking a campaign promise very early in his term, which "will hurt your overall standing and your overall ability to get your legislative program through the Congress." Wendy Borcherdt, Associate Director of Presidential Personnel, reiterated that the "women's constituencies" were keenly aware that there were no women in Cabinet and very few senior women in the administration, which fed a general perception that Reagan and his advisors were "anti-women." Even the influential anti-feminist Phyllis Schlafly had commented negatively on the small number of women in the administration. Nominating a woman to the Supreme Court would thus "strengthen our base among women," an important task given the gender gap in Reagan's electoral appeal. While Reagan was not aiming to win the feminist vote, his advisors knew he needed to maintain and preferably expand his popularity among married female voters.[5] Reagan's advisors were thus tasked with finding an outstanding female candidate who had "demonstrable conservative political and judicial views." Crucially, despite Reagan's public reputation as a staunch social conservative, he did not want a "single-issue litmus test" on abortion or ERA to automatically exclude a candidate. This ran counter to the pro-life view that opposition to abortion was the bedrock upon which all other aspects of the "community of values" rested.[6]

Choosing a Nominee

As the White House worked on the list of nominees, O'Connor's name quickly emerged as the frontrunner. She was recommended by Senator Barry Goldwater (R-AZ) and by Associate Justice William Rehnquist. O'Connor thus had the imprimatur of the godfather of the post-WWII Right, as well as the backing of the most conservative member of the Supreme Court. O'Connor was a 51-year-old Arizonian, a longtime Republican with political and legal experience, having served as an Arizona state Senator, as Senate Majority Leader, and on the Arizona State Court of Appeals. On 1 July, O'Connor was flown to Washington. She was the only nominee who met directly with both Reagan and his top advisors and it was her amicable meeting with Reagan that "all but clinched her nomination." When asked about her stance on abortion, O'Connor replied that she was "personally opposed" to the procedure. After a one-hour interview, Reagan was confident she would make a worthy Supreme Court justice, and he officially announced his choice six days later.[7]

While media speculation raged about the nomination, numerous opponents of legal abortion contacted the White House. Several proposed Schlafly, while most simply reminded Reagan that he had made multiple guarantees about judicial nominations.[8] Nellie Gray of MfL requested assurance that any nominee would have a positive pro-life record. In a telegram, representatives from 25 anti-abortion, Religious Right, and New Right groups expressed their confidence that Reagan would propose an individual for the Supreme Court who respected family values and the sanctity of human life.[9] Pro-lifers were initially certain the President would fulfill his promises to them.

This equanimity was shattered when leaks to the media indicated O'Connor was a serious contender. Almost as soon as her name surfaced, right-to-lifers began contacting the President and his staff. The most notable correspondent was Dr. Jack Willke, the new head of the NRLC, who spent two weeks reaching out to the administration with one consistent message: O'Connor did not share Reagan's social values and would be "a prolife disaster." On 26 June, the NRLC delivered a list assessing an array of potential candidates and categorized O'Connor as "not acceptable." On 3 July, Willke informed the administration that nominating her "would produce a firestorm reaction across the nation." For Willke, the selection of such a candidate was tantamount to a negation of the Republican Party Platform and Reagan's own opposition to abortion. Willke's missives were met with silence. On 6 July, Willke telephoned the White House to inform them that the NRLC was about to issue a press release that might embarrass the President. He still believed the nomination could be averted if only Reagan were provided with sufficient proof of O'Connor's past. He begged to speak to or see Edwin Meese III, Counselor to the President, within the next 24 hours.[10]

Sandra Day O'Connor: Pro-abortion, Pro-ERA, Anti-family?

The opposition to O'Connor centered on her time in the Arizona Senate. There was a great deal of difficulty in tracking down the records for all the relevant bills and when questioned in early July, she could not remember how she voted on some crucial legislation.[11] Thus, pro-lifers relied heavily on old newspaper articles and recollections of Arizona pro-lifers, most notably Gerster, the outgoing president of the NRLC. Gerster argued that while in the Senate, O'Connor "was never supportive of efforts to restore legal protection to the unborn" and had cast votes that were either "pro-abortion" or had helped to kill measures that anti-abortionists supported. Most damningly, she was alleged to have voted in favor of a sweeping 1970 bill that supported the repeal of the existing Arizona statute banning abortion. Pro-lifers felt O'Connor had a clear track record of legislative support for legal abortion and reproductive rights.[12]

In addition to claims that O'Connor had been "pro-abortion" during her time as a legislator, she stood accused of supporting feminist causes. Much was made of the fact that she was involved with the Arizona delegation to the 1977 International Women's Year Conference (IWYC), keynoting a preliminary state meeting. For social conservatives, the IWYC was shorthand for all that was wrong with Democrat President Jimmy Carter and second-wave feminism in general.[13] Willke noted that the majority of states, including Arizona, sent delegations to the IWYC that were "composed almost exclusively of people who were pro-abortion, pro-ERA, and pro-lesbian." Similarly, Representative Mark Siljander (R-MI) warned Reagan that O'Connor had been active in "the liberal" IWYC. Implicit in Siljander's and Willke's language was the assumption that if O'Connor had supported an event known for its feminist, progressive goals, she automatically could not be the kind of nominee promised by the 1980 Republican Party Platform.[14]

Gerster also emphasized that O'Connor was an early supporter of the ERA. During the 1970s, conservatives such as Schlafly had successfully convinced many Americans that the ERA was radical legislation aimed at destroying traditional gender roles and the American family. This narrative had taken particular root within the Republican Party in the late 1970s and Reagan was a well-known critic of the ERA.[15] Opponents frequently treated the amendment and abortion rights as intertwined or, as one Schlafly flyer put it, "ERA: Another way of saying Easy Rights to Abortion!" This stemmed from a discourse that presented feminism as encouraging women to avoid the "natural" roles and responsibilities associated with their sex. A December 1974 issue of *The Phyllis Schlafly Report* explained:

> Women's libbers believe that the greatest 'inequality' between men and women is that women get pregnant and men do not. They want a constitutional amendment guaranteeing a strict and doctrinaire equality which will permanently protect them against anti-abortion laws.[16]

Pro-lifers were worried by the expansive language of the ERA and they shared Schlafly's concern that an activist court might "find" unexpected rights in the broad language of the amendment.

However, for most of the 1970s, mainstream right-to-life organizations, such as AUL, ACCL, and the NRLC repeatedly resisted efforts to embed abortion in a broader agenda. Moderate pro-lifers tried to differentiate themselves from Schlafly and the Religious Right on the ERA. Before 1977, the NRLC explicitly rejected proposals to stand against the amendment. After 1977, the NRLC voted to oppose the ERA until its impact on "the rights of unborn children" was clarified. However, this position was not explained through anti-feminist or pro-family appeals. Rather, they sought "abortion neutralization" language that would let them "forget about the ERA and redirect their full energies to more affirmative goals."[17] While they agreed with social conservatives about the horror of abortion, movement leaders, such as Gerster and Willke routinely delineated between their cause and the coalition that made up the pro-family movement. Anti-abortionists wished to protect their hard-fought political territory, but there was also suspicion about the priorities of their allies. It is thus striking that in their campaign against O'Connor, pro-lifers deployed issues such as the IWYC and the ERA to discredit the nominee, representing a moment of common purpose. Gerster and Willke were presenting O'Connor as profoundly unsuitable, as both anti-life and anti-family values. Perhaps they already sensed that, on its own, abortion would not persuade the administration to act. Although they still did not conflate the pro-family, anti-feminist, and anti-abortion causes, they were attempting coalition building, trying to control and shape the political uses of *their* issue.

Certainly, the NRLC's initial claims about O'Connor, the IWYC, and the ERA were quickly taken up by others. The Council for National Policy (CNP), a Religious Right and New Right policy think tank, claimed O'Connor had been the main sponsor of the amendment in Arizona. Similarly, a telegram from MM informed Reagan that they found it "incredible that the White House would nominate a person who was pro-abortion before 'Roe versus Wade' and who spoke at the I.W.Y. Rally in Phoenix on behalf of ERA and abortion." Representative Henry Hyde (R-IL) and Senator Don Nickles (R-OK) both called the White House to protest the nomination of O'Connor, claiming that not only was she upsetting to pro-lifers, she had favored the ERA.[18] This trifecta of accusations about abortion, the IWYC, and the ERA was read as inextricable proof of O'Connor's hostility to "traditional values."

As rumors spread that O'Connor was the frontrunner, Reagan's advisors received thousands of letters and telegrams opposing her, including from anti-abortion Congressmen, such as Nickles, Hyde, Siljander, Senator Jesse Helms (R-NC), and Senator Steven Symms (R-ID). Leading right-to-life Protestant theologian Dr. Harold O.J. Brown of CAC telephoned to warn that the nomination of O'Connor would profoundly damage evangelicals' "trust in the President." Cardinal John Krol of Philadelphia, a prominent member of the US Catholic hierarchy, forwarded Attorney General William French Smith negative information on O'Connor's abortion record. Jim McFadden of AHCDL, publisher of *Lifeletter*, which was very influential in DC circles, informed Special Assistant to the President Michael Uhlmann that the nomination would confirm the "worst suspicions" of pro-life activists.[19] The passionate right-to-life reaction to this Supreme Court vacancy reveals that by 1981, the judicial strategy was an emotive and broadly held movement goal. Well before the official announcement, opponents of abortion were united in their message to the White House.

After the meeting between Reagan and O'Connor on 1 July, there was no question she was the choice. Reagan felt the criticisms of O'Connor were a "matter of interpretation, that it wasn't enough to be a red flag … [and] that she was going to pass the test of time." Thus, the administration focused on managing the announcement rather than addressing pro-life and pro-family concerns. On 6 July, White House Counsel Fred Fielding advised James Baker III, Reagan's Chief of Staff, that the initial leaks had "probably surfaced all potential problems (pro-lifers, etc.)." Fielding pushed to make the announcement quickly, noting that "if confirmation [is] held over, opponents can muster forces." In other memos, White House staff reiterated to Meese that they were receiving many distressed calls from pro-life citizens and leaders. Uhlmann warned that the White House was about to face "a nasty political protest" and reminded Meese that whatever one might think of their ideas, "the intensity of right-to-lifers on the issue of judicial power should not be underestimated."[20] Reagan's most senior advisers were repeatedly warned that opponents of abortion found O'Connor completely unacceptable.

Divisions Among Conservatives

Pro-lifers and social conservatives viewed the selection of O'Connor as an explicit rejection of their political value and of the issues that had helped mobilize them as new constituencies for the Republicans. However, most did not blame Reagan. Rather, they attributed the nomination to the dismissive attitude of the White House toward anti-abortion, Religious Right, and New Right leaders. Howard Phillips, a

New Right luminary, explained to *Time* magazine, "We've been challenged. The White House has said we're a paper tiger. They've left us no choice but to fight." Richard Viguerie, another prominent New Right figure, informed the *Washington Post*, "The White House slapped us in the face. The White House is saying you don't have a constituency we're concerned about." Judie Brown told ALL members that the President and his aides "must be told straight out that we cannot be taken for granted." Gray warned Reagan, "pro-lifers find it offensive that we must picket the White House to bring your attention to this matter." The entire August edition of *Conservative Digest* was devoted to the O'Connor nomination.[21]

If national figures felt they were not being taken seriously, grassroots activists felt personally betrayed. Some wrote to the President directly. Most repeated the trio of criticisms first proffered by Willke and Gerster—that O'Connor was anti-family, pro-abortion, and pro-ERA—and then went on to condemn Reagan and the political status quo. Adelaide Kowansky warned that "the United States is becoming a Sodom and Gomorrah world and since your election, Mr. President, even faster and faster." She ended by declaring, "Personally, I am sorry each day I voted for you." Anne Culhane, a longtime Reagan supporter, saw the nomination as proof positive that "THERE IS NO DIFFERENCE between the two major political parties in this country." In a letter that prompted a personal response from the President, Marie Craven, a former Democrat who worked in the 1980 election for Reagan, told him that he had "betrayed pro-life" and "the power of your office has taken precidence [*sic*] over your party platform and your campaign promises."[22]

From the moment O'Connor was announced, abortion dominated the news coverage. The mainstream media regularly ran quotes from anti-abortion and socially conservative leaders attacking the decision. Paul Brown of LAPAC announced that right-to-life forces felt "betrayed," noting "we took the G.O.P. platform to be the Bible." Gerster reiterated that O'Connor was "unqualified because she's pro-abortion [*sic*]. We're going to fight this one on the beaches." Peter Gemma of NPLPAC declared the nomination an insult. Schlafly noted acerbically, "some of the people who are praising President Reagan's appointment of this judge are people who would never vote for him ... [and] who are not his friends." In his diary, the President tersely commented, "Already the flack is starting and from my own supporters.

Rite [sic] to life people say she's pro-abortion. She declares abortion is personally repugnant to her. I think she'll make a good Justice."[23]

The O'Connor nomination fed into a breach within the Right, illustrating the divergence between traditional conservatives and the new breed of social and religious conservatives. While the New Right, the Religious Right, and the pro-life movement railed against O'Connor, Goldwater was one of her earliest and most vigorous supporters. His 1964 bid for the presidency was a formative moment in modern Republican history. Although Goldwater was roundly defeated by Democrat Lyndon Johnson, his candidacy helped inspire the next generation of conservatives and strengthened their commitment to capturing the party from moderate and liberal Republicans.[24] While Goldwater was a staunch anti-communist, a fierce opponent of big government, and a critic of the liberal consensus, he was openly contemptuous of the new allies who had helped deliver the White House to Reagan. In 1973, he praised the Supreme Court's decision in *Roe*, and when O'Connor was attacked he sprang to her defense, describing abortion as "the biggest humbug issue" and insisting, "Abortion is not a conservative issue. ERA is not a conservative issue." When the press reported that MM's Reverend Jerry Falwell had suggested "every good Christian ought to express concern over O'Connor's nomination," Goldwater responded tersely that "every good Christian ought to kick Falwell right in the ass." For these comments, he was criticized by former allies, dismissed as having "all but tuned out of relevant conservative politics for many years now." Republicans with impeccable conservative credentials were deemed out of touch if they did not prioritize the social issues that dominated the New Right's agenda. As MM smugly put it, "time has passed him."[25]

Although pro-lifers, the New Right, and the Religious Right wielded power when it came to the new party line, they were not as successful when it came to shaping domestic policy or influencing Reagan's agenda. O'Connor was clearly the problem, but so too was the way the White House selected her. Even before Reagan won the election, New Right leaders worried about the level of influence that moderates wielded in his administration. First Reagan selected George H.W. Bush as his running mate. Then he appointed Baker, Bush's campaign manager, as Chief of Staff. Baker was a Washington insider and offered plum jobs to people Nofziger later bitterly described as "liberal, moderate, and non-Reaganite cronies."[26] The New Right spent the first months of Reagan's presidency engaged in pitched battles over appointments and White House priorities. They believed important information about O'Connor's record was deliberately kept from the President, and that conservatives in the White House were explicitly shut out of the decision-making process. *Lifeletter* mused that while Reagan had no "desire to alienate his 'social conservative' supporters...maybe his 'Moderate Mafia' did."[27]

Opponents of abortion had less reason for concern in the first months of Reagan's presidency, but they also had naive expectations. In his 3 July letter, Willke asked that he or another member of the NRLC be allowed a top-secret review of all names being considered before the administration reached its final stages of deliberation, chiding that "such an almost catastrophe as this could easily have been prevented." On 6 July, Gerster telegrammed the White House requesting the administration hold off on making any decisions until a package of information about O'Connor arrived. After the nomination became public, social conservatives such as evangelical preacher James Robison expected personal accountability from Reagan.[28]

For their part, Reagan and his aides did a poor job of assuaging fears. In a question and answer session with the press, the administration provided brief summaries of O'Connor's history on various controversial issues and spent time rebutting some of the claims about abortion and the ERA.[29] However, this information was based upon a contested Justice Department memorandum composed by Kenneth Starr, which anti-abortionists believed was a deliberate misrepresentation of O'Connor's past. In particular, the White House completely ignored the major charge that she had voted in 1970 to repeal Arizona's abortion law. When Starr asked O'Connor about the bill, she had "no recollection" of how she voted. Starr did not investigate the matter further.[30]

In addition to defending the flawed Starr memorandum, the White House also reached out to select critics, with mixed results. Intriguingly, pro-family, Religious Right, and New Right figures, such as Schlafly, Falwell, Viguerie, Phillips, Paul Weyrich, and Terry Dolan merited confidential personal phone calls, but anti-abortion leaders, such as Willke, Gerster, and Gray did not. Only Gemma of NPLPAC warranted a call, and in the initiating White House memo his name was misspelt. Similarly, the President dictated a personal letter to Marie Craven, the grassroots activist who had accused him of betraying the right-to-life movement. He attributed all criticism of O'Connor to one Arizona right-to-life leader who had "a record of being vindictive." This portion of the letter was quoted in Patrick Buchanan's nationally syndicated newspaper column, and it angered many anti-abortion activists because it seemed to be a thinly veiled and unprovoked attack on Gerster and a direct repudiation of her assistance and support while she was president of NRLC. Shocked, Gerster wrote to Reagan, declaring "I do not believe that you wrote the letter to Mrs. Craven, but if so, it was because you were given seriously misleading information." She requested a meeting with the President, but the White House refused, perhaps because Reagan's diary reveals he did believe that the entire "bonfire among the Right to Life people" was started by "a woman—Dr. Gersten [*sic*] in Phoenix." The White House's desultory efforts to pacify pro-lifers are best explained by an aide's prediction to the *New York Times* that despite the "sound and fury ... it will wind up signifying little or nothing when it's all over." [31]

At the heart of the White House response was an assumption that the personal assurances of the President should be enough. The administration did not engage with criticisms of the Starr memorandum or other elements of right-to-life opposition, instead emphasizing that Reagan was "completely satisfied" with O'Connor's position on abortion. In statements to the press, the White House argued that Reagan "was interested in the whole shape of her legal thought—not just a single issue." This did not quiet those who felt that the 1980 Republican Party Platform had clearly outlined issues on which a candidate should have a clear ideological and judicial position. The *NRL News* summed up anti-abortion sentiment by noting that even if O'Connor was opposed to abortion, only Reagan could know why "a prolife President would choose such [an] ambiguous, lukewarm prolifer as his first selection to the court."[32]

Opposing the Nomination

Once the announcement was made, anti-abortionists were faced with some hard truths as there was no serious expectation that Reagan would withdraw O'Connor's name. Furthermore, right-to-lifers and members of the New Right acknowledged that they had little to no chance of defeating O'Connor. After all, as *Lifeletter* put it, "who wants to be the only guy to vote against the First Justiceperson?" However, this did not stop most leaders from working against O'Connor. They wanted to keep the issue in the public eye. As Gemma of NPLPAC explained, displaying their displeasure would send the message to the President that "his next court appointment had better be pro-life." Protest and activism were also aimed at an audience well beyond Washington, DC Challenging the O'Connor nomination until the bitter end helped to demonstrate to the grassroots that movement leaders were resisting cooption into the game-playing of Capitol Hill. Thus, the anti-O'Connor movement held rallies, campaigned and picketed, condemned her in their own publications, and spoke to the mainstream media. They also produced newsletters and guides instructing the grassroots on where and how to protest her selection, and New Right financier Viguerie produced several issues of a special bulletin called *The O'Connor Report*.[33]

Despite the anti-feminist and pro-family criticisms of O'Connor, abortion remained the core point of controversy throughout August and September. By and large, the broader social conservative and Religious Right movements were not part of that conversation. Schlafly did not play any notable role in the public protests or in lobbying the White House. Her criticisms remained relatively limited and were restricted to ERA-related matters. Indeed, Schlafly chided the New Right for its criticism of Reagan, believing that conservatives "had to maintain a united front if there was to be any hope for progress." She opposed abortion but remained aloof from right-to-life politics, rarely working with existing anti-abortion organizations and leaders. She generally stayed out of debates over the Human Life Amendment. Falwell, who was very confrontational at the start of the nomination process, "fell into line" after a call from the President, and thereafter refused to take a stand. Indeed in September 1981, as the Senate held nomination hearings for O'Connor, he told reporters that Reagan was "the greatest President we've had in my lifetime and history may say the greatest President ever." Falwell and Schlafly both had broad legislative agendas and presumably did not wish to sacrifice influence for an obviously lost cause. At a White House briefing for pro-family groups in October, both EF and MM assured the White House that the *Family Protection Act* was "their principal affirmative legislative program in this Congress" and promised that if the White House supported it they would reinvigorate the grassroots for the 1982 midterms. No anti-abortion leaders attended the meeting.[34]

Of the original coalition that spoke out against O'Connor, only anti-abortion organizations saw the fight through to its conclusion. To involve the grassroots, the NRLC asked activists nationwide to send letters and telegrams to the White House and Senate on 4 September so that a deluge of anti-O'Connor mail would arrive as the Senate hearings began. Prominent right-to-life leaders also went to Washington, DC, despite acknowledging that confirmation was a *fait accompli*. Gray organized anti-abortion pickets of the Senate and the White House during the hearings. At the end of the second day she complained to the press that O'Connor might have "fine lady manners and temperament," but when pushed by Senators on "her view of the paramount right to life ... She won't answer." Gerster and Willke testified before the Senate Judiciary Committee on behalf of the NRLC. Gerster summarized O'Connor's time in the Arizona State Senate and repeated the public and private pledges made by Reagan and the Republicans during the 1980 campaign. Willke called on the Senate to view support for abortion as an inherently disqualifying position for a Supreme Court nominee because, like slavery, it attacked a "fundamental right." Gerster and Willke saw themselves as bearing witness, and reassured the grassroots that "whatever else happened, the confirmation hearings gave [them] a national forum for two hours to champion the rights of the unborn." They also hoped to establish a precedent whereby a nominee's position on abortion would automatically be treated as a serious issue in future Supreme Court vacancies.[35]

THE SENATE VOTES

During the Senate nomination hearings, O'Connor confirmed that pro-lifers had been correct about much of her Arizona legislative history, including the fact she had voted for repeal in 1970. She tempered her past actions by stressing that in the intervening decade, her "knowledge and awareness" of abortion issues had increased. She emphasized that she personally found abortion repugnant. However, during the two and half days of questioning, she accepted the constitutional notion of a right to privacy, refused to indicate her position on *Roe* or how she might rule on abortion, and made it clear that her personal views would not enter into her judicial rulings. In the opinion of *NRL News*, O'Connor's testimony did little "to dispel prolife fears that ... she is favorably disposed towards legal abortion."[36]

Sandra Day O'Connor was approved 17–0 by the Senate Judiciary Committee and 99–0 by the Senate. Well before the September votes, it was clear that anti-abortion Senators would not pose a problem.

In early July, Hyde cautioned Reagan against picking O'Connor, but by the middle of the month, he told the Justice Department that the protests against O'Connor were damaging to right-to-life groups. Hyde even agreed to work for the nomination by calling on "the eight 'problem' Senators with the following line: Mrs. O'Connor is going on the Court, she cannot be defeated, so why make an enemy." Reagan also provided "cover" for those Republicans who felt the need to defend their actions to anti-abortionists, reaching out to undecided Senators to assure them that a vote for O'Connor would not "in any way be inconsistent with the [anti-abortion] commitments both of us made during our successful campaigns in 1980."[37]

These efforts were effective. Although several anti-abortion Senators were frustrated by O'Connor's vague responses during the Senate Judiciary Committee hearings, no one voted against her and only Senator Jeremiah Denton (R-AL) abstained. Several Senators associated with the New Right felt compelled to issue statements justifying their votes, and they linked their decision to their "faith in the President." Senator Charles Grassley (R-IA) noted that, after speaking to Reagan, he was confident "in his own mind that the President feels as I do on the subject of abortion." He hoped this would "satisfy some doubts [that] the leaders of the prolife forces in this country may have that the President is not honoring statements he made in the election." Senator John East (R-NC) explained that he knew in his "heart of hearts" O'Connor must disagree with *Roe* "because she is the nominee of Ronald Reagan."[38] Right-to-life Senators fell into line behind the President.

Pro-life views on O'Connor underwent a dramatic shift after the 1983 case of *City of Akron v. Akron Reproductive Health, Inc.* O'Connor wrote the dissenting opinion and claimed the trimester framework established in *Roe* was on a "collision course with itself."[39] Pro-lifers rejoiced, with Doug Badger of CAC interpreting the decision as a call to reverse *Roe* and a major blow to second-wave feminists and reproductive rights supporters who assumed O'Connor was on their side.[40] *Lifeletter* commented approvingly on her "strongly worded dissent" and captioned a photograph of O'Connor "Best Man on the Court?" Pro-lifers were further heartened by her vote and dissenting opinion in *Thornburgh v. American College of Obstetricians and Gynecologists* (1986). O'Connor seemed to be a clear anti-*Roe* vote. Over the course of Reagan's presidency, the judicial strategy became paramount for right-to-lifers, the sole path to ending legal abortion. Thus the protests and disappointments of 1981 were erased. In the NRLC's 1988 overview of "the Reagan legacy," the nomination of O'Connor was listed as the first "landmark pro-life accomplishment" of his administration. However, she ultimately proved that right-to-life fears had merit. Twice her vote was a decisive factor in upholding *Roe*.[41]

INSIGHTS

The right-to-life reaction to the O'Connor nomination offers telling insights into the inherent instability of the relationship between opponents of abortion, President Reagan, and the Republican Party. During the nomination process, a core problem was that there was no definitive record of O'Connor's past votes. Thus, the struggle over the nomination became, in part, a struggle over trust and confidence. The White House repeatedly told opponents of abortion to put aside their concerns and trust Reagan's judgment—an approach that persuaded right-to-life Senators. One reading is that pro-life politicians genuinely believed in Reagan's commitment to the cause. A more pragmatic interpretation is that these positive votes were the product of a simple calculation that voting against O'Connor was a waste of political capital and might put them at odds with their fellow Republicans. As *Lifeletter* put it, "the anguished howls sent up [by anti-abortionists] over the President's 'breaking faith' reminded every-one that their greatest strength—passionate dedication—can be a weakness: they want to treat abortion as a purely moral issue, whereas to win they must keep it a political one."[42]

For anti-abortion activists, Reagan's selection of O'Connor and the White House's dismissive reaction to their concerns were distressing examples of politics in action. Abortion seemed to be no more important than Reagan's need to satisfy the moderate wing of the Republican Party or, confusingly, to appease women's groups. In a scathing article subtitled "Reagan Goofs," NPLPAC summed up the sentiments of many anti-abortionists, declaring that since the election, "pro-life considerations seem to have become afterthoughts to other, more orthodox, political soundings."[43] The behavior of Republicans in the Senate also indicated that anti-abortion influence was relatively shallow.

The reality of federal politics—the compromises, shaky coalitions, and competing demands—was a dramatic anti-climax after the heady days of the 1980 presidential campaign. The tensions and fissures over

O'Connor, which appeared less than six months into Reagan's presidency, exposed the complicated nature of the alliance that elected him. Unfortunately for pro-lifers, this was but a foretaste of a period of intense disillusionment and bitterness. If pro-lifers focused their ire on an external target during their campaign against O'Connor, when confronted with how best to use Congress to end legal abortion, they turned their anger and frustration inward.

NOTES

1. "Transcript of Remarks by Reagan and Nominee to High Court," *New York Times*, 8 July 1981, A12; Ed Magnuson et al., "The Brethren's First Sister: Sandra Day O'Connor," *Time*, 20 July 1981.
2. For examples of this tendency, see Critchlow, "Mobilizing Women: The 'Social Issues,'" in *The Reagan Presidency*, 341–3; McKeegan, *Abortion Politics*, 132–3; Self, *All in the Family*, 376–7; and Ziegler, *After Roe*, 55–6.
3. Roger Mall, "The Hatch-Ashbrook Federalism Amendment," Box 1, Abortion (2), DJ; Ray White to NRLC Board of Directors, 13 November 1975, Box 10, NRLC Board of Directors 1975 (5), ACCL; Linda Greenhouse, "Justice John Paul Stevens as Abortion-Rights Strategist," *U.C. Davis Law Review*, Volume 43, Number 3 (2010): 751.
4. "Is Reagan Scuttling Pro-lifers?"; "Republican Party Platform of 1980"; "Statement by Governor Ronald Reagan," 14 October 1980, Box 18, Supreme Court Nomination (1), Fred Fielding Files (hereafter FF), Ronald Reagan Presidential Library.
5. Henry Abraham, *Justices, Presidents, and Senators: A History of U.S. Supreme Court Appointments from Washington to Bush II*, Fifth edition (Lanham: Rowman and Littlefield, 2008), 266; Lyn Nofizger to Ronald Reagan, 22 June 1981, FG 051, #019695, WHORM; Lynn Schafran, "Reagan vs. Women," *New York Times*, 13 October 1981; Wendy Borcherdt to Fred Fielding, 26 June 1981, Box 18, Supreme Court Nominations (5), FF; Critchlow, "Mobilizing Women," 293–4.
6. Abraham, *Justices, Presidents, and Senators*, 268; Magnuson et al., "The Brethren's First Sister," 5.
7. Barry Goldwater and John Rhodes to Ronald Reagan, 23 June 1981, FG 051, #029858, WHORM; Abraham, *Justices, Senators, and Presidents*, 266–8; Mark Tushnet, *A Court Divided: The Rehnquist Court and the Future of Constitutional Law* (New York: W. W. Norton and Company, 2005), 52.

8. Norma Russell to Ronald Reagan, 30 June 1981, FG 051, #030586, WHORM; Eva Scott to Ronald Reagan, 25 June 1981, FG 051, #030235, WHORM.
9. Nellie Gray to Ronald Reagan, 25 June 1981, FG 051, #030119, WHORM; Telegram to Ronald Reagan, 2 July 1981, Box 21, Supreme Court (2), FF. The telegram was a veritable "who's who" of conservative pro-life, New Right, and Religious Right organizations, but older national groups such as NRLC, MfL, AUL, and ACCL were not signatories.
10. Jack Willke to Ronald Reagan, 1 July 1981, FG 051, #019837, WHORM; Jack Willke to Ronald Reagan, 3 July 1981, Box 18, Supreme Court (4), FF; Marilee Melvin to Edwin Meese, 6 July 1981, Box 3, Appointments—Supreme Court—O'Connor, (2), Edwin Meese Files (hereafter EM), Ronald Reagan Presidential Library.
11. She was accused of casting between four and eight "pro-abortion" votes, of supporting population control, of supporting the ability of minors to access contraceptives and surgical family planning procedures without parental consent, and supporting taxpayer funding of abortion.
12. Carolyn Gerster to Ronald Reagan, received 6 July 1981, Box 18, Supreme Court (5), FF; Jack Willke to Ronald Reagan, 1 July 1981, FG 051, #019837, WHORM; Jack Willke to Ronald Reagan, 3 July 1981, Box 18, Supreme Court (4), FF.
13. For the role of the IWYC in the emergence of family values politics, see Marjorie Spruill, *Divided We Stand: The Battle Over Women's Rights and Family Values That Polarized American Politics* (New York: Bloomsbury, 2017).
14. Jack Willke to Ronald Reagan, 1 July 1981, FG 051, #019837, WHORM; Representative Mark Siljander to Ronald Reagan, 2 July 1981, FG 051, #030839, WHORM.
15. For more on the movement to stop the ERA, see Donald Critchlow, *Phyllis Schlafly and Grassroots Conservatism: A Woman's Crusade* (Princeton: Princeton University Press, 2005); Donald G. Matthews and Jane Sherron De Hart, *Sex, Gender and the Politics of ERA: A State and the Nation* (New York: Oxford University Press, 1990); Taranto, *Kitchen Table Politics*; and Young, *We Gather Together*.
16. "ERA: Another Way of Saying Easy Rights to Abortion!" flyer, Box 5, Folder 9, Phyllis Schlafly, PM; "E.R.A.'s Assist to Abortion," *The Phyllis Schlafly Report*, Volume 8, Number 5, December 1974, 3, Box 25, Phyllis Schlafly Folder, ACCL.
17. Ziegler, *After Roe*, 201; Douglas Johnson, 'Aborting the E.R.A.,' *American Politics*, May 1987, Box 144, Folder 11, National Right to Life Committee 1982–1991, CLC.

18. Louis (Woody) Jenkins to Board of Governors of Council for National Policy, 8 July 1981, Box 148, Council for National Policy—Correspondence and Memoranda, 1981, William A. Rusher Papers (hereafter WAR), Library of Congress; Moral Majority to Edwin Meese, 2 July 1981, FG 051, #032502, WHORM; Max Friedersdorf to Jim Baker, Ed Meese, Mike Deaver, Fred Fielding, and Pen James, 6 July 1981, Box 3, Appointments—Supreme Court—O'Connor (2), EM.
19. Max Friedersdorf to Edwin Meese, 6 July 1981, Box 3, Appointments—Supreme Court—O'Connor (2), EM; Mark Siljander to Ronald Reagan, 2 July 1981, FG 051, #030839, WHORM; Marilee Melvin to Ed Thomas, 6 July 1981, and Thomas Kelly to Myra Tankersley, 6 July 1981, both in Box 3, Appointments—Supreme Court—O'Connor (2), EM; Michael Uhlmann to Edwin Meese, 6 July 1981, Box 3, Appointments—Supreme Court—O'Connor (1), EM.
20. Martin, *With God on Our Side*, 228; Fred Fielding to James A. Baker III, 6 July 1981, Box 18, Supreme Court Nomination (1), FF; Marilee Melvin to Ed Meese, 6 July 1981, Box 3, Appointments—Supreme Court—O'Connor (2), EM; Michael Uhlmann to Edwin Meese, 6 July 1981, Box 3, Appointments—Supreme Court—O'Connor (1), EM.
21. Magnuson et al., "The Brethren's First Sister," 3; Bill Peterson, "For Reagan and the New Right, the Honeymoon is Over," *Washington Post*, 21 July 1981; Judie Brown to Dear Friend, BMS 479/1, Folder 3, GHW; "Conservatives Criticize Choice," *Conservative Digest*, August 1981, 9, BMS 479/1, Folder 4, GHW.
22. Adelaide Kowansky to Ronald Reagan, 4 August 1981, Box 1, Sandra Day O'Connor (2), Mary Quint Files (hereafter MQ), Ronald Reagan Presidential Library; Anne Culhane to Ronald Reagan, 8 July 1981, Box 1, Sandra Day O'Connor (1), MQ (emphasis in original); Marie Craven to Ronald Reagan, 7 July 1981, Box 18, Supreme Court (2), FF.
23. "Transcript of Remarks by Reagan and Nominee to High Court," *New York Times*, 8 July 1981; Francis Clines, "Baker Vows Support for Nominee," *New York Times*, 8 July 1981; Magnuson et al., "The Brethren's First Sister," 3; Schlafly quote in Gregory Schneider, "Conservatives and the Reagan Presidency," in *Reassessing the Reagan Presidency*, 74; Ronald Reagan, "6 July 1981," in *The Reagan Diaries*, 28.
24. For discussion of Goldwater's significance in post-WWII conservatism, see Mary Brennan, "Winning the War/Losing the Battle: The Goldwater Presidential Campaign and Its Effects on the Evolution of Modern Conservatism," in David Farber and Jeff Roche (eds.), *The Conservative Sixties* (New York: Peter Lang, 2003), 63–78.

25. Abraham, *Justices, Senators, and Presidents*, 267; Magnuson et al., "The Brethren's First Sister"; "High Court Nominee Disturbs Conservatives," *Human Events*, 18 July 1981, Box 148, Council for National Policy—Correspondence and Memoranda, 1981, WAR; "Goldwater: Time Has Passed Him," *Moral Majority Report*, 21 September 1981, 6.
26. Nofziger quoted in Christopher Maynard, "The Troika: James Baker III, Edwin Meese III, and Michael Deaver," in Andrew Johns (ed.), *A Companion to Ronald Reagan* (Malden: Wiley-Blackwell, 2015), 533.
27. "Interviews with Meese, Others Make Clear President Uninformed on O'Connor Record," and Rowland Evans and Robert Novak, "Conservatives in White House Were Shut Out on O'Connor," *Conservative Digest*, August 1981, 18, 19, 23, BMS 479/1, Folder 4, GHW; *Lifeletter*, Number 11, 12 August 1981, 2, Box 1, Abortion—General (1), Papers of Stephen Galebach (hereafter SG), Ronald Reagan Presidential Library (emphasis in original).
28. Jack Willke to Ronald Reagan, 3 July 1981, Box 18, Supreme Court (4), FF; Peterson, "For Reagan and the New Right, the Honeymoon is Over"; Ed Thomas to Edwin Meese, 27 July 1981, Box 3, Appointments—Supreme Court—O'Connor (1), EM.
29. The White House addressed three bills: SB 1190, a 1973 family planning bill that would have provided family planning information to minors; HCM 2002, a 1974 resolution calling on Congress to amend the constitution to outlaw abortion; and SB 1245, a 1974 amendment to an appropriations bill that banned the University of Arizona hospital from performing abortions. According to the White House, SB 1245 was the only bill on which O'Connor voted, and her negative vote was because she believed the amendment violated the state constitution. On the ERA, the White House argued that in 1974, O'Connor had "supported a conservative alternative to ERA." "Official Statement on Sandra D. O'Connor," Box 18, Supreme Court Nomination (5), FF.
30. Kenneth Starr to Attorney General, 7 July 1981, Box 1, Sandra Day O'Connor (5), MQ; "The Kenneth Starr Memorandum—And the Important Data It Omitted," *Conservative Digest*, August 1981, 12–13, BMS 479/1, Folder 4, GHW.
31. Elizabeth Dole to James Baker, 7 July 1981, Box 3, Appointments—Supreme Court—O'Connor (1), EM; Reagan to Marie Craven, 3 August 1981, Box 8 [Pro-Life/Continued-#2] (1), Morton Blackwell Files (hereafter MBL), Ronald Reagan Presidential Library; Carolyn Gerster to Ronald Reagan, 9 September 1981, Box 8 [Pro-Life/Continued-#2] (2), MBL; Critchlow, "Mobilizing Women," 308; Reagan, "7 July 1981," *The Reagan Diaries*, 28; Smith, "Reagan's Court Choice."

32. "Official Statement on Sandra D. O'Connor," Box 18, Supreme Court Nomination (5), FF; "Walking Softly," *NRL News*, 28 September 1981, 8.
33. *Lifeletter*, Number 11, 1981, 2, Box 1, Abortion—General (1), SG (emphasis in original); Gemma quoted in Clines, "Baker Vows Support for Nominee"; *The O'Connor Report* undated, *The O'Connor Report* (August 1981), *The O'Connor Report* (September 1981), all in BMS 479/1, Folder 4, GHW.
34. Critchlow, *Phyllis Schlafly and Grassroots Conservatism*, 282; Heineman, *God is a Conservative*, 131; Williams, *God's Own Party*, 195–6; Elizabeth Dole to Ronald Reagan, 19 October 1981, Box 2, Women appointees/Issues (2), DJ.
35. *The O'Connor Report* (undated), BMS 479/1, Folder 4, GHW; Gray quoted in Ed Rogers, "Sandra Day O'Connor Today Finished Testifying at Her Confirmation," *United Press International*, 11 September 1981; Jack Willke, "So Now What?" and "Chronology of a Confirmation," *NRL News*, 28 September 1981, 1, 10.
36. Willke, "Chronology of a Confirmation," 1.
37. Max Friedersdorf to Ronald Reagan, 18 July 1981, FG 051, #019961, WHORM; Reagan quoted in Sheldon Goldman, *Picking Federal Judges: Lower Court Selection from Roosevelt Through Reagan* (New Haven: Yale University Press, 1997), 316.
38. Willke, "Chronology of a Confirmation," 11; Fred Barbash, "O'Connor Approved by Senate Committee," *Washington Post*, 16 September 1981.
39. *City of Akron v. Akron Center for Reproductive Health*, 462 US 416 (1983).
40. Abraham, *Justices and Presidents*, 346; Martin Mawyer, "Pro-life Leaders Optimistic Despite Setbacks," *Moral Majority Report*, August 1983, 6; David O'Steen, "Facing the Challenge of 1988," 20 March 1988, Box 144, Folder 11, National Right to Life Committee—1982-1991, CLC.
41. James Clarity and Warren Weaver, "Briefing," *New York Times*, 14 July 1983.
42. *Lifeletter*, Number 11, 1981, 2, Box 1, Abortion—General (1), SG.
43. "O'Connor ... 'A Symbol for All Seasons?' Reagan Goofs," *Pro-Life Political Reporter*, August 1981, 3, Box 7, NPLPAC/POTUS—Pro-Life Coalition—Cabinet Room—23 January 1984 (2), MBL.

CHAPTER 4

"A Movement in Disarray": The Hatch/Helms Fight

Abstract In Reagan's first term, the triumph of the New Right and the new Republican majority in the Senate made it seem that the executive and legislative branches would provide fertile ground for the ultimate anti-abortion goal, a Human Life Amendment to the US Constitution. However, the pro-life movement was plunged into chaos in the early 1980s as two competing models emerged in the Senate. This chapter examines movement turmoil, charting the complicated religious, ideological, and strategic schisms which erupted and that were indicative of deeper divisions within the movement over the past and future of the cause. This struggle over the movement's constitutional strategy also revealed the divisions within the Republican Party over economic and social conservatism. Neither measure was successful, and the constitutional strategy effectively came to an end in 1983. These experiences forced anti-abortionists to confront the question of compromise and just what they could expect from their allies in Washington, DC.

Keywords Abortion politics · Social movements · Constitutional amendment · Legislation · Catholic Church · Republicans

---

Paul Brown quoted in Leslie Bennetts, "Antiabortion Forces in Disarray Less than a Year After Victories in Election," *New York Times*, 22 September 1981.

© The Author(s) 2019
P. Flowers, *The Right-to-Life Movement, the Reagan Administration, and the Politics of Abortion*, Palgrave Studies in the History of Social Movements, https://doi.org/10.1007/978-3-030-01707-1_4

On 22 September 1981, one day after Sandra Day O'Connor was unanimously confirmed to the Supreme Court, Paul Brown of LAPAC told the *New York Times*, "political reality has come home to the pro-life movement, and it has been totally unpleasant."[1] He was speaking not about O'Connor, but about the general divisions within the movement and between allies in Congress. Ronald Reagan's victory in 1980, combined with the triumphant self-aggrandizing of the New Right and the new Republican majority in the Senate, made the legislative branch appear like fertile ground for an anti-abortion amendment to the US Constitution. In 1981, the 97th Congress was presented with multiple models for how to outlaw abortion. By the end of the year, two key pieces of legislation divided the movement: the Human Life Bill and the Human Life Federalism Amendment.

The push in the early 1980s to use the legislative branch to end abortion has attracted specialist scholarly interest, although it often serves to illustrate a broader story. Older work by political scientists, such as Edward Keynes, Randall Miller, Barbara Craig, and David O'Brien, used it to explore the dynamics between the branches of government.[2] Recently, Mary Ziegler framed the fight as part of the ongoing tactical struggle between pro-life incrementalists and absolutists. Neil Young presented it in the context of clashes between Catholics, the New Right, and the Religious Right. Young and Ziegler agree that the divisions among pro-lifers "doomed both bills." In examining the conflict as a distinct case study, I find that the splits in the movement were not along simple religious, ideological, or strategic lines, nor did they remain fixed. Although it was a competition over movement authority, some leading factions were willing to compromise, and actions by the Reagan administration were what helped prolong the turmoil. I also disagree that pro-life conflict caused both measures to fail, suggesting instead that dynamics among Republicans doomed them from the outset.

A Congressionally mandated end to abortion was a rare goal that, at least in the abstract, united the whole movement. Neither of the 1981 measures reflected the standard model that pro-lifers endorsed, yet an acrimonious war of words broke out. Right-to-lifers grappled with questions of compromise, pragmatism, and expediency, and the place of institutional religious bodies in the abortion struggle. They struggled to make sense of the silence from the White House and the significant gap between their goals and Republican priorities. For most of Reagan's first two years in office, the defining features of the national right-to-life movement were the tension, enmity, and ill will among allies. This conflict tells us a great deal about the struggle within social movements when competing claims emerge over who has the right to speak and strategize on behalf of the cause.

ABORTION AND THE LEGISLATIVE BRANCH

From 1973, right-to-lifers wanted to end legal abortion. There were two ways to achieve this: a contrary Supreme Court decision or a constitutional amendment. Most in the movement saw an amendment as the faster and more direct path to protecting fetal life. Almost as soon as *Roe* was handed down, the NRLC declared that its first priority was developing a "political campaign" for passage of a constitutional amendment. In the 1970s, the two core approaches were "states' rights amendments" and "personhood amendments."

A states' rights amendment returned the issue of abortion to the state legislatures. It said nothing about the fetus as a constitutional subject, in effect viewing *Roe* as a problem because the courts had circumvented the democratic process. This approach was popular among politicians and, in the 1976 election, Republican President Gerald Ford attempted to court the anti-abortion vote by endorsing a states' rights amendment. It was an unsuccessful strategy because, as Frances Frech of USCL explained, "most pro-lifers won't accept it; pro-abortionists don't want it, either." Right-to-lifers believed that with such an amendment, abortion would still be available, dependent on geography and income. Furthermore, there was nothing to stop the issue being revisited when partisan interest or popular will demanded it. It provided no meaningful protection for fetal life and misunderstood the ethical arguments made by the movement. As Frech asked, "What if the majority of the people voted to let the innocent be killed (and many times in the history of the world they have done so)—would that make it right?"[3]

Most anti-abortionists preferred the personhood amendment. The amendment repeatedly introduced by Senator James Buckley (C-NY) exemplified the basic goals of the movement, declaring simply that the term person applied "to all human beings, including their unborn offspring at every stage of their biological development, irrespective of age, health, function, or condition of dependency." Another common approach was to declare that fetuses were to be considered "persons" under the existing language of the US Constitution and were thus afforded protection through the 14th Amendment.[4]

Although the movement embraced the personhood amendment, this approach had problems of its own. Political allies insisted that right-to-life amendments needed to include "exceptions"—instances where abortion would be permitted. Even before reform of state abortion laws began in the mid-1960s, therapeutic abortions were allowed in cases where the life of the mother was at stake. Some Protestant pro-lifers accepted that rape, incest, maternal health, or fetal defect also warranted access to legal abortion. This was not the attitude of absolutists (many of whom were Catholic), who believed abortion was never acceptable. Similarly, there was no consensus about whether life began at the moment of fertilization or implantation, which had consequences for the oral contraceptive pill and the intrauterine device.[5] Despite anti-abortion agreement that a constitutional amendment was urgently needed, there was no uniformly accepted model. At the start of Reagan's presidency, rival pro-life meetings were held by the NRLC and ALL that endorsed competing language for a personhood amendment—one that included an exception for the life of the mother and one that did not.[6]

In the 1970s and early 1980s, the pursuit of an anti-abortion amendment operated in the shadow of the ERA, which functioned as both inspiration and cautionary tale. The ERA, first proposed in the aftermath of female enfranchisement, was introduced in every congressional session between 1921 and 1972. After sustained lobbying by second-wave feminists, it finally received the requisite two-thirds majority in both houses of Congress and was sent on to the states. The ERA had a seven-year deadline to be ratified by three-quarters of the states. Initially, it experienced dizzying success, approved by 33 state legislatures in two years. It was tantalizingly close to being added to the constitution, until the intervention of Phyllis Schlafly and her grassroots campaign to STOP-ERA. Schlafly's success at the state level demonstrated the power of family values politics and suggested that some states would be politically receptive to a right-to-life amendment, but she also proved that a small, organized contingent could derail a large and sophisticated ratification campaign.

The Senate held intermittent hearings on anti-abortion amendments in 1974 and 1975, and the House held hearings in 1976. No concrete gains were made, but this did not reduce right-to-life enthusiasm for amending the constitution. Between 1973 and 1980, Human Life Amendments were introduced in Congress through 266 independent proposals. None went beyond subcommittee review.[7] While right-to-life efforts to ban abortion via the legislative branch stalled, several anti-abortion measures were enacted via amendments to other bills. The Church Amendment, the Helms Amendment, and the Hyde Amendment placed abortion in broader contexts such as religious freedom or negative rights discourses and managed to attract support from some normally pro-choice legislators.[8] They limited the scope and impact of *Roe* and helped engender movement loyalty toward specific politicians, but they were not an outright ban. In 1981, when reliable allies backed competing Senate models to end *Roe*, the passion associated with this goal exacerbated preexisting tensions.

THE HUMAN LIFE BILL AND THE HUMAN LIFE FEDERALISM AMENDMENT

In the first days of the 97th Congress, Senator Jesse Helms (R-NC) introduced an anti-abortion statute known as the "Human Life Bill." Despite the enthusiasm of grassroots activists, most pro-life politicians were cognizant that their side did not have the numbers, and Helms' statute was a canny response to this fact. It used traditional personhood arguments, declaring that the 14th Amendment to the Constitution "protects all human beings" and that the states must not "'deprive persons of life' … from the time of conception." It also removed abortion and related issues from lower court review.[9] It allowed for the implementation of the strongest version of right-to-life language via the simple majority required for passage of a bill. Pro-lifers did not immediately rally behind the bill, viewing it as a diversion from the true goal of a Human Life Amendment. In February 1981, ALL's message to the grassroots was to "not bother with this at all and urge your Congressmen and Senators to simply not support it."[10]

Although Helms' approach offered an expedited path to outlawing abortion, it was legally dubious. In 1981, Helms and his allies introduced over 30 "court-stripping" bills in Congress, focusing on abortion, busing, and school prayer. The goal was to remove a controversial issue from the jurisdiction of the lower federal courts via legislation rather than by the more laborious constitutional amendment process. The legal community condemned this as a dangerous attack on the independence of the judiciary. Six former Attorneys General issued a joint statement to

Congress noting that, while they differed on the Supreme Court's finding in *Roe*, they agreed that Helms' statute was unconstitutional. David Brink, president of the American Bar Association, warned that passage of these bills might lead to a "constitutional crisis that could prove the most serious since our great Civil War." Even the strict constructionist Robert Bork, no fan of *Roe*, warned that court-stripping bills would "create chaos."[11] However, Professor Charles Rice, one of the pro-life movement's leading legal thinkers, argued that the approach was not inherently unconstitutional, for Section 5 of the 14th Amendment gave broad enforcement powers to Congress.[12]

The deluge of legal criticism made important segments of the right-to-life movement uneasy, as did the fact that Helms had introduced the bill without movement consultation. Anti-abortion opponents believed it was a "faulty, ill-timed piece of legislation tying up precious pro-life resources" and that when it was inevitably struck down, the "movement would have to start again ... in mobilizing the public." The Catholic hierarchy was an early critic, declaring in March 1981 that only a constitutional amendment could protect fetal life. David O'Steen, the executive director of the long-running and influential state group Minnesota Citizens Concerned for Life (MCCL), was also a crucial opponent. In a confidential memorandum circulated among movement leaders, O'Steen argued that since the numbers were not there for a traditional personhood amendment, the movement should embrace a two-amendment strategy. This approach proved persuasive for Senator Orrin Hatch (R-UT), who warned the Senate Judiciary Committee that Congress was "attempting to enact a law in the face of an absolutely contrary Supreme Court decision." In September 1981, after months of debate, Hatch proposed his Human Life Federalism Amendment.[13]

Hatch's amendment was inherently pragmatic, for, as he told the *New York Times*, "We just don't have the votes" for a constitutional ban on abortion. His amendment did not discuss the morality of abortion, did not deal with exceptions, and did not specify when life began.[14] It simply declared, "a right to abortion is not secured by this Constitution. The Congress and the several States shall have the concurrent power to restrict and prohibit abortions." Even here there was some legal controversy, for Hatch's amendment reversed the traditional logic that afforded Congress the supreme power to legislate, specifying that a "law of a State which is more restrictive than a law of Congress shall govern."[15]

Given that Hatch's approach was a slightly more elaborate states' rights amendment, its defenders worked hard to explain why the movement should support it. They presented it as an interim step before the ultimate goal. To convince grassroots activists that this approach had historical precedent, MCCL framed it as further evidence of the historical parallel between the pro-life and abolitionist causes, for "slavery was abolished through one amendment and citizenship granted in another."[16] Privately, some leading right-to-lifers feared it would take decades before there would be any chance of passing a personhood amendment and the longer abortion on demand went unchallenged, the more "hopelessly ingrained in the fabric of society" it would become. Hatch supporters viewed the Human Life Federalism Amendment as a way of creating a new pro-life climate. They presented passage of the amendment as the "only realistic chance" the movement had to change the culture before it was too late. Helms' supporters disagreed. When the two-amendment strategy was first circulated, ALL warned that this was a "quick fix" designed to "please" politicians who did not support movement goals. Judie Brown accused pro-life leaders who endorsed the strategy of "playing political games with babies' lives."[17] She became a dedicated advocate of the Human Life Bill.

Both measures had a complicated journey in Congress. Helms' bill passed the Subcommittee on Separation of Powers in July 1981 with a narrow victory, but was blocked from consideration by the Senate Judiciary Committee because defeat was almost certain. In March 1982, Helms introduced an expanded version of the bill that also contained a permanent ban on the use of federal funds for abortion. The full Senate was forced to consider Helms' approach in September 1982 when he offered it as an amendment to the debt ceiling bill. It was instantly blocked by a filibuster and, after several cloture votes, tabled. Hatch's amendment was voted 10-7 out of the Senate Judiciary Committee in March 1982—the greatest level of success of any anti-abortion constitutional amendment to date. However, it then stalled. In September 1982, Hatch unexpectedly withdrew the amendment after the Senate Majority Leader privately promised him a full vote in 1983. When it was reintroduced in the 98th Congress, the language was pared back even further, but it still suffered a resounding defeat.

The Movement Divides

By 1982, right-to-life politicians understood that there would be no anti-abortion ban enacted, but pro-life organizations and activists did not. Although neither measure reflected core movement goals, the flaws and limitations were ignored as leaders struggled to compel unified endorsement of one approach. Both sides claimed that victory was possible in the 97th Congress. Helms' supporters were confrontational and combative, believing that Hatch had needlessly shattered the unity of the movement. Paul Brown of LAPAC and Judie Brown of ALL were the fiercest public critics of the Human Life Federalism Amendment, describing it as "foolhardy," "a sellout of our principles," and "morally unacceptable." Backers of Hatch dismissed Helms' bill as unconstitutional, but their engagement was subtler. Frequently, they simply did not mention Helms' bill, refusing to treat it as warranting serious consideration.[18] Both sides were adamant they were pursuing the only option that could realistically protect fetal life.

The NRLC originally supported Helms' bill and experienced internal divisions over the Hatch model. However, in November 1981, its board voted to endorse the Human Life Federalism Amendment over all others and subsequent votes in 1982 had ever larger majorities supporting it. Of the other major national anti-abortion groups, NPLPAC, ACCL, and AUL backed Hatch's amendment. Many of the older state organizations threw their weight behind it. The Catholic hierarchy vociferously supported Hatch. Father Charles Fiore of NPLPAC claimed to the White House that at least 80% of "rank-and-file pro-lifers" backed it (either alone or in combination with Helms' bill).[19] Supporters of Helms' bill included MfL, AHCDL, PLAL, HLI, CAC, ALL, LAPAC, and a minority faction within the NRLC. High-profile New Right and Religious Right groups also supported Helms' bill, notably MM, RR, and the Conservative Caucus (CC).

Older, often more moderate, elements of the right-to-life movement strongly favored Hatch's legislation. In contrast, Helms' supporters often self-identified as conservative and some groups had significant ties with the New Right and Religious Right. They tended to be quite new and, apart from MfL, ALL, and MM, lacked the profile and influence of the NRLC and AUL. Many of Helms' supporters were absolutists, meaning they supported only outright bans on abortion. In contrast, several of Hatch's most prominent supporters embraced incrementalism, working for compromise solutions that restricted but did not ban abortion.[20] However, these categories do not completely explain what happened to the pro-life movement in 1981 and 1982. NPLPAC and the Catholic hierarchy were normally absolutist in their orientation, AHCDL was normally incrementalist, and conservative religious groups, such as CAC, MM, and RR were inconsistent when it came to abortion legislation. Differences in strategy were important but did not dictate how the movement splintered.

THE CATHOLIC CHURCH

The Catholic hierarchy's vocal support for Hatch was particularly divisive within the movement. Helms' backers often focused their ire on the bishops rather than on Hatch, a Senate ally. Many maintained that Hatch only introduced his amendment after strong encouragement from the bishops, who had been explicitly consulted about the amendment. The bishops were also accused of working behind the scenes against Helms' bill. According to Curtis Young of CAC, the "courageous and principled advocacy" of the Catholic clergy had helped bring millions of evangelicals to the right-to-life cause in the 1970s, yet when success was at hand the hierarchy had inexplicably backed "a radical departure from pro-life principles."[21] From this perspective, the Catholic hierarchy was directly responsible for pro-life turmoil and had profoundly damaged the cause. While the clash offers fascinating insights into competing claims to spiritual and political authority, the sharpest divisions occurred within religious groups rather than between them.

The loudest and most scathing criticism of the Catholic hierarchy came from conservative American Catholics. Despite the language of *Humane Vitae*, there was a large gap between doctrine and behavior, with one 1970 study revealing that 78% of young married Catholic women limited their family size by means that violated Church teaching. After Vatican II and *Griswold*, the US Catholic hierarchy began to treat birth control as an issue of private morality rather than a matter for state regulation, focusing instead on abortion.[22] For theologically devout Catholics, this was morally bankrupt. In their eyes, the devaluation of sex that accompanied the "contraceptive mentality" led inexorably to sexual promiscuity, disease, divorce, and abortion.

Conservative Catholics were deeply suspicious of the motivations and conduct of the hierarchy during the Helms/Hatch fight.[23] Catholic newspaper *The Wanderer* offered months of acerbic commentary, arguing that the bishops had moved against Helms because they were alarmed by the evolution of abortion politics. After having "done nothing of consequence in the pro-life movement since 1973," the bishops now wanted to steer the movement away from the influence of evangelicals, conservatives, and Republicans. Father Paul Marx of HLI claimed that through their support of Hatch, they had "lined up against [them] ... at least 80% of the pro-life leaders and active workers." William Buckley, a prominent Catholic and doyen of the Old Right, diagnosed the intervention as the problem: "The bishops should not be concerned with process, tactics, dealings, wheelings. It is the bishops' task, pure and simple, to tell us what they are consecrated to study, namely the moral issue."[24]

Part of this bitterness also stemmed from the increasing activism of the USCC and NCCB on social justice issues. As political historian Lawrence McAndrews has shown, the hierarchy was a significant political actor in the 1980s, weighing in on divisive topics such as nuclear disarmament and social welfare. The bishops were a source of irritation to many conservatives, who rejected their deployment of ethical and moral claims in support of secular goals. In 1983, Cardinal Joseph Bernardin called for American Catholics to embrace a "consistent ethic of life," presenting abortion as part of a range of life issues including nuclear war, capital punishment, and economic inequality. As the hierarchy worked to broaden the meaning of pro-life, *A.L.L About Issues* sarcastically quipped that Bernardin, aka "Cardinal Quixote," should "leave the quagmire of nuclear hypotheses to those who have time. Preborn babies run out of time at a rate of one every 20 seconds."[25] The Reagan administration was particularly frustrated by efforts to link nuclear freeze and opposition to abortion. White House aides formulated a broad strategy to ensure that Reagan and the Republicans enjoyed the same level of Catholic electoral support in 1984 as they had in the 1980 election, operating from the base assumption that the "USCC is, in its staff, essentially opposed to our strategies." As Michael Uhlmann of the Justice Department put it, the administration needed to frame "the pro-life issue in our terms rather than the political opposition's" (referring to the Catholic hierarchy). This culminated in the 1983 publication of "Abortion and the Conscience of the Nation" in *Human Life Review*, carefully timed to be printed before the final version of the bishops' "Challenge of Peace" pastoral letter.[26]

For many Helms' supporters, the Catholic hierarchy's meddling in legislative matters was proof the bishops engaged in pragmatic politics and should not be making claims to spiritual leadership of the cause (or indeed, the United States). Some conspiratorial elements believed a broader plot was afoot. *The Wanderer* suggested that a failed Congressional vote on an abortion amendment would allow the "Catholic *apparat*" to ditch "an albatross-issue" that kept them from their true interests. Conservatives viewed the bishops' support for Hatch as part of their liberal bias. In a scathing column titled "Bishops Take a Dive," the *National Review* described the hierarchy as "irrelevant," "short-sighted," and embracing a "number of intellectually bankrupt positions." Their support for the Hatch amendment was dismissed as a "tactically defensible stand, though utterly lacking in moral definition." This commentary embarrassed long-time editor William Rusher, who had promised Hatch quite different coverage after the beleaguered Senator complained about the harsh criticism he was receiving from fellow right-to-lifers.[27]

For its part, the Catholic hierarchy did not shy away from criticizing supporters of Helms' bill. Officially, the hierarchy claimed it "had no desire to pick a fight with other people in the pro-life movement or with members of Congress." Early leaks undermined this goal, with oddly pointed attacks on Nellie Gray of MfL, who was described as "not relevant to saving the lives of unborn children." More broadly, USCC officials condemned pro-lifers who wouldn't back Hatch as not being "interested in saving babies." The bishops viewed Helms' bill as nothing more than an attempt to "link the pro-life effort with various 'New Right' concerns." After the failure of both measures, the bishops ignored claims they had divided the movement, instead blaming Helms for the turmoil of the early 1980s.[28]

"Name-Calling, Backbiting, Threats, and Scurrilous Behind-the-Scenes Intrigue"[29]

From its inception, the national right-to-life movement was prone to internal fighting and acrimony. In the early 1970s, both AUL and the NRLC experienced bitter conflicts over strategy. The dramas in NRLC triggered a lengthy report on organizational styles, which concluded that "the most vicious personal attacks on Right to Life people often come from other Right to Life people."[30] This time, however, the bitterness spread among organizations. Each side believed there was only one piece of legislation worth backing, each called on their opponents to fall into line and, when this did not happen, accused them of damaging the cause. Pro-lifers attacked and insulted one another in public and in private.

In general, supporters of Hatch positioned themselves as speaking for the "most sophisticated, experienced, and broad based" groups. Their "outstanding pro-life credentials," coupled with support from scholars and lobbyists with "unassailable intellectual integrity," meant they spoke for the "mainstream." In response, Helms' supporters claimed to be the future of the cause, representative of the new energy that had delivered the White House to Reagan and turned abortion into an important political issue. They savaged supporters of the Hatch amendment for their pragmatism. CAC argued that "attempting to gain votes at the expense of principle has proven the death knell of every movement that has adopted such tactics."[31]

Both sides insisted that everyone else had a "great deal to learn about coalition building and effective congressional politics." In practice, neither side demonstrated much savviness and there was a striking degree of naivety. Hatch supporters frequently claimed that the amendment would be successful because of its muted language and states' rights approach, despite the lack of evidence to support this assertion. Indeed, Hatch's legislative assistant Stephen Markman wrote a cynical memorandum suggesting that pro-life Senators could "harmlessly vote" for the amendment "because it had no chance of passage" in the House. Helms' supporters immediately leaked this "smoking gun" statement to the press, but Hatch supporters ignored the Markman memo and continued to treat the amendment as viable. While Hatch supporters tried to court ambivalent political votes, Helms supporters attacked Congressional allies, attempting to compel unity through threats and insults. ALL told Hatch, the Chair of the Subcommittee on the Constitution, that his approach was "a sham" and "in political terms … going nowhere." At the same hearing, Paul Brown called on Hatch to withdraw his amendment for "the good of prolife efforts in this nation." Brown later telegrammed Senators announcing that LAPAC, which normally targeted liberal and pro-choice politicians, would consider a vote for the Hatch Amendment "a total anti-life vote." Young of CAC launched a campaign against pro-life ally Senator Mark Hatfield (R-OR) for equivocating.[32] The behavior of some pro-life groups and leaders during the early 1980s revealed a cause that was divided, unpredictable, and politically ungrateful.

The chaos confused the New Right. Paul Weyrich of Heritage Foundation (HF), along with other New Right leaders in the Library Court (LC), concluded that pro-lifers needed to be stopped "from destroying themselves." LC was a multi-issue forum that wielded a great deal of influence within conservative circles in Washington, DC. At a gathering in early 1982, LC pushed right-to-life leaders to sign a "human life covenant" that emphasized "solidarity" in the cause. Connie Marshner, the head of LC and the NPFC, warned that if the fighting continued:

> The average politician will throw up his hands and say, "A pox on both your houses—don't any of you ask me to do anything for you ever again." If that happens, the right-to-life movement will have pulled the trigger on its own heart.

Judie Brown, a leading figure in LC, was shocked and angered by this attempt to broker peace and wept when confronted with the covenant, which she refused to sign.[33]

Republican Priorities

As right-to-lifers fought among themselves, most of their political allies stayed silent. In late 1982, the *New York Times* described the abortion issue as one that "Congressional leaders and the White House have been trying to avoid for the last 18 months." Some pro-life leaders shared this perspective and tried to educate the grassroots about the motives of the New Right and Republicans. Douglas Johnson of the NRLC concluded that Senate Majority Leader Howard Baker (R-TN) had exploited movement divisions to "delay floor action on any pro-life initiative." CAC warned that although the New Right opposed *Roe*, it primarily valued "the abortion issue as an effective tool to arouse voter hostility to political liberals." Pro-lifers wanted to "secure legal protection for unborn children," but the core goal for strategists, such as Viguerie and Weyrich was "a conservative Republican majority in Congress."[34]

There was also the problem of Republican priorities. In early March 1981, Reagan told the Conservative Political Action Conference that "conservatives do not have a separate social agenda, a separate economic agenda, and a separate foreign policy agenda. We have one agenda."

Yet only a few months later, Senate Majority Leader Baker told Republicans, "I want the big controversial social issues to wait for next year. I want this year to be Ronald Reagan's year." Republican Senators were directed to focus on passing Reagan's sweeping neo-liberal economic, welfare, and tax reforms.[35] Although pro-lifers understood the dire economic situation in the United States, they were still shocked by the decision. As Cal Thomas of MM told James Baker III, White House Chief of Staff, "If we clean up the economy, but are still allowing the slaughter of one and one-half million babies a year, I will not be able to say that we are better off at all." By 1982, core administration goals like the *Economic Recovery Act* of 1981 and deep budget cuts had been passed, yet Reagan's silence and inaction on abortion continued. The CAC lamented the "apparent [policy] schizophrenia" in the White House and warned that "the Administration—and its slate of Republican congressional candidates—may pay the price of ignoring the 'social agenda' this November."[36]

Anti-abortionists had expected leadership and guidance from the President. Some, such as Fiore of NPLPAC, wondered why their most high-profile ally had not tried to "assist in healing what divisions exist among his supporters." Instead, they got inaction and blame, and the message from the administration exacerbated some of the internecine conflict. Aides routinely claimed that Reagan was avoiding "urging specific actions" because he was waiting for pro-lifers to unite behind a single approach. By early 1982, groups such as the NRLC, NPLPAC, and MM had decided to endorse both the Hatch and the Helms measures, meaning that moderate, conservative, and Religious Right elements were all willing to compromise. Fiore suggested to Edwin Meese III, Counselor to the President, that if Reagan pledged his "enthusiastic support" for both measures he would "put the ball precisely back where it belongs, i.e. into the Congress' court." Instead, the White House continued to insist that the movement needed to unify behind one piece of legislation. At the annual White House gathering on 22 January 1982, Reagan's advisors told movement leaders to "get their act together" if they wanted the administration's support. Some pro-lifers found this "most offensive," pointing out that Reagan did not demand consensus when pursuing other controversial goals. One explanation is that throughout 1982, White House summaries of public opinion polls clearly indicated that most Americans opposed constitutional efforts to ban abortion.[37]

A broader issue was intraparty dynamics. Republicans like Reagan, Helms, and Hatch were prominent opponents of abortion. However, the party was still sharply divided over abortion and there were several powerful pro-choice Republicans, including Baker, the Senate Majority Leader. Reagan was willing to wield presidential influence in his dealings with Congress to advance his economic and foreign policy goals, but did not try and remake his own party when it came to the social issues. Political historian Robert Mason argues that despite the political realignments occurring in the 1980s, Reagan's leadership of the Republican Party was "neutral." He was often a dedicated champion for candidates, but did not tie his support to "a particular course that [the party] should take." Reagan also delegated electoral strategy to his advisors. In his first term, some of the most powerful members of the White House were Republican moderates, and thus short shrift was given to the interests of social conservatives. Throughout Reagan's presidency, anti-abortionists complained that his loyalty to Republicans trumped his loyalty to the unborn. His passive stance on the Helms and Hatch measures helped avoid a potentially damaging confrontation between the White House and pro-choice Republicans in the Senate, but it also meant that the President did not take a leadership role on abortion. In 1981 and 1982, pro-life congressional efforts were doomed to failure partly because Reagan did not use rhetorical or heresthetical influence to try and shape the legislative debate.[38]

Only the threat of negative electoral repercussions prompted action from the White House. In March 1982, faced with rumors of an imminent floor vote on the Hatch Amendment, Office of Policy Development staffer Gary Bauer insisted the President needed to be "on record" about the proposed measures to ensure that the "defeat of anti-abortion legislation on Capitol Hill is not placed on the door step of the White House." On 5 April, Reagan wrote to leaders in the Senate and the right-to-life movement. He walked a careful line, asserting that it was "most important ... that the Congress consider one or more of the proposals in the near future." He also reiterated that divisions among pro-life activists undermined the pursuit of "the common goal."[39]

This vaguely worded missive did not back any specific approach, nor did Reagan suggest he might have a role in working with Congress. Instead, he simply offered his prayers and best wishes for success, emphasizing debate as a goal in and of itself. Nevertheless, MM rejoiced at "the strongest commitment toward anti-abortion legislation the White

House has ever acknowledged," noting that for the first time, Reagan had included Congressional leaders in his call for right-to-life legislation. Those pro-life groups that still refused to endorse both measures claimed that Reagan's letter supported their preferred approach. The USCC quickly issued a press release announcing that Reagan had "fostered unity in the pro-life movement and elicited new support among major Protestant groups and leaders for the Human Life Federalism Amendment." Supporters of the Human Life Bill pushed Helms to pursue "immediate action" on his legislation so "we will not miss this long delayed opportunity."[40] Both measures remained deadlocked in Congress.

Reagan's tepid interventions on abortion were thrown into even starker relief by his sudden decision in May 1982 to champion the School Prayer Amendment. Within a month, the President moved from declaring a National Day of Prayer to formally announcing that he endorsed the goal of an amendment to sending a draft amendment to both houses of Congress. The language submitted to Congress declared, "Nothing in this Constitution shall be construed to prohibit individual or group prayer in public schools or other public institutions. No person shall be required by the United States or by any state to participate in prayer." Although religious organizations were deeply divided about language, the President was willing to take a leadership role on this legislation. *Christianity Today* later noted that after his initial burst of activity Reagan expended "very little political capital" on the School Prayer Amendment, which was ultimately defeated in 1984. Nevertheless, this example stood in marked contrast to his approach to the abortion legislation.[41]

Curiously, most pro-life leaders did not contrast their situation with supporters of school prayer. It seems they genuinely believed that the movement was solely to blame for the inaction in Washington, DC. As Joseph Lampe of ACCL surmised, pro-lifers have "probably self-forfeited any chance to pass major restrictive proposals." He expressed the shame felt by many, noting that the "movement has been its own worst enemy." Roger Mall of Iowa Right to Life Committee echoed Lampe's despair and concern about the movement, worrying that pro-lifers had become too concerned with questions of political influence and power and had forgotten their true calling—the "business of protecting the unborn."[42]

Abortion in the Senate

The abortion issue came to a head in the Senate in the last weeks of the 1982 legislative session. In August, Helms added an amendment that attached fetal personhood language to the debt-ceiling bill. The White House had worried about this possibility back in March, viewing it as posing "special difficulties" because "something of prime importance to us could be held up by a side fight on abortion."[43] Senator Bob Packwood (R-OR), who had been a major pro-choice voice in the Senate since 1970, led a coalition of Republicans and Democrats in an epic filibuster of Helms' amendment that lasted for almost five weeks. There was significant time pressure, as the debt-ceiling bill needed to be approved by 1 October, otherwise, the government would be out of money.

White House aides again pushed for the President to show that he was "keeping faith" on the abortion issue. Morton Blackwell, Special Assistant to the President for Public Liaison, warned:

> Politically the President has benefited greatly by the efforts of the pro-life activists. Reluctantly they have accepted kind words but few actions from this Administration because they were divided as to abortion remedy priorities. Now ... their attention is riveted on the White House to see if the President's actions speak as loudly as his words.

Finally, on 8 September, one day before a scheduled cloture vote, Reagan announced to the NRLC that "one can tiptoe around principles only so long." He wrote to nine Republican Senators encouraging them to vote to end Packwood's filibuster. This intervention was not overly burdensome or time-consuming, but the White House knew that failure to act would "read as a betrayal" to pro-lifers. The imminent midterms were the primary motivation, with Blackwell promising that if Reagan intervened, the "political fallout ... would be very beneficial."[44]

Although *Lifeletter* lauded Reagan for his "all-out support," this was a rather generous reading of his actions. Reagan did not urge Senators to vote for Helms' measure, but simply to invoke cloture. Lee Atwater, Deputy Assistant to the President for Political Affairs, made a list of "political pros and cons" to help inform strategy about Helms' amendment, listing procedural action that was "not about abortion per se" as a distinct positive.[45] In the pages of *Moral Majority Report*, grassroots activists such as Anna Hohl sarcastically noted that the President was "strangely silent" during the filibuster, waiting until the final moment to "openly declare his support and fight actively" for pro-life legislation. The Catholic hierarchy completely ignored Reagan's intervention, with the NCCB attributing the dismal pro-life record of achievement at the close of the 97th Congress to "Senators unsympathetic to the pro-life cause, as well as the President of the United States, [who] were all too willing to seize on pro-life disunity as an excuse for inaction." Some White House staff were furious about this "piece of slander," with William Gribbin, Deputy Director of the Office of Legislative Affairs, warning Blackwell that the USCC and NCCB "cannot be trusted, cannot be worked with, cannot be placated."[46]

The fight over the two approaches came to a sudden and anticlimactic end, and there was no on-the-record abortion vote before the midterm elections. The cloture vote failed three times and Helms' amendment was tabled by one vote on September 15, 1982. On the same day, Hatch withdrew his Human Life Federalism Amendment, having been assured by Baker that if he introduced it in the next session it would be brought to the floor for a full vote. Although White House advisors believed in May that "the abortion issue will be a positive issue for us in the vast majority of cases where it is a factor," the 1982 elections were a setback for both right-to-lifers and the Reagan Revolution.[47] Pro-life candidates achieved few victories against pro-choice candidates. In the House, Republicans experienced enough defeats to effectively end the working conservative majority between Republicans and Southern Democrats. In a 1983 document, Blackwell attributed these setbacks to the White House's focus on fiscal matters at the expense of social issues such as pornography, busing, abortion, and school prayer. He suggested that because these issues—which had helped politically activate millions of people—were "virtually absent" from the media, huge numbers of conservative voters stayed home on election day.[48]

Hatch reintroduced his amendment in the 98th Congress, but this version was even less satisfactory for the right-to-life movement. After an intervention by pro-life ally Senator Thomas Eagleton (D-MO), the proposed text simply stated that "a right to abortion is not secured by this Constitution." The provisions allowing the states to restrict abortion were dropped. Baker kept his word and the Hatch–Eagleton Amendment had two days of debate on the Senate floor. On June 28, 1983, it was defeated 50-49, failing to receive even a simple majority and falling 17 votes shy of the two-thirds majority required. Just over one-third of Senate Republicans voted against it. Helms voted "present" to indicate his "manifest disagreement" with both sides. Right-to-lifers were not surprised by this result. Even Willke, in an internal memo to NRLC officials, was frank that the amendment was "extremely unlikely" to obtain a two-thirds majority; the question was how to present the Senate defeat to the media. Paul Brown, who also opposed the Hatch-Eagleton Amendment, declared that in pursuing a floor vote, the NRLC and the Catholic hierarchy had "handed the pro-life movement the greatest single legislative setback in its 10-year history and have driven a mammoth wedge into the movement itself." This was the high point of right-to-life Congressional activity on an abortion ban. Indeed, the bruising quality of the debate left some political allies claiming that the Senate needed a "little relief" from controversial social issues like abortion.[49] Although other right-to-life constitutional amendments were introduced in the 1980s, none came close to the "success" experienced by the Hatch and Helms measures. The dream of a legislative or constitutional end to abortion was over.

Aftermath

The events of 1981–1983 challenged and transformed the anti-abortion movement. After almost two years of vicious internal fighting, right-to-life leaders were left reeling. Each side had positioned itself as supporting the realistic approach, yet neither measure came close to victory. The fight over the Human Life Federalism Amendment and the Human Life Bill ultimately illustrated the weak bonds that connected opponents of abortion. Newly assertive factions tried to capitalize on the growing national profile of the movement, positioning themselves as the true leaders of the cause. Multi-issue New Right and Religious Right groups were but one element in this turmoil; more important were the clashes between Catholics and among moderate and conservative single-issue groups. Although the Hatch/Helms split did not end the working alliance between opponents of abortion, some groups remained suspicious and even dismissive of the motivations of their allies.

The political implications were also profound, for this experience confirmed the fears that had emerged during the O'Connor nomination: abortion was not a make-or-break issue for their new allies. Rather than assisting the newcomers to Washington, DC to find their feet, Reagan and the Senate Republican leadership used right-to-life turmoil as an excuse to do nothing. Worse, two stalwart allies had introduced compromise measures doomed to fail. At every turn, Senate Republicans had stymied their legislative efforts, yet Reagan's primary contribution was to blame the movement for its divisions.

In the short term, the national movement had several pressing concerns. It needed to quickly heal and rebuild alliances, lest it render itself obsolete. Leaders needed to restore their credibility and demonstrate that federal access was meaningful and they could achieve victories. They had to reassert that they were politically (rather than merely symbolically) important to the White House. While pro-life groups continued to claim that their primary goal was a Human Life Amendment, they quickly reoriented, searching for new unifying issues. One obvious consequence was the new significance of the judicial strategy; overturning *Roe* was now the only way for pro-lifers to end legal abortion in the United States. However, in the short-term, right-to-lifers seized on the issue of international family planning and population aid, and in so doing found a level of consensus that eluded them when fighting abortion at home.

Notes

1. Brown quoted in Bennetts, "Antiabortion Forces in Disarray Less Than a Year After Victories in Election."
2. Edward Keynes and Randall Miller, *The Courts vs. Congress: Prayer, Busing, and Abortion* (Durham: Duke University Press, 1989), 281–3, 296–8; Barbara Craig and David O'Brien, *Abortion and American Politics*, 137–47; Ziegler, *After Roe*, 84–9; Young, *We Gather Together*, 212–5.
3. Frances Frech to Marjory Mecklenburg, 22 October 1976, Box 45, Ford (1), ACCL (emphasis in original).
4. Mark Herring, *The Pro-life/Choice Debate* (Westport: Greenwood Press, 2003), 110.
5. Paige, *The Right to Lifers*, 119.
6. "Anti-abortion Groups Spar Over Amendment Tactics," *Christianity Today*, 6 February 1981, 84; NRLC press release, 5 October 1981, Box 76.1-6, National Right to Life Committee, Inc./National Right to Life Educational Fund, Hall–Hoag Collection, John Hay Library at Brown University.

7. For further details on Human Life Amendments in the 1970s, see Alisa Von Hagel and Daniela Mansbach, *Reproductive Rights in the Age of Human Rights: Pro-life Politics from Roe to Hobby Lobby* (New York: Palgrave Macmillan, 2016), 62; Keynes with Miller, *The Court vs. Congress*, 281–5.
8. Sara Dubow, "'A Constitutional Right Rendered Utterly Meaningless': Religious Exemptions and Reproductive Politics, 1973–2014," *Journal of Policy History*, Volume 27, Number 1 (2015): 1–35; Craig and O'Brien, *Abortion and American Politics*, 118–27.
9. United States, *The Human Life Bill—S. 158: Report, Together with Additional and Minority Views to the Committee on the Judiciary, Made by Its Subcommittee on Separation of Powers* (Washington, DC: US Government Printing Office, 1981); Keynes and Miller, *The Courts vs. Congress*, 296.
10. Judie Brown, "Please Do Not Be Confused," *A.L.L. About Issues*, February 1981, 14.
11. Craig and O'Brien, *Abortion and American Politics*, 140; Brink quoted in Stuart Taylor, "Bar Leaders Fear Crisis Over Curbs on Courts," *New York Times*, 12 November 1981; Bork quoted in Tom Wicker, "Court-Stripping," *New York Times*, 24 April 1981.
12. Charles Rice, "The Human Life Bill," *A.L.L. About Issues*, July 1981, 12–3.
13. "Human Life Bill Now in Perspective," *Pro-Life Political Reporter*, August 1981, 5, Box 7, NPLPAC/POTUS—Pro-Life Coalition—Cabinet Room—28 January 1984 (2), MBL; MCCL, "The Hatch Human Life Amendment," pamphlet, Box 44, Hatch Amendment clippings (4), ACCL; Lawrence McAndrews, *What They Wished For: American Catholics and American Presidents, 1960–2004* (Athens: University of Georgia Press, 2014), 231; United States, *Human Life Bill*, 36.
14. Hatch quoted in Bennetts, "Antiabortion Forces in Disarray Less Than a Year After Victories in Election"; Mall, "The Hatch–Ashbrook Federalism Amendment," Box 1, Abortion (2), DJ; "Bishops' Opposition to HLB Hit," *The Wanderer*, 5 November 1981, Box 44, Hatch Amendment clippings (4), ACCL.
15. United States, *Constitutional Amendments Relating to Abortion Hearings before the Subcommittee on the Constitution of the Committee on the Judiciary, United States Senate, Ninety-Seventh Congress, First Session, on S.J. Res. 17, S.J. Res. 19, and S.J. Res. 110 … October 4, 14, 19, November 4, 5, 12, 15, December 7, and 16, 1981* (Washington, DC: US Government Printing Office, 1983), 13.
16. Bennetts, "Antiabortion Forces in Disarray Less Than a Year After Victories in Election"; MCCL, "The Hatch Human Life Amendment," pamphlet, Box 44, Hatch Amendment clippings (4), ACCL.

17. "Warning," *A.L.L. About Issues*, July 1981, 2.
18. Bennetts, "Antiabortion Forces in Disarray Less Than a Year After Victories in Election"; ALL, "Comment on September 21, 1981 NCHLA Newsletter Analyzing Hatch Amendment F. J. Res. 110," 15 October 1981, Box 8 [Pro-Life/Continued] (1), MBL; NCHLA Newsletter, 21 September 1981, and MCCL Newsletter, September 1981, Box 44, Hatch Amendment clippings (4), ACCL.
19. Father Charles Fiore to Edwin Meese, 4 February 1982, Box 7, NPLPAC/POTUS—Pro-Life Coalition—23 January 1984 (2), MBL.
20. For further discussion of incrementalism as a strategy, see Ziegler, *After Roe*, 58–91.
21. *Action Line*, 8 October 1981, 3, 4, the Pro-Life Newsletter Collection, Schlesinger Library at the Radcliffe Institute (hereafter PLN).
22. John D'Emilio and Estelle Freedman, *Intimate Matters: A History of Sexuality in America*, Second edition (Chicago: University of Chicago Press, 1997), 252. For further discussion of the American response to *Humanae Vitae*, see Leslie Tentler, *Catholics and Contraception: An American History* (Ithaca: Cornell University Press, 2004), 264–80; and Williams, *Defenders of the Unborn*, 58–87.
23. For more on conservative Catholicism as an intellectual and spiritual position, see Michael Cuneo, *The Smoke of Satan: Conservative and Traditionalist Dissent in Contemporary American Catholicism* (New York: Oxford University Press, 1997).
24. Robert Mauro, "Bishops Seeking to Mobilize Catholics to Support Hatch," *The Wanderer*, 14 January 1982, Box 44, Hatch Amendment clippings (3), ACCL; Paul Marx, "Hatch, Helms, and the Catholic Bishops," Box 51, Folder 57, PM; William Buckley, "Anti-Nuke Sentiment Great—But Soviets Aren't Getting the Message," *Arizona Republic*, 5 December 1981, A7.
25. "At Deadline," *A.L.L. About Issues*, January 1981, 46.
26. For more on the bishops' political activity in the 1980s, see McAndrews, *What They Wished For*, 198–248. For more on the nuclear freeze movement, see Kyle Harvey, *American Anti-nuclear Activism, 1975–1990: The Challenge of Peace* (New York: Palgrave Macmillan, 2014). Joseph Bernardin, "A Consistent Ethic of Life: An American–Catholic Dialogue," 6 December 1983, in Alphonse Spilly (ed.), *Selected Works of Joseph Cardinal Bernardin*, Volume 2 (Collegeville: The Liturgical Press, 2000), 81–90; Elizabeth Dole to Edwin Meese, James Baker, Michael Deaver, Box 7, Catholic Strategy (1), MBL; Michael Ullman to Edwin Harper, 22 March 1983, Box 7, Pro-Life File, MBL; Critchlow, "Mobilizing Women," 309.

27. "Bishops' Opposition to HLB Hit," Box 44, Hatch Amendment clippings (4), ACCL; "Bishops Take a Dive," *National Review*, 11 December 1981, 1461–2; William Rusher to Orrin Hatch, 8 December 1981, Box 38, Hatch, Orrin 1976–1987, WAR.
28. Paul A. Fisher, "Hatch Hints Defeat of Bishops-Backed Amendment," *The Wanderer*, 10 December 1981, 9, Box 44, Hatch Amendment clippings (4), ACCL; CAC News Release, 16 December 1981, Box 44, Hatch Amendment clippings (2), ACCL; Richard Doerflinger to Pro-Life and Respect Life Coordinators, 17 September 1982, Box 8, Pro-Life (1), MBL.
29. Bill Peterson, "Worries for New Right," *Washington Post*, 16 February 1982.
30. Prudence Flowers, "Fighting the 'Hurricane Winds' of Abortion Liberalization: Americans United for Life and the Struggle for Self-Definition Before *Roe v. Wade*," *The Sixties: A Journal of History, Culture, and Politics* (2018); Arlene Doyle, "Do You Need Permission to Save an Unborn Baby? A Pro-life Study of Struggles Within the Right to Life Movement and a Comparison of Two Kinds of Organization, Directorship vs. Coalition," 1977, preface, The United States Coalition for Life Archive.
31. Mall, "The Hatch–Ashbrook Federalism Amendment," Box 1, Abortion (2), DJ; "Statement of NPLPAC on SJR 110," 7 December 1981, Box 7, NPLPAC/POTUS—Pro-Life Coalition—Cabinet Room—28 January 1984 (2), MBL; *Action Line*, 3 December 1981, 4, Box 44, Hatch Amendment clippings (2), ACCL.
32. Joseph Lampe to Victor Seavulle, 3 February 1982, Box 16, Miscellaneous Correspondence 1982 (1), ACCL; McAndrews, *What They Wished For*, 234; Peterson, "Worries for New Right"; Testimony of Charles Rice and Paul Brown in United States, *Constitutional Amendments Relating to Abortion, 1981*, 1239, 1214; Beth Spring, "Down Go the Abortion and School Prayer Bills," *Christianity Today*, 22 October 1982, 57.
33. Peterson, "Worries for the New Right."
34. Steven Roberts, "Reagan Backs Anti-abortion Bill as Opponents Resume Filibuster," *New York Times*, 9 September 1982; Douglas Johnson, "Filibuster Kills Pro-life Bill," *Moral Majority Report*, October 1982, 6; *Action Line*, 7 May 1981, 3, PLN.
35. For more on Reagan's economic agenda in his first term, see Kim Phillips-Fein, "Reaganomics: The Rebirth of the Free Market," in Gil Troy and Vincent Cannato (eds.), *Living in the Eighties* (New York: Oxford University Press, 2009), 125–38.

36. Critchlow, *Phyllis Schlafly and Grassroots Conservatism*, 273; C.J. Bailey, *The Republican Party in the US Senate, 1974–1984* (New York: St. Martin's Press, 1988), 94; Thomas quoted in Williams, *God's Own Party*, 196; *Action Line*, 12 June 1982, 2, PLN.
37. Charles Fiore to Edwin Meese, 4 February 1982, Box 7, NPLPAC/ POTUS—Pro-life Coalition—23 January 1984 (2), MBL; Morton Blackwell to Elizabeth Dole, 20 August 1982, Box 7, Pro-Family Activists (3), MBL; Gary Bauer to Edwin Harper, 29 March 1982, WE 003, Box 3, #087082, WHORM; Lee Atwater to Edwin Harper, 2 September 1982, WE 003, Box 3, #087082, WHORM.
38. Robert Mason, "Ronald Reagan and the Republican Party: Responses to Realignment," in Cheryl Hudson and Gareth Davies (eds.), *Ronald Reagan and the 1980s: Perceptions, Politics, Legacies* (New York: Palgrave Macmillan, 2008), 152. For more on presidential influence, see Kimberly Maslin-Wicks, "Two Types of Presidential Influence in Congress," *Presidential Studies Quarterly*, Volume 28, Number 1 (1998): 108–27.
39. Gary Bauer to Edwin Harper, 11 March 1982, Box 16, OA9447, Abortion (1), EM; Gary Bauer to Edwin Harper, 23 March 1982, Box 1, Abortion—Memos (2), SG; Ronald Reagan to Jesse Helms, 5 April 1982, Box 1, Abortion (3), RJ.
40. Deryl Edwards, "Helms, Hatch Proposals Gain Momentum," *Moral Majority Report*, 26 April 1982, 3; USCC press release, "Hatch Amendment Supporters See New Unity Among Pro-life Groups," 30 April 1982, Box 8 [Pro-Life/Continued-#2] (1), RRL, MBL; Petition to Jesse Helms, 19 April 1982, Box 7, American Life Lobby (2), Mariam Bell Files (hereafter MBE), Ronald Reagan Presidential Library.
41. Ronald Reagan, "Message to the Congress Transmitting a Proposed Constitutional Amendment on Prayer in School," 17 May 1982, http:// www.presidency.ucsb.edu/ws/index.php?pid=42527; Young, *We Gather Together*, 215–8; Beth Spring, "Rating Reagan," *Christianity Today*, 7 October 1983, 50.
42. Joseph Lampe to Victor Seavulle, 3 February 1982, Box 16, Miscellaneous Correspondence 1982 (1), ACCL; Mall, "The Hatch–Ashbrook Federalism Amendment," Box 1, Abortion (2), DJ.
43. Gary Bauer to Edwin Harper, Michael Uhlmann, Roger Porter, 24 March 1982, Box 1, OA9101, Abortion—Memos (2), SG.
44. Morton Blackwell to Elizabeth Dole, 20 August 1982, Box 7, Pro-Family Activists (3), MBL; Reagan quoted in Craig and O'Brien, *Abortion and American Politics*, 145.
45. Lee Atwater to Edwin Harper, 2 September 1982, WE 003, Box 3, #087082, WHORM.

46. *Lifeletter,* Number 12, 1982, 1, Box 8, Pro-Life (1), MBL; Anna Hohl, "By One Vote" [Letter to the Editor], *Moral Majority Report,* 22 October 1982, 12; Richard Doerflinger to Pro-Life and Respect Life Coordinators, 17 September 1982, and William Gribbin to Morton Blackwell, undated, both in Box 8, Pro-Life (1), MBL.
47. Gary Bauer to Edwin Harper, 18 May 1982, WE 003, Box 3, #087082, WHORM.
48. Morton Blackwell, "Reviving the Winning Coalition," 11 January 1983, Box 11, Blackwell, Morton 1970–1984, WAR.
49. United States, *Legal Ramifications of the Human Life Amendment: Hearings Before the Subcommittee on the Constitution of the Committee on the Judiciary, United States Senate, Ninety-Eighth Congress, First Session on S.J. Res. 3 ... February 28, and March 7, 1983* (Washington, DC: US Government Printing Office, 1983); Willke quoted in Wesley Pippert, "Anti-abortion Amendment 'Going Down in Flames,'" *United Press International,* 26 June 1983; Brown quoted in Michael Wright, Carlyle Douglas, and Caroline Herron, "Abortion Foes Overreach in the Senate," *New York Times,* 3 July 1983; Beth Spring, "New Problems in Congress for the Antiabortionists," *Christianity Today,* 4 February 1983, 51.

CHAPTER 5

"Voodoo Demographics": The Right-to-Life Movement Confronts the Population Establishment

Abstract In the early 1980s, anti-abortionists experienced several important defeats, and national groups struggled to find ways to work with the Reagan administration and yet still achieve victories. The chapter explores the broadening of the right-to-life agenda and the growing anti-abortion interest in foreign policy. Pro-lifers capitalized on revelations about China's one-child policy to offer a fiery and emotive critique of international population organizations and the uses of American aid dollars. Right-to-life leaders experienced rapid success when they experimented with new types of arguments and were more calculating about the electoral cycle. These efforts culminated in the Mexico City Policy of 1984 and the defunding of major population NGOs. In Reagan's second term, the movement monitored the bureaucracy, Congress, and the White House to ensure that policy implementation was truly pro-life. National right-to-life groups shaped their agenda to suit Reagan's needs, but insisted that rhetoric must be translated into action.

Keywords Right-to-life movement · Population aid · One-child policy · Mexico City Policy · Agency for International Development · Ronald Reagan

---

Population Crisis Center, quoted in Richard Meislin, "Delegate to Mexico Meeting Says U.S. Still Backs Family Planning," *New York Times*, 11 August 1984.

© The Author(s) 2019
P. Flowers, *The Right-to-Life Movement, the Reagan Administration, and the Politics of Abortion*, Palgrave Studies in the History of Social Movements, https://doi.org/10.1007/978-3-030-01707-1_5

The most significant right-to-life achievement during Reagan's presidency occurred in foreign policy. A controversial new approach to population aid, announced at the August 1984 United Nations (UN) International Conference on Population in Mexico City, gave the US anti-abortion movement a sweeping victory on a global stage. Historians such as Barbara Crane, Jason Finkle, Matthew Connelly, and Kathryn Slattery agree that Reagan's population policy was shaped by the pro-life movement and short-term domestic concerns about the 1984 election.[1] Less explored is right-to-life activity before and after the UN Conference, a period when the movement experimented with new tactics.

This chapter teases out why right-to-lifers looked to the international scene for movement victories and how they persuaded the White House and Congress to act. Anti-abortion voices increasingly targeted international family planning in the early 1980s, eventually seizing on China's one-child policy to discredit the entire population establishment. This new arena for action was crucial for the movement after previous disappointments. Right-to-life leaders experienced rapid success because they experimented with new arguments and were more calculating about the electoral cycle. After 1984, the movement monitored the bureaucracy, Congress, and the White House to ensure that policy implementation was truly pro-life. National right-to-life groups shaped their agenda to suit Reagan's needs, but insisted that rhetoric must be translated into action.

PRO-LIFERS AND POPULATION AID

For almost two decades, the United States was a global leader in efforts to combat the impending "population bomb" in the developing world. In 1967, Congress added Title X Programs Relating to Population Growth to the *Foreign Assistance Act* (1961). Between 1965 and 1982, the Agency for International Development (AID) distributed over $2 billion in funding for population assistance—roughly half of the global total. Funding population programs had near-unanimous support from Republicans and Democrats, religious leaders, and scientists. In 1973, shortly after *Roe*, Senator Jesse Helms (R-NC) successfully added an amendment that declared, "No foreign assistance funds may be used to pay for the performance of abortion as a method of family planning or to motivate or coerce any person to practice abortions." Subsequent amendments emphasized the importance of voluntarism in population efforts and barred the use of US funds for abortion lobbying. Such was the consensus that neither chamber of Congress held a recorded floor vote on international family planning issues until 1984.[2]

Despite the Helms Amendment, a small number of right-to-life leaders were skeptical about the use of US dollars, specifically the fact that AID-funded groups such as the UN Fund for Population Activities (UNFPA), the Pathfinder Fund (PF), International Planned Parenthood Federation (IPPF), and PP. These organizations advocated for and supported abortion services, and some provided abortions with non-US funds. In 1980, Patrick Trueman of AUL accused AID of being "foremost among the abortion-promoting organizations" and crucial to the "propagation of abortion" worldwide.[3] Randy Engel of USCL and Father Paul Marx of HLI shared this view. However, at the start of the 1980s most opponents of abortion did not pay attention to AID or the international population establishment.

Reagan's own views were contradictory. While Governor of California, he challenged neo-Malthusian ideas, yet also suggested that the United States might help lead other countries "toward population stabilization."[4] Once in office, neither Reagan nor the Republicans were concerned by population funding. In mid-1981, Engel chastised Reagan for proposing a 33% increase in funding for AID's "anti-people crusade." She also condemned Congress for excluding right-to-life testimony from population hearings. At the start of Reagan's presidency, Engel and Trueman called on the movement to unite against the use of US tax dollars to promote abortion overseas.[5] These calls went unheeded because pro-lifers wanted victories at home. Domestic failure and an increasingly limited scope for federal action caused the movement to broaden its horizons. By the end of 1983, attacks on AID and the international population establishment attracted unified support from across the movement.

Right-to-life leaders opposed the major population organizations because they included abortion services as part of family planning programs. It did not matter that these services were paid for by non-US dollars. From their perspective, AID's funding decisions meant US dollars normalized abortion overseas and covered the operating costs of the international abortion industry. Right-to-lifers were also suspicious of AID's claims to stringently monitor grants. A common claim was that aid dollars were inherently fungible. Government audits conducted at the start of Reagan's presidency did not reveal any transgressions by population NGOs, but pro-lifers such as Engel were unpersuaded, insisting that "there is no realistic method of stopping anti-life double dipping since abortion is such an intrinsic part of their operations." Conservative Catholic activists such as Marx, Engel, and Judie Brown of ALL also opposed population NGOs because they distributed contraceptives, and Brown referred to family planning as "the funnel of filth." However, this stance was generally kept out of movement lobbying.[6]

Complaints about indirect support for abortion were sometimes coupled with a more dramatic accusation—namely, that AID deliberately circumvented the Helms Amendment. Right-to-lifers argued that the agency relied on euphemisms such as "menstrual regulation" and "menstrual extraction" to mask its support for abortion, and that intermediary groups such as IPPF and UNFPA were used to "launder" abortion funds. John Cavanaugh-O'Keefe of HLI claimed that AID used "fraudulent accounts" to directly fund abortion. Engel told readers of *The Wanderer* that the agency was deliberately working "to kill babies" as part of a long-term "anti-life crusade" funded by American tax dollars. The opaque language of government reports and complicated relationships within the population establishment meant that most were in the dark about AID's activities. Americans were exporting abortion to the rest of the world, unaware of what a federal agency was doing in their name.[7]

When right-to-lifers initially attacked AID, they received formulaic responses from the Reagan administration that quoted agency administrators and reiterated official guidelines. Cavanaugh-O'Keefe dismissed self-reporting, comparing it to asking whether "the fox had been eating the chicken and [getting] a denial." On their own, arguments about direct and indirect support for abortion did not move the White House to action. Secretary of State George Shultz and UN Ambassador Jeane Kirkpatrick supported the United States' leadership role in international family planning efforts, and for three years, Reagan issued favorable statements at international forums echoing this sentiment. As late as February 1984, Reagan personally assured Bishop Antonio Quarracino of Buenos Aires that the law was very clear that US funds could not be used for abortion services.[8] The campaign against population aid might have suffered the same fate as other right-to-life efforts during Reagan's first term, if not for a potent combination of international events and electoral expediency.

THE ONE-CHILD POLICY

In 1979, the People's Republic of China, faced with a looming demographic problem, announced a new one-child policy to halt population growth by the year 2000. While coercion was not an explicit part of the program, in rural communities, overzealous officials sometimes relied on compulsion rather than voluntarism. UNFPA and IPPF were aware that the Chinese program involved "very strong measures," yet they provided grants for technology, consultant visits, and population institutes. By 1983, all Chinese couples with a second child were sterilized and all unauthorized pregnancies were aborted. That same year, UNFPA gave the first annual UN Population Award to Qian Xinzhong, head of the Chinese Family Planning Commission, and Indira Gandhi, Prime Minister of India during that country's forced mass-sterilization campaign. The award was a public relations misstep.[9]

Although the Chinese program was newsworthy because it was exceptional, it became an easy shorthand for pro-lifers to convey their broader concerns about US foreign aid. Beyond the specific allegations about forced abortions, right-to-lifers were particularly focused on the one-child policy because of the connections between China, UNFPA, IPPF, and AID. In the early 1980s, America provided about a quarter of the total budget for UNFPA and IPPF. As the one-child policy became increasingly controversial, AID continued to fund them at the same level. Both UNFPA and IPPF insisted that their Chinese contributions were for technical support, while AID argued that its grants were lump sums that were not connected to any one program. Dr. Jack Willke of the NRLC scoffed at the idea that US population funds were insulated from "coercive activities."[10]

The one-child policy offered a rare opportunity for the right-to-life movement. In the United States, the policy attracted broad criticism, and pro-lifers were delighted that even supporters of population control and reproductive rights condemned it. The NRLC consistently reminded the grassroots that they needed to lobby broadly on population aid, as even pro-choice politicians might "recoil" from China's program. Antiabortionists were also thrilled that the mainstream media, which they generally viewed as the enemy, was very negative about the policy. The NRLC compiled information packs for the White House and Congress that relied exclusively on excerpts from news sources such as the *New York Times*, *Wall Street Journal*, *Washington Post*, *60 Minutes*, and PBS.

State leaders were encouraged to reference reputable mainstream news sources rather than reports in anti-abortion, conservative, or religious publications. They wanted to convey the reliability and neutrality of the accounts, hoping to counteract the broad perception that pro-lifers were "notoriously hysterical."[11]

Right-to-lifers were quick to recognize that China's one-child policy disrupted the traditional configurations of domestic abortion politics. As Cavanaugh-O'Keefe put it, the Chinese program was not "respectful of 'the right to choose' or … the recent Harvard elitist invention entitled 'the right to privacy.'" Although pro-lifers opposed abortion at any stage of pregnancy, lobbying material on China focused almost solely on second and third-trimester abortions and eschewed the traditional emphasis on the fetus. It relied heavily on appeals to emotion, focusing on "ruthless" implementation and the suffering of women. Chinese women were "red-eyed from lack of sleep and crying"; were "herded" into vehicles where their "wailing noises" filled the air; or were "handcuffed, tied with ropes and placed in pig's baskets."[12] While pro-lifers highlighted coerced abortions late in pregnancy, they also argued that the disincentives used in the Chinese program undermined any notion of meaningful consent. By articulating new themes of choice and freedom, they tried to solidify their long-running claim that they were both pro-life and pro-woman.[13]

Conscious of the interests of the White House, pro-life leaders incorporated conservative arguments about policy implementation, taxpayer rights, and neo-liberalism. They simplified arrangements between multiple NGOs, noting how much money AID allocated to UNFPA and IPPF and how much money those two organizations gave to China's program. AID was thus guilty by financial association. When pro-lifers referred to the complexity of population funding arrangements it was only to insist that this was why allies in Congress were "under the misimpression that the U.S. could not possibly be supporting the Chinese program." ALL focused heavily on the fact that taxpayers had not consented to the uses of population aid, and would not if they knew what truly went on. A consistent pro-life theme was that the government had an obligation to heed the concerns of taxpayers because they were morally implicated in the decisions of the state. Right-to-lifers also called upon the Reagan administration to apply the principles of supply-side economics to international population funding, calling for the "policy schizophrenia" to end. Others argued that forcing AID to adhere to a stricter interpretation of the Helms Amendment would stop the tacit support of abortion while saving millions of dollars. Gary Curran of ALL went much further, telling the *New York Times* that money spent on international family planning was "wasted" as "all of this talk about a population crisis is basically myth."[14]

Anti-abortionists also used the one-child policy to advance their claim that abortion was the ultimate human rights abuse. Father James McHugh, founder and first leader of the NRLC, believed right-to-life arguments had to be grounded in the US Constitution and the international human rights tradition. Well before the one-child policy, Engel described AID as a "vehicle for the violation of fundamental human rights including the right to life of pre-born children." Anti-abortionists thus emphasized that China was relying on "grave and obvious human rights abuses" and that UNFPA was "subsidiz[ing] human rights violations."[15] These types of statements had a dual meaning.

This rhetorical blurring fit well with the Reagan administration's interest in co-opting human rights discourse. In the late 1970s, Reagan was hostile to human rights policy, echoing neo-conservatives such as Kirkpatrick, who argued that President Jimmy Carter's moralist approach weakened America's standing in the world.[16] Public and political backlash forced Reagan to have a human rights policy, but the administration ensured that it served Cold War ends, with human rights narrowly defined as democracy and individual freedom. Only totalitarian (communist) governments would be sanctioned for abuses. Commentators believed Reagan spent his first term attempting to "ignore human rights as much as possible." However, the Reagan administration was happy to take on pro-life uses of human rights rhetoric. In 1986, Reagan reminded the NRLC's annual convention that "the promotion of abortion and the use of forced abortion … are direct attacks upon the values which are the foundation of Western civilization … This is the ultimate human rights issue." Similarly, Carl Anderson, the Office of Policy Development staffer who helped craft the Mexico City Policy, argued in *Human Life Review* that *Roe* ignored the United States' history as a "society committed to a legal order grounded in the recognition of fundamental human rights."[17]

While human rights rhetoric was swiftly incorporated into the debate, other foreign policy concerns were more contentious. When writing to the grassroots, anti-abortion leaders used the term "Red China." However, when engaging with the White House, they generally avoided this type of language, which would not have been well received.

Reagan's hawkish Cold War foreign policy was primarily targeted at the "evil empire," the Soviet Union. His relationship with China, in contrast, was blossoming. In January 1984, Chinese Premier Zhao Ziyang visited Washington, DC, and in April Reagan visited Beijing. The White House saw these visits as vital to building relations with China on the "foundation of mutual trust, mutual respect, and a mutual interest in promotion of peace and prosperity." China was also a vital part of an anti-Soviet containment strategy.[18] The one-child policy was not mentioned during either visit.

This put the goals of right-to-lifers out of step with the Reagan administration. By 1984, attacks on international population funding were a core legislative priority for the movement, with China at their heart. In April, the NRLC supported a Congressional attempt to cut off AID contributions to UNFPA because it funded population control programs that included forced abortions. The Reagan administration was divided in its response. Stephen Galebach of the Office of Policy Development took the NRLC seriously and recommended the White House "support or at least not … oppose" the legislation.[19] At the same time, UN Ambassador Kirkpatrick assured Chinese officials that the administration opposed these Congressional efforts.[20] Given that the Office of Policy Development was simultaneously working on the Mexico City Policy, it is clear the White House did not have a unified sense of what the new approach to population would mean.

An Expedient New Policy

Although the focus on China was diplomatically awkward for the administration, the general interest in international population funding was extremely useful. Before the annual right-to-life meeting in January 1984, Reagan's advisors reminded him of the disappointing history of pro-life legislative efforts. To placate attendees, he should remind them that there were a "variety of ways to make progress for the right to life," including, of course, via the ballot box. Anti-abortion leaders came to the White House prepared to demand something more concrete. They reiterated their ongoing complaints about AID and presented the administration with a thick briefing book of newspaper reports on China's one-child policy and UNFPA. However, this time they offered a problem and a solution. According to Jean Doyle, the new head of the NRLC, the 1974 UN population conference had launched the promotion of abortion in the Third World. It was thus "essential" the government send individuals who "reflect the Administration's pro-life policies" to the second UN International Conference on Population, being held in Mexico City from 6 to 14 August 1984.[21] Previous anti-abortion activism had generally involved endless lobbying and meetings, frequently with little or no result. Now, anti-abortionists were requesting something the President could do without legislative or judicial cooperation, which would not cost him serious domestic political capital, and which would occur just three months before the election.

Until March 1984, the State Department led US preparations for the conference. After March, the White House proceeded "unilaterally and under great secrecy," with the Office of Policy Development playing a primary role. Anderson, a conservative Catholic with links to right-to-life groups, was alleged to have written the entire first draft of the new population statement. It was a dramatic repudiation of 20 years of US policy and the broader Western consensus about the perils of population growth in the developing world. Now, population growth was seen as a "neutral phenomenon." The solution to rapidly increasing population (if one was required) lay not in family planning and birth control but in free markets and the spread of laissez-faire capitalism. The United States would encourage "developing countries to adopt sound economic policies," for the liberation of "individual initiative through the market mechanism" was crucial to any population strategy. This new stance was at odds with contemporaneous Central Intelligence Agency (CIA) analysis, which warned that in coming years, tension around population and resources could exacerbate the Cold War.[22]

The neo-liberal outlook was coupled with a strong new right-to-life condition for population aid, offering a palatable package for both elements of the Reagan Revolution. Pro-life arguments that had been ignored for several years were suddenly embraced. The administration reaffirmed its commitment to voluntarism and called for coercive family planning measures to be "shunned," a nod to the China issue.[23] More dramatically, any population NGO that received US population funds was to refrain from providing advice, counseling, or information about abortion, even if abortion was legal in that country, and even if the NGO used non-US funds for these services. The administration was banning actions that were legal for domestic recipients of federal family planning grants, expanding the abortion war in a way that was calculated not to affect US voters. The provisions on abortion were quickly dubbed the "global gag rule" because of their impact on speech.

When the policy was leaked by State Department officials in late May, it was widely condemned. In July, the House held hearings on population assistance that were filled with expert testimony defending past US efforts and deploring the new approach. Sixty members of Congress, representing both pro-life and pro-choice views from both parties, sent a petition to the White House warning that the policy could "actually increase unwanted pregnancies and abortions." The State Department, the National Security Council, and AID all worked behind the scenes trying to modify it, concerned by the implications of appearing to interfere in the reproductive policies of other countries. AID viewed the global gag rule as "unnecessarily controversial." After the White House ignored its suggestions for an alternative resolution about family planning, AID's head M. Peter McPherson met several times with key stakeholders to try to exempt UNFPA from the new policy.[24]

Right-to-lifers and social conservatives were delighted by the new provisions and the factional conflicts playing out between and within the legislative and executive branches, taking this as proof that Reagan had proposed a meaningful disruption to the status quo. In the early 1980s, pro-lifers such as Engel, Brown, and Marx had concluded that the bureaucracy was a major impediment in the quest for anti-abortion victories. By 1984, most pro-lifers would have agreed with the *Family Protection Report*'s assertion that it was "common knowledge" that opponents of abortion had "few friends in State or AID, and none at the top."[25] Although news articles about machinations within the federal bureaucracy agitated anti-abortionists, they also served to keep the issue alive. In June and July, movement leaders engaged with Reagan's advisors, pushing the White House to stay firm. When the press indicated there might be exemptions granted for UNFPA, Paul Brown warned that if the White House "back[s] off, there's going to be hell to pay." However, most pro-life correspondence and rhetoric relied on encouragement rather than threats. Curran assured Chief of Staff James Baker III that other countries had also considered cutting off funds for population control organizations. The CAC suggested the White House should simply argue that the new abortion provisions were an extension in kind of bans on racial and sexual discrimination in domestic grants—clauses liberals strongly supported. The *Moral Majority Report* both complimented and insulted the administration, noting "New Right leaders rarely have the opportunity to praise any Administration officials for sound conservative policies, but it appears ... Baker may deserve a pat on the back."[26] There was silence from the Catholic hierarchy, but this did not mean disapproval. The new stance fit well with the Vatican's long-standing opposition to international family planning programs. Furthermore, the Holy See had permanent observer status at UN conferences as a "non-member state," and Catholic views were thus fully represented without lobbying.

The Mexico City Conference and the 1984 Election

Movement leaders were pleased by the leaked draft but insisted that it needed to be introduced by a properly right-to-life conference delegation. They worried that the White House would undermine its bold new statement by sending the usual State Department and population experts to Mexico City. Doyle wrote repeatedly to the administration about "persistent rumors" that a "predominantly pro-abortion delegation" would be sent. Pro-lifers were thus gratified when James Buckley, one of their initial suggestions, was announced as the delegation head. As a Senator in the 1970s, Buckley had a long history of right-to-life political activity, and in his post-Senate career he attacked population aid and reproductive rights from within the bureaucracy. Buckley took the role on the proviso that he would not be "required to defend any policy that runs counter to his beliefs." National groups continued lobbying to try to ensure that the White House sent only "pro-life, pro-family people" to Mexico City, but the most notable thing about the rest of the delegation was that they were high-ranking government officials and conservatives who did not have expertise in population or family planning. A few days before the conference, after pressure from the State Department, the White House agreed to send additional specialist advisors to assist the delegation.[27]

Although right-to-lifers did not get their dream delegation, they managed to exclude a bureaucratic enemy. Richard Benedick, the Coordinator for Population Affairs in the State Department, was responsible for opening US talks with the Vatican on population issues and supported giving AID grants to groups promoting natural family planning, but he was also a staunch defender of population programs. He had attended every preparatory meeting for the Mexico City conference since 1981 and was strongly opposed to the new policy. Benedick was thus subjected to a "vicious campaign" by right-to-lifers, which culminated in an article in *A.L.L. About Issues* that described him as "the single most dangerous anti-life official in the Reagan administration" and warned that sending him to the conference "would be like sending Adolph [*sic*] Eichmann to a holocaust memorial." Although Benedick's allies on the National Security Council fought back against the pro-life attacks, the White House denied him a place in the delegation because it was "widely believed he leaked the draft document" in May. Benedick characterized this experience as "humiliating" and a "personal trauma" and requested reassignment. In 1985, when he was up for a role as Deputy Assistant Secretary of State for Environment, Health, and Natural Resources, right-to-lifers unsuccessfully tried to block his career advancement.[28]

Once the final policy statement was released and the delegation confirmed, movement leaders lavished praise on the President. In February 1984, when reflecting on the upcoming election, Judie Brown told ALL's members that while Reagan "cares a great deal" about abortion, he did not "lobby hard enough" or use the press on behalf of the cause. However, in July she wrote an unusually glowing letter to the President, lauding him for his "display of courage and conviction" and offering him the "sincerest thanks and best wishes" of right-to-lifers worldwide. Willke let the White House know that the NRLC directly credited Reagan with "taking a position of leadership in promoting more humane alternatives." Shortly after the conference, Marx wrote from Mexico, assuring the President that "the statement ... is finding more and more good press outside the United States."[29]

Despite the controversy surrounding the new population policy, the US did not have a huge impact on the conference's recommendations. Of the 140 countries represented, only Costa Rica, Chile, and the Vatican expressed support for the new policy. Buckley's delegation forced clashes over controversial topics such as disarmament and settlements in occupied territories, but did not propose any amendments on abortion. Instead, guided by the recommendations of the State Department, they supported compromise language that maintained the tacit agreement at international forums to treat abortion as a matter for sovereign states. The most notable thing about the US presence at the conference was that domestic drama continued to play out. Six members of Congress flew to Mexico City to hold an unusual press conference announcing that the new policy did not represent the views of most Americans.[30]

Buckley, reflecting the desires of the Reagan administration, presented the policy as a continuation of the status quo. In a press briefing before the conference, he claimed that it did "not reflect any radical, new departures" and was simply a matter of "tightening existing policy." He also ignored right-to-life arguments about fungibility and suggested that "segregated funds" would be sufficient to ensure American dollars did not promote or provide abortion. During the conference, Buckley refused to name any countries engaged in "forcible coercion" and made it clear that Reagan would still fund voluntary family planning programs.[31]

The Mexico City Policy was widely understood as a product of the looming presidential election. When the draft leaked, the *New York Times* explained that Reagan's "conservative supporters believe they are entitled to some substantive victories." Sacrificing population control was a concession to this base. During the conference, delegates from other countries dismissed the new US policy as a craven appeal to domestic voters. Buckley argued that Reagan's views on abortion were already well established, but this defense ignored the fact the policy was clearly intended to maintain rather than gain supporters. The conference also ended one week before the Republican National Convention began, meaning efforts to shape the final population statement were doomed to fail. As one Reagan aide anonymously told the press, "We don't want to have to explain [compromise] to a convention with a number of people who have strong views on the subject." Although Reagan insisted in the presidential debates that "scientific and solid figures" proved that talk of a population explosion had been "vastly exaggerated," he did not address what the Mexico City Policy meant in practice.[32] While abortion was an issue in the 1984 campaign, most of Reagan's re-election strategy was oriented around national optimism and economic recovery.[33]

The Mexico City Policy appealed to American right-to-lifers on two levels. For the grassroots, it was a striking statement of principle from the President on an international stage. The United States was leading the fight to restore dignity to the unborn and was disavowing its long-standing role in "promoting" abortion in the developing world. For movement leaders, it represented a rare tangible victory and a means to achieve broader changes. Although the White House did not seem to envisage major shifts in the distribution of population aid, right-to-life leaders understood the Mexico City Policy as a significant weapon.

This was contingent on Reagan being re-elected and Republicans maintaining their power in Washington, DC. Reagan's landslide victory in 1984, coupled with gains in the House and continued Republican control of the Senate, put anti-abortion leaders in a prime position to push for AID to fundamentally alter its approach to population aid.[34]

Defunding the Population Establishment

The first high-profile population scalp was IPPF, which had enjoyed bipartisan support for 17 years. Less than 1% of IPPF's budget went to abortion-related services, but its failure to comply with the global gag rule meant it was defunded in 1985. The status of funds for UNFPA was less clear as the policy applied to NGOs (and subsequent US Court of Appeals rulings would find it applied only to international NGOs, meaning that PP was exempt).[35] At the Mexico City conference, the United States caused disquiet by demanding "concrete assurances" that UNFPA was not supporting abortion or coercion, but accepted a simple written statement from executive director Rafael Salas about its practices.[36]

Right-to-life groups did not trust UNFPA or AID to voluntarily adhere to the policy and feared Reagan's second term would be business as usual. In July 1984, even as he praised the new policy, Willke warned, "the practical impact ... will depend to large degree on the procedural mechanisms which are established to implement it." He warned that the policy would be meaningless if it relied on "mere 'assurances.'" That same month, Cavanaugh-O'Keefe wrote a column in the *National Catholic Register* decrying the ongoing population "cover up," demanding to know when the White House would "take action and clean house at AID?"[37] From mid-1984 onwards, right-to-lifers kept up a constant drumbeat of opposition to UNFPA and the autonomy of AID.

In the mid-1980s, funding for UNFPA was earmarked in foreign aid legislation, so Congress was a key site for the next phase of the population struggle. Movement leaders and allied politicians focused on appropriation bills, building on the example of past anti-abortion funding restrictions such as the Hyde Amendment. The NRLC was establishing itself as the legislative and lobbying arm of the right-to-life movement, and from 1984 a significant part of its agenda focused on foreign aid. Initially, it concentrated on the Senate, which was narrowly held by Republicans and "closely divided on the abortion issue."

After success in 1985, pro-lifers focused on staving off more general attacks by the "pro-abortion coalition" in the House and Senate. They closely monitored relevant committees and called on the grassroots to bombard members whenever a relevant measure was considered. They encouraged anti-abortionists to emphasize their status as taxpayers, reminding politicians that the general public had a direct stake in the distribution of aid. The NRLC's frequent legislative alerts also functioned as civics lessons, offering detailed histories of the power of Appropriations Committees and the uses and abuses of riders and amendments.[38]

In 1985, conservatives introduced several pieces of population legislation in Congress. The House passed Representative Chris Smith's (R-NJ) amendments to the *Foreign Assistance Authorization Act*, which explicitly condemned China's one-child policy and granted the President extremely broad discretion over UNFPA funding. Smith's approach was rendered moot in August after Representative Jack Kemp (R-NY) and Senator Bob Kasten (R-WI) successfully added a pro-life amendment to the FY 1985 *Supplemental Appropriations Act*. This did not mention China, simply prohibiting the use of appropriated funds in programs that supported or participated in the management of coercive abortion or involuntary sterilization. The Senate Appropriations Committee endorsed the amendment with an important modification made by Senator Daniel Inouye (D-HI), a UNFPA supporter. The final power to determine whether a program was compliant lay with the President. Reagan's advisors viewed Inouye's clause with suspicion, believing it distorted the issue and worrying it might provoke a confrontation with China.[39] Reagan quickly delegated the authority to Shultz, Secretary of State, who in turn delegated it to McPherson.

Monitoring AID

In the aftermath of the UN conference, McPherson attempted to pacify AID's critics. In 1985, he withheld $10 million of the $46 million committed to UNFPA—the amount that would have gone to programs in China. He ultimately reallocated this money, which angered both UNFPA's supporters and its critics. Population NGOs filed a lawsuit arguing that the re-delegation of authority under the Kemp–Kasten Amendment was illegal and violated the will of Congress. However, an August 1986 Federal Appeals Court upheld the process by which authority had been transferred to McPherson. For their part, right-to-lifers opposed the power given to their long-time foe, complaining McPherson had not gone far enough. In their opinion, UNFPA should not receive any US dollars unless it completely broke with the Chinese population program.[40]

In 1986, the White House again delegated the UNFPA funding decision to McPherson, reiterating its view that the President did not need to personally determine compliance with the Kemp–Kasten Amendment. This was troubling for movement leaders, because at a 1985 meeting, Don Regan, Chief of Staff, assured them that future determinations of compliance would be made by the President. In May 1986, Patrick Buchanan, Assistant to the President and Director of Communications, advised Regan that strong "personal reassurances to prolife leadership" would be necessary to overcome the sense that the White House had gone back on its word, which was "even more important than it was last year."[41]

By mid-year, many right-to-life leaders were convinced that McPherson was preparing to reapprove funding for UNFPA. They were suspicious of his focus on program management, since the Kemp–Kasten Amendment also barred support for programs using coercive abortion. The NRLC worried that if UNFPA simply told AID that it was no longer involved in managing the one-child policy, McPherson would reinstate all US funding. In April, McPherson refused to guarantee to anti-abortion members of Congress that UNFPA would not be funded. In July, *Lifeletter* hysterically claimed McPherson's continued silence was a "sure sign" AID was working to "torpedo ... Reagan policy" and reinstate funding for "Red China's ... forced abortion/infanticide population programs." McPherson was engaged in closed-door negotiations with Chinese officials and UNFPA, but ultimately announced that no American dollars would go to UNFPA in 1986.[42]

At the start of 1987, McPherson left AID for the role of Deputy Secretary at the Department of Treasury. *Lifeletter* approvingly noted that during his six-year tenure he was the "target of relentless attacks from anti-aborts." However, in a surprising twist, it labeled him "our de facto New Friend" and the kind of "imperfect victory" that pro-lifers should aspire to—because he also oversaw the implementation of the Mexico City Policy and eventually defunded UNFPA. Right-to-lifers assumed that McPherson's experiences would provide a cautionary example for both the White House and any future head of AID.[43]

Anti-abortionists were greatly concerned about the identity of McPherson's replacement. In April 1987, Willke had a letter hand-delivered to Reagan after the press reported that Iowa Governor Robert Ray, a pro-choice Republican, might head the agency. Having reluctantly given up on having the President determine UNFPA compliance, movement leaders now had to spell out to the White House that it was vital that the head of AID could "effectively exercise administrative discretion in the 'pro-life' direction." Although the NRLC went public with its opposition, Ray was offered the job only to turn it down. McPherson was ultimately replaced with Michael Woods, a Republican moderate with no recorded position on abortion. For six years, the movement had insisted to the White House that appointees to key executive and bureaucratic roles should have a strong "pro-life commitment."[44] The Woods appointment was proof that Reagan was still willing to leave the implementation of his policies in the hands of people who did not have a clear position on the social issues. However, the implications of this were not explored by movement groups, which were distracted by Reagan's sudden spate of right-to-life activity in 1987.

UNFPA's funding was not reinstated until 1993, but right-to-life organizations remained acutely focused on potential shifts in Congress and the bureaucracy. For the rest of Reagan's presidency, their message to the grassroots was that eternal vigilance was necessary. The NRLC repeatedly warned that the population establishment was lobbying to restore funding to UNFPA and frequently told the grassroots they needed to "fight to save" the Mexico City Policy and the Kemp–Kasten Amendment.[45] The movement's actions on population after 1986 were both educational and performative. Urgent legislative alerts and close coverage in pro-life publications pushed activists to see themselves as part of an international struggle, and touted the credentials and influence of right-to-life leaders.

The global gag rule and the ban on UNFPA funding are a particularly controversial and contested element of Reagan's legacy. Implementation has been strictly partisan. Democratic Presidents Bill Clinton and Barack Obama swiftly rescinded the Mexico City Policy, and Republican Presidents George W. Bush and Donald Trump moved equally rapidly to reinstate it. Incoming presidents generally announce the fate of the policy on their second or third day in office, often timed to coincide with the anniversary of *Roe*. Cumulatively, the Mexico City Policy and the Kemp–Kasten Amendment force international population NGOs to choose between accepting US money and behaving as though abortion does not exist or offering abortion counseling and referrals and being denied US funds. Both choices have significant consequences for the health care and family planning services available in the developing world, and primarily impact poor women of color. Although right-to-lifers believe the policy reduces the number of abortions performed, scientific studies indicate the opposite is true. In 2017, Trump dramatically broadened the scope and impact of the Mexico City Policy. Previously, the policy applied specifically to US funds for family planning and population aid; now it applies to the $8.8 billion in US funds dedicated to global health initiatives and assistance.[46]

Exporting the Abortion War

In the early 1980s, China's one-child policy allowed right-to-lifers to translate their suspicion of international family planning programs into something palatable for their political allies. This shift to foreign policy had complex roots. Their opposition to China's program was clearly based on the traditional principles of right-to-life, but it was also a pragmatic turn. Unable to attain substantive victories at home, they strove to offer Reagan and his advisors different types of anti-abortion initiatives. They honed new arguments and rhetorical strategies and refined their lobbying approach, aiming to achieve significant change without passage of explicitly right-to-life legislation. They also worked together with a striking degree of harmony.

There has been relative agreement about the short-term ideological and political underpinnings of the Mexico City Policy. However, the struggle over population aid also offers insights into the dynamics between right-to-lifers and the White House. For several years, right-to-life leaders railed against the uses of American population aid, to no avail. Once the White House was interested, it took the lead and anti-abortionists functioned essentially as cheerleaders. Long after the UN conference, movement leaders worked to maintain pressure on the Reagan administration. Although the Mexico City Policy originated in the White House, right-to-lifers made it their own.

NOTES

1. Matthew Connelly, *Fatal Misconception: The Struggle to Control World Population* (Cambridge: Harvard University Press, 2008); Barbara Crane and Jason Finkle, "Ideology and Politics at Mexico City: The United States at the 1984 International Conference on Population," *Population and Development Review*, Volume 11, Number 1 (March 1985): 1–28; Barbara Crane and Jason Finkle, "The United States, China, and the United Nations Population Fund: Dynamics of US Policymaking," *Population and Development Review*, Volume 15, Number 1 (March 1989): 23–59; Kathryn Slattery, "Building a 'World Coalition for Life': Abortion, Population Control and Transnational Pro-life Networks, 1960–1990," PhD Thesis, University of New South Wales, 2010.
2. Ruth Dixon-Mueller, *Population Policy and Women's Rights: Transforming Reproductive Choice* (Westport: Praeger, 1993), 71; John Sharpless, "World Population Growth, Family Planning, and American Foreign Policy," *Journal of Policy History*, Volume 7, Number 1 (1995): 87; Luisa Blanchfield, "Abortion and Family Planning-Related Provisions in U.S. Foreign Assistance Law and Policy," *Congressional Research Service*, January 2017; Sharon Camp, "The Politics of U.S. Population Assistance," in Laurie Mazur (ed.), *Beyond the Numbers: A Reader on Population, Consumption, and the Environment* (Washington, DC: Island Press, 1994), 124.
3. Patrick Trueman, "Abortion and American Foreign Policy," 1980, Box 1 [Abortion—Agency for International Development] (2), SG.
4. Thomas Robertson, *The Malthusian Moment: Global Population Growth and the Birth of American Environmentalism* (New Brunswick: Rutgers University Press, 2012), 209; Ronald Reagan, "Statement on World Population Day," 24 October 1974, 1, Chronological Files, 1984 System I case files, 8403775, National Security Affairs Files, Ronald Reagan Presidential Library.
5. Randy Engel, "It's Time to Kill the Title X Twins," *The Wanderer*, 30 April 1981, Box 1 [Abortion—Agency for International Development] (3), SG; Randy Engel, "U.S. Aid Population Control Programs: A Basic Q & A Fact Sheet," *A.L.L. About Issues*, April 1981, 13; Trueman, "Abortion and American Foreign Policy," Box 1 [Abortion—Agency for International Development] (2), SG.
6. Engel, "U.S. Aid Population Control Programs"; Brown quoted in Erick Eckholm, "Population Growth: How U.S. Policy Evolved," *New York Times*, 11 August 1984.
7. John Cavanaugh-O'Keefe, "AID's Abortion Abuses," *National Catholic Register*, 15 July 1984, FO 006 #232238PD, WHORM; Engel, "It's Time to Kill the Title X Twins," Box 1 [Abortion—Agency for International Development] (3), SG.

8. Morton Blackwell to Randy Engel, 6 April 1982, Box 61, Chron Letters January 1982–June 1982 (1), MBL; John Cavanaugh-O'Keefe, "Report on Meeting with Dick Durham and John White of USAID," March 1984, 5, Box 51, Folder 124, PM; Crane and Finkle, "Ideology and Politics at Mexico City," 16; Ronald Reagan to Bishop Quarracino, 13 February 1984, Box 8, United Nations Population, Aid, Abortion (6), JS.
9. McConnelly, *Fatal Misconception*, 342–5, 347, 350.
10. Jack Willke to James Baker, 18 July 1984, FO 006 #232238PD, WHORM.
11. Douglas Johnson, "Legislative Alert: Forced Abortions in China," 27 April 1984, Box 1 [Abortion—Agency for International Development] (1), SG; Cavanaugh-O'Keefe, "AID's Abortion Abuses," FO 006 #232238PD, WHORM.
12. John Cavanaugh-O'Keefe, "Abortion Will Destroy the Left," 1984, Box 74, Folder 25, PM; Johnson, "Legislative Alert," Box 1 [Abortion—Agency for International Development] (1), SG; Engel, "It's Time to Kill the Title X Twins," Box 1 [Abortion—Agency for International Development] (3), SG.
13. For more on their claim to be pro-woman, see Haugeberg, *Women Against Abortion*; Melody Rose, "Pro-life, Pro-woman? Frame Extension in the American Antiabortion Movement," *Journal of Women, Politics, and Policy*, Volume 32, Number 1 (2011): 1–27; and Ziegler, *After Roe*, 95–127.
14. Johnson, "Legislative Alert," Box 1 [Abortion—Agency for International Development] (1), SG; Judie Brown, "Why the U.S. Must Stop Supporting Population Control Now" and "Four Types of Recommended Action That You and Those You Educate Can Take Now," both in *A.L.L. About Issues*, June 1984, 21, 28; Carl Anderson and William J. Gribbin quoted in Slattery, "Building a 'World Coalition for Life,'" 127; Judie Brown to Robert Kasten, 6 June 1983, Box 1 [Abortion—Agency for International Development] (3), SG; Curran quoted in Stephen Engelbert, "Conservatives Hope to Link Abortion with Overseas Aid," *New York Times*, 24 June 1984.
15. Williams, *Defenders of the Unborn*, 90–1; Engel, "U.S. AID Population Control Programs"; Johnson, "Legislative Alert," Box 1 [Abortion—Agency for International Development] (1), SG; Engelbert, "Conservatives Hope to Link Abortion with Overseas Aid."
16. For further discussion of human rights and US foreign policy, see Barbara Keys, *Reclaiming American Virtue: The Human Rights Revolution of the 1970s* (Cambridge: Harvard University Press, 2014).
17. Tamar Jacoby, "The Reagan Turnaround on Human Rights," *Foreign Affairs*, Volume 64, Number 5 (June 1986): 1072; Clair Apodaca,

Understanding U.S. Human Rights Policy (New York: Routledge, 2006), 82–6; Peter Smith, "Reagan's Anti-Human Rights Policies," *Boston Globe*, 14 March 1984; Ronald Reagan, "Taping: National Right to Life Convention," 2 June 1986, Box 1, Abortion (6), Carl Anderson Files (hereafter CA), Ronald Reagan Presidential Library; Carl Anderson, "After *Roe*: You Can't Go Home Again," *Human Life Review*, Volume 49 (Spring 1987): 61, Box 1, Abortion (1), CA.
18. Engel, "It's Time to Kill the Title X Twins," Box 1, [Abortion—Agency for International Development] (3), SG; "Special Warning to All Islamic Pro-lifers: These Men Are Dangerous to Your Health!" *A.L.L. About Issues*, July 1984, 10; Suggested reply to Beryl Walbert, RAC Box 25, China—Social—Population [1984], Davis Laux Files, Ronald Reagan Presidential Library; Apodaca, *Understanding U.S. Human Rights Policy*, 84; Rosemary Foot, *Rights Beyond Borders: The Global Community and the Struggle Over Human Rights in China* (Oxford: Oxford University Press, 2000), 94.
19. Stephen Galebach to Bob Reilly, 7 May 1984, Box 1 [Abortion—Agency for International Development] (1), SG.
20. Crane and Finkle, "The United States, China, and the United Nations Population Fund," n. 42.
21. "Meeting with National Leaders of Pro-life Movement," 23 January 1984, Box 7, [NPLAC] POTUS—Pro-Life Coalition—Cabinet Room—23 January 1984 (1), MBL; Connelly, *Fatal Misconception*, 352; Jean Doyle to Ronald Reagan, 10 February 1984, FO 006 #237720, WHORM.
22. Crane and Finkle, "Ideology and Politics at Mexico City," 16; Constance Holden, "A 'Prolife' Population Delegation?" *Science*, 22 June 1984, 1321; "Policy Statement: International Conference on Population," 13 July 1984, Box 8, United Nations, Population Aid, Abortion (1), JS; Robert Gates to John Poindexter, 14 February 1984 and *Population, Resources, and Politics in the Third World: The Long View*, iv, January 1984, Box 82, Population (1), Executive Secretariat, NSC Subject Files (hereafter ESNSC), Ronald Reagan Presidential Library.
23. "Policy Statement," Box 8, United Nations, Population Aid, Abortion (1), JS.
24. Michelle Goldberg, *The Means of Reproduction: Sex, Power, and the Future of the World* (New York: The Penguin Press, 2009), 97; Petition from Sander Levin to Ronald Reagan, 8 August 1984, FO 006, #234566, WHORM; Richard Levine to Robert McFarlane, 11 July 1984, Box 82, Population (1), ESNSC; Phil Gailey, "White House Urged Not to Bar Aid to Countries Supporting Abortion," *New York Times*, 20 June 1984.
25. "The Mexico Population Conference: A High Stakes Turf Fight," *Family Protection Report*, July 1984, Box 8, United Nations Population, Aid, Abortion [Articles], JS.

26. Brown quoted in Loretta McLaughlin, "Right-to-Life Groups Vow to Blunt Talks on Population," *Boston Globe*, 12 July 1984; Gary Curran to James Baker, 28 June 1984, Box 8, United Nations Population, Aid, Abortion (3), JS; "Thank You, Jim Baker," *Moral Majority Report*, August 1984, 16.
27. Jean Doyle to James Baker, 19 April 1984, FO 006 #237720, WHORM; Holden, "A 'Prolife' Population Delegation?"; James Buckley to James Baker, 12 July 1984, Box 82, Population (1), ESNSC; Bob Kimmitt to Jack Svahn, 15 May 1984, Box 82, Population (2), ESNSC; Jim Cicconi to Becky Norton Dunlop, 11 July 1984, FO 006 #237720, WHORM; Crane and Finkle, "Ideology and Politics at Mexico City," 14.
28. "A Population Aide Tells of Attacks," *New York Times*, 16 August 1984; Jean Doyle to James Baker, 19 April 1984, FO 006 #237720, WHORM; "Special Warning to All Islamic Pro-lifers"; Richard Levine to Robert McFarlane, 17 July 1984, Box 82, Population (1), ESNSC; Jack Willke to Ronald Reagan, 6 August 1985, Regan and Willke Meeting—8/06/1985 Chinese Abortion Situation, CA.
29. Judie Brown, "What About President Reagan?" *A.L.L. About Issues*, February 1984, 3; Judie Brown to Ronald Reagan, 20 July 1984, FO 006 #233370, WHORM; Jack Willke to James Baker, 18 July 1984, FO 006 #232283PD, WHORM; Paul Marx to Ronald Reagan, 17 August 1984, FO 006 #235191, WHORM.
30. Crane and Finkle, "Ideology and Politics at Mexico City," 13, 15.
31. Slattery, "Building a 'World Coalition for Life,'" 153; Crane and Finkle, "Ideology and Politics at Mexico City," 9–12.
32. Engelbert, "Conservatives Hope to Link Abortion with Overseas Aid"; Laura López and Janice Simpson, "A Debate Over 'Sovereign Rights,'" *Time*, 29 August 1984, 32; Gailey, "White House Urged Not to Bar Aid to Countries Supporting Abortion"; "The Candidates Debate; Transcript of the Reagan–Mondale Debate on Foreign Policy," *New York Times*, 22 October 1984.
33. For more on the 1984 election, see Rossinow, *The Reagan Era*, 161–80.
34. Finkle and Crane, "Ideology and Politics at Mexico City," 20.
35. The two cases were *DKT Memorial Fund Ltd v. Agency for International Development* (1988) and *Planned Parenthood Federation of America v. Agency for International Development* (1990).
36. Camp, "The Politics of U.S. Population Assistance," 127; Crane and Finkle, "Ideology and Politics at Mexico City," 12.
37. John Wilke to James Baker, 18 July 1984, FO 006, #232283PD, WHORM; Cavanaugh-O'Keefe, "AID's Abortion Abuses," FO 006, #232283PD, WHORM.

38. NRLC Legislative Alert, "Senate Action on Tax-Funded Abortions Likely in September," 12 August 1985, and NRLC Legislative Alert, "Will Funds Again Go to U.N. Agency That Supports Forced Abortions?" 28 April 1986, both in Box 5, Chinese Abortion 1986 (4), MBE.
39. Carl Anderson to Pat Buchanan, 30 April 1986, Box 5, Chinese Abortion 1986 (4), MBE.
40. Crane and Finkle, "The United States, China, and the United Nations Population Fund," 37–9.
41. Carl Anderson to Pat Buchanan, 30 April 1986 and Carl Anderson to Pat Buchanan, 8 May 1986, both in Box 5, Chinese Abortion 1986 (4), MBE.
42. "AID Chief Awards Big Bucks to PP's 'Population' Mag," *Lifeletter*, Number 8, 1986, Box 5, Abortion (Federal Funding of) (1), MBE; Crane and Finkle, "The United States, China, and the United Nations Population Fund," 39–40.
43. "White House Taps 'Moderate' to Replace AID's McPherson," *Lifeletter*, Number 4, 1987, Box 2, C. Everett Koop (1), MBE.
44. Jack Willke to Ronald Reagan, 8 April 1987, Box 2, Abortion—AID [Agency for international Development], CA; "White House Taps 'Moderate' to Replace AID's McPherson," Box 2, C. Everett Koop (1), MBE.
45. Douglas Johnson, "Urgent Legislative Alert," 6 March 1987, Box 10, Prolife Bill Chronology—Summary (5), MBE; Douglas Johnson, "Planned Parenthood Attack on Mexico City Policy Suffers Sharp Setback in Key House Committee," *NRL News*, 13 August 1987, 1, 10.
46. Eran Bendavid, Patrick Avila, and Grant Miller, "United States Aid Policy and Induced Abortion in Sub-Saharan Africa," *Bulletin of the World Health Organization*, Volume 89, Number 12 (December 2011): 877; "Presidential Memorandum Regarding the Mexico City Policy," 23 January 2017, https://www.whitehouse.gov/the-press-office/2017/01/23/presidential-memorandum-regarding-mexico-city-policy.

CHAPTER 6

Cultivating Reagan's Abortion Legacy: His Last Years in Office

Abstract In 1987, the White House embarked on abortion initiatives in the legislative, bureaucratic, and judicial realms. The administration introduced the President's Pro-Life Bill, demanded strict new regulations on domestic family planning grants, and nominated Robert Bork, a staunch opponent of *Roe*, to the Supreme Court. The chapter locates these actions in the social and political context. It suggests that Reagan's sudden debut as a pro-life champion was political theatre intended to rebut the perception he was a "lame duck" and to embed social conservatism in the Republican Party. It analyses the range of pro-life reactions to Reagan's interventions, concluding that the movement was still divided over strategy and most organizations were judicious in their response to White House initiatives. However, major national groups also consciously chose to treat some defeats like victories, crafting a pro-life legacy for Reagan before he left office.

Keywords Right-to-life movement · Legislation · Family planning · Supreme Court · Republicans · Ronald Reagan

On July 30, 1987, the White House hosted a gathering of pro-life leaders and members of Congress, culminating in a rousing 20-minute speech by Ronald Reagan. In front of an audience of 200, Reagan praised right-to-lifers for their "conscience," "conviction," and "integrity," and reiterated his commitment to the cause. He outlined four "practical steps" his administration was taking to advance the right-to-life agenda. Most of these steps were familiar: the introduction of the Mexico City Policy and the defunding of UNFPA, a call to enforce the Hyde Amendment more strictly in Washington, DC, and a piece of anti-abortion legislation initiated by the White House. The fourth was a surprising change to domestic family planning regulations, added to the speech only the previous day. Jean Doyle, former head of the NRLC, described the speech as "one of the most exciting moments of my almost seventeen-year involvement in the movement." However, the policy promises (half of which were not achieved in 1987) were less significant than the timing and symbolism. Although Reagan had discussed his opposition to abortion many times, according to Carl Anderson, Special Assistant to the President for Public Liaison, this was his "first major Presidential address on the prolife issue." The gathering was part of a vigorous campaign to forge a pro-life legacy for the President, and the events of 1987 were vital in solidifying right-to-life loyalty to Reagan and the Republican Party.[1]

Anti-abortionists spent much of Reagan's presidency longing for him to act. They valued his rhetoric and appreciated their relationship with the White House, but this did not supplant their desire for him to lead. They presented Reagan's advisors with a huge number of ways the President could do something on abortion, ranging from the legal and policy oriented to the cultural and social. Because a constitutional amendment was not an option after 1983, staff in the Offices of Public Liaison and Policy Development tried to find ways to position the President in a "role of moral leadership" on abortion.[2] However, during Reagan's first term, he had only two clear pro-life achievements: publication of "Abortion and the Conscience of the Nation" in 1983 and the introduction of the Mexico City Policy in 1984—neither of which changed the status of abortion in the United States.

In 1987, right-to-lifers were thus delighted by a flurry of abortion-related activity from the White House in the legislative, bureaucratic, and judicial realms. Between March and July, the administration introduced the President's Pro-Life Bill, called for strict new regulations on domestic family planning grants, and nominated a conservative icon to the Supreme Court. The CAC exulted that the "broader war against abortion" was suddenly advancing on multiple fronts. Political historian Lawrence McAndrews has argued that this was the moment when

Reagan "decided to lead" the pro-life cause and dared to "propose a new paradigm for the abortion debate."[3] I come to a different conclusion, suggesting Reagan was engaged in political theater, performing the role of pro-life champion but with no real skin in the game. Intriguingly, Reagan did not need to be successful. Two of the three initiatives were roundly defeated, but the movement publicly treated them like wins because Reagan was finally working for the cause.

In the Doldrums

Reagan's right-to-life actions came at an important moment for the movement. New elements such as Randall Terry and OR posed a profound challenge to the strategies and leadership of some older organizations. OR presented protest, or more specifically, illegal protest that temporarily shut down abortion clinics, as an action that directly saved fetal lives. OR was founded in 1986 and held its first out-of-state protest in New Jersey in 1987. Within a year, over 10,000 right-to-lifers had been arrested during OR protests; by 1991 that number stood at more than 40,000. The NRLC, deeply committed to respectability politics, rejected this type of direct action. In 1986, pro-lifers who engaged in acts of civil disobedience were evicted from the NRLC's annual convention. As OR gained notoriety, Dr. Jack Willke and the NRLC studiously ignored the group. In 1990, Father Paul Marx of HLI sarcastically challenged Willke about his years of silence, pointing out that *NRL News* had still never reported on OR or the broader rescue movement. Willke claimed that this was because of legal advice, and that if the NRLC commented on OR it might be open to federal conspiracy charges for encouraging illegal activity. Many anti-abortionists dismissed this defense, instead attributing the NRLC's stance to its long-standing belief that it was "the movement" and had a right to police the behavior and strategies of other pro-life groups. For his part, Terry regularly claimed that the right-to-life movement was "failing" before he intervened. The intense popularity of clinic rescues and direct action in the Reagan years reveals the broad discontent of grassroots pro-lifers. OR offered many anti-abortionists a sense of meaning and purpose at a time when victory seemed elusive; its rapid rise demonstrates that despite the claims of the NRLC, many right-to-lifers had lost confidence in mainstream movement strategies and the political status quo.[4]

More broadly, the national right-to-life movement was floundering. Groups at both the state and local level, including LAPAC and the NRLC, were in "serious crisis" because of debt. These financial difficulties were coupled with a stalled political agenda. After the defeat of the Hatch-Eagleton Amendment in 1983, the NRLC and many other national groups focused their political lobbying on the minutiae of amendments, riders, and lawsuits. Despite their dedicated efforts, domestic victories were still few and far between. Anti-abortion leaders who believed in the power of the ballot box to effect social change insisted that "staying strong with the basics" meant focusing on the three branches of government. However, they struggled to explain why the movement's significant political access had not translated into meaningful change. On the eve of the 1986 midterm elections, Douglas Johnson of the NRLC felt compelled to address the question of whether "past pro-life electoral efforts [have] really made any difference?" After the election, which was a rout for Republicans, *Lifeletter* described the grassroots as "admittedly discouraged" by politics and lobbying.[5]

This discontent was not just about democratic engagement in the abstract. Pro-lifers had been deeply excited by the publication of "Abortion and the Conscience of the Nation," the announcement of the Mexico City Policy, and Reagan's landslide re-election in 1984. This amplified their disappointment when the White House and Republicans in Congress reverted to ignoring most of the right-to-life agenda. In 1987, Paul Brown of LAPAC jeered that the NRLC was thoroughly compromised, so enmeshed with the Reagan administration that it was just "an arm of the Republican Party. Whatever the White House says, they do." Some grassroots activists lashed out directly at the President. Teresa Ashcraft told Reagan:

> Please quit with the talk, the smile and the wave of the hand to pro-lifers each January 22. Please take pro-life action off the back burner where it has been for the past six years of your administration.

In an even more public act of dissent, Nellie Gray filled the opening pages of the 1987 MfL program with biting commentary, noting that while "the President talks prolife," his actions did not follow his words, reflecting the "kind of conduct which makes citizens distrust politicians." Gray also articulated a core source of discontent. Anti-abortionists spent a lot of energy petitioning their allies in Washington, DC, when "there should be no need for grassroots prolife Americans to lobby any prolife public official—we should be able to rest assured that … [they] would do [their] duty."[6] There was broad dissatisfaction with the priorities of politicians.

The Reagan Revolution also seemed to have stalled. In the 1986 midterm elections, Democrats regained the Senate. Religious Right, New Right, and national right-to-life groups attributed this to the political timidity of Republicans on abortion and the social issues. With Democrats now in control of both houses, passage of conservative legislation in the 100th Congress was unlikely. Historian Doug Rossinow describes the period from late 1986 to 1988 as "a crisis of legitimacy for conservatism." There were parallel scandals amongst televangelists and Wall Street financiers. Reagan's approach to domestic and foreign policy was also under attack; he was booed by scientists because of the administration's silence about AIDS, while the Iran–Contra affair threatened to be a second Watergate crisis.[7] The Tower Commission Report into Iran–Contra did not press the issue of impeachment, instead portraying Reagan as "a confused and remote figure" who had little control over White House staff. Incoming Chief of Staff Howard Baker was warned that senior White House aides viewed Reagan as "lazy," "inattentive and inept." Some in the administration even called for him to be removed from office via the invocation of the 25th Amendment.[8]

Baker, who was appointed the day after the Tower Commission Report was released, was instrumental in Reagan's political resurrection. In late 1986, Reagan had identified two core agenda items for the remainder of his presidency: US–Soviet arms control and deficit reduction. Baker quickly made these a central priority. However, conscious of the short period in which to realize these ambitious goals, Baker developed a second strategy focused upon "values." Because of the Democratic dominance in Congress, this approach did not rely on legislative initiatives, instead showcasing Reagan's "stylistic strengths" and rhetorical fervor. This was explicitly understood as "framing the debate for 1988," part of broader Republican electoral strategy.[9] While Baker was Republican Senate Majority Leader in the early 1980s pro-lifers attacked him for being pro-choice, but he was the political operator who oversaw the most vigorously anti-abortion moment of the Reagan presidency. The White House's combative actions in 1987 served to rededicate multiple elements of Reagan's base while demonstrating that the President might be down, but he was not out.

The President's Pro-life Bill

For several years, White House advisors had suggested that if Reagan proposed his own abortion bill he could take a position of leadership while combatting anti-abortion pessimism. In 1985, Office of Policy Development staffer Stephen Galebach began planning, arguing that the numbers in the House and Senate meant pro-life legislation was "do-able, with work." A draft of the bill was produced in early 1986. By mid-year, Anderson framed introduction of the bill as "necessary for the 1986 election" because it would have a substantial impact on grass-roots pro-lifers, Catholic voters, and the Religious Right. At the June NRLC convention, Representative Jack Kemp (R-NH) announced the existence of the bill to "enthusiastic cheers," but the legislation became "bogged down" by divisions within the White House and was not introduced. After the rout in the midterms, right-to-lifers urged the White House to take its stalled legislation off the "back burner." *Lifeletter* argued that it would allow Reagan to fulfill his long-running promise to do "something" about abortion in his final term, while also proving that he would still "vigorously push his own agenda".[10] In the last days of 1986, the White House gave right-to-life and pro-family leaders a draft of the bill, seeking feedback. Some groups concluded that this consultative process was a sham. Significant anti-abortion concerns were not acknowledged, there was no serious effort made to reconcile divergent responses, and suggestions were ignored. The administration proceeded with its initial approach, but the President's Pro-Life Bill did not receive the unified endorsement of the movement.[11]

The bill was introduced in 1987 and 1988. In 1987, it had three parts. First, in a symbolic move, it declared that the constitution did not secure a right to abortion and the Supreme Court had erred in denying the humanity of the fetus. If approved, Congress would be on record opposing *Roe*—an approach that mirrored the "findings" in Helms' 1981 Human Life Bill. Second, it barred the allocation of federal Title X family planning funds to private recipients who provided or referred for abortions. The core aim of the bill was to permanently enact the Hyde Amendment's ban on using federal funds to pay for abortions. In 1988, the bill was reduced to just the Hyde Amendment provisions.[12]

The prospects for the legislation were bleak and even Congressional supporters thought its chances were "pretty slim." Some national anti-abortion leaders let the White House know that they "appreciate this effort by the Administration, but understand that the bill does not stand a good chance of passage." Groups such as the NRLC expended very little energy on the bill, and it did not even make the front cover of *NRL News* when Representative Henry Hyde (R-IL) introduced it on March 19, 1987. The bill attracted 141 co-sponsors in the House and 14 in the Senate, over 31 of whom were Democrats. However, it remained stuck in committee.[13]

Although Reagan requested vigorous support from the pro-life movement, he did not get it. The AHCDL was the strongest and loudest right-to-life backer of what it dubbed the "Superbill," believing the movement had been presented with an "incredible opportunity" because, in contrast to every other piece of pro-life legislation Congress had considered, this bill had "President Reagan's clear support and authorship." If right-to-lifers did not work for the bill, it "would deliver a devastating message about the anti-abortion movement's political will." AHCDL used its newsletter *Lifeletter* to shame other groups for their tepid or critical reactions to the bill. The NRLC endorsed the legislation but was explicit that this was because it was "consistent" with its own long-running policies. In an obliquely worded message to state leaders, Johnson explained that there were always measures in Congress that were not on the "front burner" and the group only concentrated on "goals which may be achievable."[14] The NRLC provided updates on the bill's fortunes but did not try to mobilize the grassroots on its behalf.

The bill's most notable pro-life opponent was ALL. On January 22, 1987, it called on Reagan to support "in word and action" the traditional Human Life Amendment model. No reference was made to the President's Pro-Life Bill, which ALL already believed was weak and would do nothing to "stop the slaughter." ALL was appalled that the bill did not define when life began, was vague about exceptions, and seemed to use states' rights language. Once the legislation was introduced, ALL circulated a 12-point critique and called on all "responsible groups" to "bitterly complain" about it. Judie Brown claimed the White House was deliberately misleading allies in Congress by assuring them that the pro-life movement fully endorsed the measure. In the early 1980s, politicians accused the movement of wasting precious political resources and good will; now ALL charged the President's advisors with the same thing. *The Wanderer* also published a highly critical column from movement elder statesman Professor Charles Rice, who dismissed the legislation as relying on "failed formulas of compromise."[15]

For most of 1987, the Catholic hierarchy was silent on both the bill and the proposed Title X reforms. This was particularly surprising, given that Reagan had a high-profile visit to the Vatican in June. That same month, *Lifeletter* gossiped that the Catholic bishops "have shown no support—nor even thanked the President … for his Lincolnesque anti-abortion initiative." It attributed this to the fact that the hierarchy had been "very quiet on The Issue" since the Hatch amendment debacle, and those Cardinals and Bishops who were strongly anti-abortion pushed for a "seamless garment" rather than a single-issue approach. The bishops' only positive on-record comments came in September, when the Pope had a 10-day tour of the United States. The USCC, NCCB, and NCHLA did not play a lobbying role in any of the case studies discussed in this chapter. In contrast, Religious Right and Protestant groups such as the CWA, CAC, FotF and MM were extremely enthusiastic about the bill. CWA led Congressional lobbying efforts, forming a taskforce to attract co-sponsors and push for a discharge petition. CWA and MM both used this moment to present themselves as "the mainstream portion of the pro-life movement," yet single-issue pro-lifers were frequently oblivious to what their allies were doing. *Lifeletter*, approvingly outlining CWA and CAC's actions, commented to readers that "you may not have heard of such groups, but Congress knows 'em well."[16] *Lifeletter* was aimed at pro-lifers interested in political activism and yet it assumed that its readers were completely unaware of CAC, the major evangelical anti-abortion group, and CWA, the largest women's group in the Religious Right. Historical narratives emphasize the significance of fundamentalists and evangelicals in the pro-life movement in the 1980s, but in practice, groups often functioned in isolation.

The President's Pro-Life Bill highlighted the continued limitations of right-to-life political access. AHCDL complained that since the 1980 election, pro-lifers had tried to get Reagan's backing for legislation and yet "RR's men always answered 'get your act together.'" It blamed insider opposition in the GOP and former White House Chief of Staff "Don 'Don't' Regan" for the almost two-year delay in introducing the bill. Judie Brown pointed out that Republicans still did not have an overarching legislative strategy when it came to abortion, but expected pro-life groups to sign on to anything they proposed.[17]

The bill also led to dysfunctional public squabbling that was uncomfortably reminiscent of the chaos of the early 1980s. When the NRLC was incorrectly accused of opposing the bill, it retorted that other pro-life groups "often demonstrated their unreliability." Even after the NRLC went on record with its support, AHCDL publicly dismissed its efforts as "luke warm." Most of the drama centered on ALL, which MM, CWA, and AHCDL blamed when the bill quickly stalled, accusing Brown of providing politicians with an excuse to do nothing because they could point to divisions within the right-to-life movement. In an article titled "Pro-Life Family Feud," Brown lamented the constant internal disputes amongst pro-lifers. Given her combative role within the movement, she offered a degree of self-awareness when she acknowledged, "each of us has savaged some other group, oftentimes without provocation and without a single fact."[18]

In 1988, the White House pushed to reintroduce the legislation, consulting again with movement leaders about wording and intent. At the behest of right-to-lifers, who believed a purer bill made it easier to summarize voting records, the bill was stripped to one core goal. The President's Pro-Life Bill was reintroduced by Hyde on July 29, 1988, attracted 125 co-sponsors in the House, and was again read only in subcommittee. This did not matter, because in 1988 all parties saw the legislation as a vehicle for other ends. The administration used sweeping language, promising that the bill would protect the unborn child's "rights to life, liberty, and the pursuit of happiness."[19] In reality, it primarily allowed Reagan to reassert his pro-life credentials. For right-to-life leaders, the bill helped position abortion as a prominent issue in an election year. They supported the White House's desire to reintroduce the bill, but most still did not actively lobby for it. Instead, with an eye on the presidential primaries, they wove it into their emerging narrative about Reagan's presidency.

Rewriting Title X

Reagan's next 1987 action focused on the bureaucracy. From 1970, Title X of the *Public Health Service Act* ensured that low-income and poor Americans could access family planning and sexual health services, including contraception, at little or no cost. Throughout the 1970s there was bipartisan political support for federal funding of family planning and the budget for Title X grew to almost $162 million by FY 1981.[20] At the start of the decade, most national pro-life organizations did not focus on the grants because Title X funds could not be used to provide abortions. The leading voice against them came from Judie Brown of

ALL, who spent several years conducting a one-woman crusade against the Title X program and its major beneficiary, PP.

Funding for Title X programs fell by 25% for FY 1982, but this was in line with broad budget cuts. Brown was not satisfied. She spent years calling on Reagan to be "mean as a junk yard dog on waste and abuse" so as to stem the "budget deficit hemorrhage."[21] She claimed that PP used tax dollars to attack the traditional family by offering minors' birth control and sex education without parental consent. She also argued that because Title X funds were used to counsel and refer for abortion, the government was effectively in the "abortion advocacy business." Title X's funding needed to be slashed and strict new regulations needed to be implemented. After the movement's successful attack on international population aid, other right-to-life groups began to view domestic family planning as ripe for action. In 1985, the NRLC condemned Title X as the "largest single funding source" for organizations "that aggressively promote abortion."[22]

Politicians spent much of the 1980s claiming that any adjustment to Title X required legislative change, but pro-life appointees managed to destabilize the program from within HHS. Marjory Mecklenburg, an early anti-abortion leader with connections to AUL, ACCL, and NRLC, was appointed Deputy Assistant Secretary for Population Affairs in Reagan's first term. In mid-1982 she introduced the so-called "squeal rule," which required family planning clinics that received Title X funds to notify parents of children under the age of 18 when they received prescription birth-control devices. The controversial regulation was invalidated by the federal courts before it came into effect. It was several more years before an anti-abortionist in HHS again tried to use the bureaucracy to directly challenge family planning. Jo Ann Gasper, a pro-family activist and publisher of *The Right Woman*, replaced Mecklenburg in 1985. On 21 January 1987, Gasper wrote to 10 regional HHS directors informing them that PP was disqualified from receiving federal Title X funds because its "general support" of abortion meant in violation of the *Public Health Service Act*. She acted without authorization, only alerting her superiors after the letters were sent. The White House was quick to take credit for her initiative, circulating copies of Gasper's letter at the annual January 22 right-to-life meeting. Movement leaders were thrilled and lavished praise on the administration.[23]

Gasper's superiors in HHS were less impressed. The letter was almost immediately rescinded, she was officially reprimanded, and her authority to administer the Title X program removed. Anti-abortion and leaders worked to rally "the troops," and the White House received almost 50,000 letters and phone calls demanding that Gasper's edict be upheld. Prominent right-to-lifers in Congress also advocated on her behalf. Behind the scenes, the White House gave, "very specific guidance" about how to respond. Bowen's "clarifying" memo, issued on February 5, declared that under the 1970 law, no recipients could provide abortion or abortion-related services. However, Bowen's chief of staff assured the press that the memo did not represent a change in policy, and Bowen later explained to Congress that unless there was a change in the law, PP was "entitled" to federal Title X funds for its family planning activities. punishment continued. She told Bowen it was "an unwarranted and outrageous insult" to be penalized for upholding the law and "trying to support agenda," but the reprimand was not lifted until the end of March. Bowen was an opponent of abortion, but his handling of the Gasper situation earned him the ire of right-to-lifers and conservatives.[24]

Gasper briefly became a minor movement celebrity. She received a "standing ovation" at the June NRLC convention. Kemp, a hopeful for the 1988 Republican nomination, claimed that if he were President, he would "summon her to the Oval Office and give her the Medal of Honor." Emboldened, she resumed her challenge to HHS protocol, even reaching out to high-profile Congressional allies to bemoan the "frustrating and unsatisfying situation" she faced in the federal bureaucracy. For two months, she refused to renew Title X grant applications for two PP affiliates. On July 2, Bowen fired Gasper because of her repeated insubordination. Gasper rejected this explanation, announcing at a press conference, "I was fired because I am pro-life ... I was fired because I stood up for my convictions." Movement leaders called for Reagan to replace Bowen, but in his diary, Reagan acknowledged that although Gasper was a "good person," Bowen "had no choice" but to fire her.[25]

As complaints poured into the White House, conservative advisors proposed the July 30 meeting with pro-lifers as a way of pacifying the base. It was at this gathering that new Title X regulations were announced. To sustained applause, Reagan announced that the administration would "immediately" pursue new guidelines to prevent counseling and referrals for abortion, to require physical and financial separation between abortion and family planning services, and to prohibit groups that advocated for or promoted abortion from receiving federal funds. Reagan repeated the pro-life claim that, in its current form, Title X "fosters the view that abortion is an acceptable and government-sanctioned method of family planning." According to CAC, July 30 was "Jo Ann Gasper Day at the White House." The new regulations, which broke with a decade-long precedent mandating nondirective pregnancy counselling, were a last-minute idea. In a gossipy account, the *New Republic* noted that Reagan was "simply presented with a final text that included the new measures." It credited the policy to behind-the-scenes maneuvering by Office of Policy Development staff Anderson, Bauer, and Dinesh D'Souza, a young conservative advisor who had only been at the White House for two months. The primary White House concern about the new regulations, outlined by Communications Director Tom Griscom, was that since they were such "simple changes" it gave rise to the question, "Why hadn't the White House ordered them before?" Luckily for the Reagan administration, pro-life leaders knew better than to dwell on such things. Instead, they were vociferously enthusiastic about the proposed changes and Reagan's "putdown" of Bowen.[26]

The new regulation, nicknamed the "gag rule," was formally proposed in September. National pro-life groups rallied the base, emphasizing that the grassroots needed to write *en masse* to demonstrate their appreciation for Reagan's tough new stance. Approximately 75,000 comments were submitted. The final regulations were released on February 2, 1988, but a preliminary injunction prevented them from going into effect. In May 1991, the Supreme Court ruled in *Rust v. Sullivan* that the regulations were an appropriate use of executive power—a clear victory for right-to-lifers. However, Republicans in the legislative and executive branches were an impediment to Reagan's Title X legacy. Representative John Porter (R-IL) and Senator John Chafee (R-RI), two moderate Republicans, twice successfully added anti-gag rule amendments to key legislation. President George H.W. Bush vetoed their efforts, but also insisted on modifying the regulations because his administration would "not be in the business of 'gagging' doctors." Pro-lifers found Bush's foot-dragging deeply frustrating. Ultimately, the new Title X rules were only in effect for a month in 1992. On November 3, the US Circuit Court of Appeals ruled that the Bush Administration had acted illegally when it rushed to introduce the revised regulations. Democrat Bill Clinton's victory on the same day spelt the end of Reagan's Title X changes. Thus, although it was a successful reform, its direct impact was extremely short-lived.[27]

THE NOMINATION OF ROBERT BORK

While these legislative and bureaucratic interventions allowed the White House to capitalize on existing areas of right-to-life interest, Reagan's most dramatic pro-life gesture was the product of chance. On June 26, 1987, Justice Lewis Powell made the "surprise announcement" that he was retiring from the Supreme Court. Powell was a moderate and a crucial fifth vote on several contentious issues, including reproductive rights. News of the vacancy electrified pro-lifers. Although they had attacked the O'Connor nomination in 1981, by 1987 they believed she was a clear anti-*Roe* vote. In Reagan's second term, he elevated William Rehnquist to Chief Justice and appointed Antonin Scalia. Right-to-lifers strongly supported these appointments and by 1986, believed that the pro-*Roe* majority had shrunk from seven to five. As Senator Gordon Humphrey (R-NH) exulted upon hearing of Powell's retirement, "We seem to be only one vote away from ending the dark night of the abortion holocaust."[28]

By the late 1980s, Supreme Court vacancies were extremely important for the pro-life movement, for the judicial strategy was now the only way to end legal abortion. In 1984, AUL organized a conference that brought together lawyers, academics, and politicians to share strategies about how to reverse *Roe* through the Supreme Court. This became the AUL edited book *Abortion and the Constitution*, published in 1987.[29] Focusing on the judicial strategy allowed right-to-lifers to gloss over their consistent clashes with pro-choice Republicans, including the fact that one-third of Senate Republicans helped defeat the Hatch-Eagleton Amendment in 1983, effectively ending the constitutional strategy. Instead, anti-abortionists rewrote their history of disappointment under Reagan, laying all blame at the feet of Democrats in the legislative branch. Emphasizing judicial appointments also allowed right-to-lifers to accept Reagan and the Republican Party's general inaction so long as they promised to appoint pro-life justices to the Supreme Court. Short-term disappointments were an acceptable price to pay if they meant *Roe* was ultimately overturned.

Even before nominees to fill Powell's seat were short-listed, right-to-lifers assumed that liberal Senators would attempt to block Reagan's pick. Democrats had narrowly failed to stop Rehnquist's elevation to Chief Justice, and after the 1986 midterm elections they had control of the Senate. On July 1, Reagan ensured that it would be a particularly bitter nomination fight when he announced that his choice was District of Columbia Appellate Court Judge Robert Bork. Bork had already been passed over for the Supreme Court, once by Republican Gerald Ford and twice by Reagan. Bork was controversial for two reasons; his conservative jurisprudence and belief in constitutional originalism, and his starring role in the Saturday Night Massacre during the Watergate crisis.[30] The Bork nomination ended in defeat, but it appealed to multiple elements of Reagan's base and amplified their perception that conservatives were outsiders and underdogs.

The administration claimed that nominating Bork was strategically sound, assuring AUL that since Bork was unanimously confirmed in 1982, "it would be tough for the Senate to go back and say it made a mistake." This was incorrect. Hours after Bork was announced, Senator Edward Kennedy (D-MA) rose on the floor of the Senate to sketch out a dystopian vision of the future:

> Robert Bork's America is a land in which women would be forced into back-alley abortions, blacks would sit at segregated lunch counters, rogue police could break down citizens' doors in midnight raids, schoolchildren could not be taught about evolution, writers and artists would be censored at the whim of government, and the doors of the federal courts would be shut on the fingers of millions of citizens for whom the judiciary is often the only protector of the individual rights that are the heart of our democracy.

While Kennedy offered the opening salvo, Senator Joe Biden (D-DE), Chair of the Senate Judiciary Committee, was the "leader of the anti-Bork campaign."[31] Mobilization was unprecedented in terms of scale and coordination. More than 80 organizations condemned Bork as a Supreme Court nominee.[32]

In contrast, opponents of abortion celebrated. Bork had a long record of criticizing the right to privacy, and in 1981 he testified before the Senate that *Roe* was "an unconstitutional decision." Most national pro-life groups had become shrewder in their approach to nominations since O'Connor, no longer demanding an explicitly pro-life stance. Thus, the NRLC and AUL celebrated Bork's judicial philosophy and praised Reagan for fulfilling his 1984 campaign promise to appoint "constructionist" justices.[33] Not all in the movement shared this belief that constitutional originalism should be accepted in lieu of a clear record on abortion, but Bork's history of hostility to *Roe* masked these divisions. When Bork was attacked, pro-lifers and religious conservatives sprang to the defense of the President and his nominee. The SBC, representing the largest non-Catholic religious denomination in the United States, officially endorsed Bork—the first time in its 140-year history it had backed a Supreme Court nominee. The NRLC, AUL, AHCDL, CAC, MM, CV, and CWA worked together to rally the base, although multi-issue Religious Right groups emphasized Bork's views on a wide range of issues. An urgent NRLC Legislative Alert warned that "the outcome of this confirmation battle cannot be predicted," so "all-out grassroots mobilization" was needed until the Senate voted. CV implored supporters to "act now" to "return the law of our land to godly foundations while we have a chance." Collectively, these groups presented the 1987 nomination fight as "the decisive battle in the Abortion War" and claimed that "the entire pro-abortion movement is throwing all of its resources" into blocking Bork.[34]

Opponents of abortion used their traditional lobbying techniques of legislative alerts and direct mailings to generate huge quantities of pro-Bork mail aimed at key Senators. SBL sent material to 26,000 pastors in 24 states encouraging individual Baptist churches to endorse and promote Bork. The Pennsylvania Pro-Life Federation (PPLF) targeted equivocating Judiciary Committee member Senator Arlen Specter (R-PA), who received mail that ran three-to-one in favor of Bork. CWA targeted Senator Howell Heflin (D-AL), a pro-life Democrat. Two weeks before the nomination hearings began, the Senate Judiciary Committee had received more than 33,000 pieces of mail, most of which supported confirmation. Pro-life and Religious Right groups were confident that playing to their "greatest strength"—namely, extensive grassroots networks and "the ability to generate ... support at the local level"—would counter the slick public relations campaign of their enemies.[35]

Bork's pro-life supporters saw all the criticism as illegitimate and "ideological." They ignored the fact that the legal community was divided.

They dismissed the range of groups working against Bork and brushed aside the controversies surrounding his views on busing and affirmative action. Historian Ethan Bronner argues that the anti-Bork coalition avoided single issues, concentrating instead on broad themes of civil rights and privacy. Anti-abortionists saw these as "excuses" that masked the real issue—Bork's stance on *Roe*. Pro-lifers viewed the campaign against Bork as proof that "the abortion lobby has become ... an integral part of left-wing activism in this country." They were particularly dismissive of Democratic opposition to Bork, derisively referring to it as the "party of abortion" and beholden to feminist and pro-choice groups. The August 1987 cover of *NRL News* depicted Molly Yard and Eleanor Smeal of NOW dragging Biden behind them via a hook in his nose. Ignoring their own campaign against O'Connor in 1981, they accused feminists and pro-choice advocates of politicizing the judicial nomination process.[36]

The strong pro-life and Religious Right interest in Bork ran counter to the White House's plan to present Bork as a "mainstream" jurist. The administration reinterpreted decades of Bork's conservative legal thought, even rewriting the Justice Department's briefing book entries on affirmative action and abortion. The New Right was discouraged from responding to liberal criticism, and Kennedy's provocative speech went largely unanswered. The National Conservative Political Action Committee conducted only one mailing on Bork's behalf. *The Phyllis Schlafly Report* focused primarily on AIDS and the Iran–Contra scandal during the crucial months of July and August, running only one small column reminding readers of the need to oppose "activist Federal judges." Dan Casey of the American Conservative Union later acknowledged, "Nobody thought there was a problem with Bork until ... it was too late."[37]

Bork was an active participant in this effort to refashion his legacy. During the Senate Judiciary Committee hearings from 15 to 30 September, he distanced himself from some of his past statements, expressed his respect for precedent, and offered concessions on how he would vote on several controversial issues. The contradictions at the heart of his five days of testimony led Specter to conclude that there was a "considerable difference between what Judge Bork has written and what he has testified he will do if confirmed." The Judiciary Committee voted 9-5 against Bork. In the full Senate vote on October 23, 1987, the vote was 58-42, the largest margin by which the Senate has ever rejected a Supreme Court nomination. Six moderate Republicans, as well as most of the pro-life and conservative Southern Democrats, joined liberal Democrats in voting against the nominee.[38]

Leading conservative Republicans such as Senator Strom Thurmond (R-SC) suggested that next time, the administration "not send someone as controversial," but Reagan defiantly vowed to pick someone who would upset Senate liberals "just as much." With guidance from Attorney General Edwin Meese III, he quickly selected District of Columbia Appellate Court Judge Douglas Ginsburg, another constitutional originalist. In a humiliating turn for all parties, nine days after he was nominated, Ginsburg was forced to withdraw his name from consideration because of his past marijuana use. Finally, on November 11, Reagan nominated the Ninth Circuit Court of Appeals Judge Anthony Kennedy. Kennedy was widely perceived to be a traditional, rather than an "ideological," conservative, and he was greeted with bipartisan praise. He had not ruled on abortion during his 12 years on the bench. The NRLC and AUL supported Kennedy because of his constitutional philosophy, but they did not work to mobilize the grassroots for him. ALL, in its usual combative way, told the press, "don't give me this judicial restraint nonsense ... we want to know where the guy stands." Indeed, ALL was deeply insulting about the difficulty Reagan had experienced filling Powell's seat, declaring "after years of trying, [the White House] have finally mastered incompetence."[39] After only three days of hearings, the Senate confirmed Kennedy 97-0 on February 3, 1988. While this level of Senate consensus now seems striking, O'Connor, Scalia, and Kennedy were all unanimously confirmed. Pro-life and pro-choice groups were correct in claiming that the future of *Roe* hung in the balance in the late 1980s. Kennedy, along with O'Connor, would form a crucial part of the majority that upheld legal abortion.

Right-to-lifers did not question their ability to mobilize the grassroots, for as Denise Neary of PPLF explained, "The operation was a success—but the patient died." Nor did they blame the President, his advisors, or Senate Republicans for Bork's defeat. They did not reflect on how the White House handled the nomination or discuss the moderate Republicans who voted against the nominee. They did not speculate about why such a controversial candidate was not put forward in 1981 or 1986 when Republicans had a majority in the Senate. Bork— one of the nations' most well-known legal critics of *Roe*—was left on the back burner until Democrats held the balance of power in the Senate.

The events of 1987 make Bork seem more like an offering to the culture wars than a viable contender for the Supreme Court. The nomination pitted liberals and conservatives against one another, triggered intense polarization around multiple controversial issues, and heightened partisan divisions. Pro-life groups focused all their ire on the Democrats, claiming that when NOW and PP announced they opposed Bork, "the Senate Democratic leadership smartly saluted and did their bidding."[40] Bork's defeat helped deepen pro-life and socially conservative commitment to Reagan and the Republicans.

National right-to-life groups seized on the Bork defeat as reaffirming the fundamental importance of electoral engagement and political lobbying. In 1988, they heartened the movement with claims that the reversal of *Roe* was all but imminent and that pro-lifers "were poised as close or closer to victory than before Robert Bork's nomination." Simultaneously, they warned of how precarious and fragile those gains were. Almost the entire January 22, 1988 edition of *NRL News* focused on the presidential election, the Supreme Court, and the future of *Roe*. Although the NRLC supported the Kennedy nomination, they focused their rhetorical energies on the moment of defeat, going so far as to describe Bork's confirmation hearings as a "lynching."[41] The NRLC repeatedly emphasized that the only way to end abortion was through the judicial branch, and that the Bork nomination had demonstrated the importance of having a Republican in the White House *and* a Republican majority in the Senate.

A Pro-life Legacy

By the beginning of 1988, despite the fact that two of Reagan's three pro-life actions stalled or were defeated, his credentials were dramatically burnished. Anti-abortion groups enthusiastically incorporated these efforts into an emerging narrative about Reagan's legacy. The NRLC praised him for introducing the "first pro-life bill ever drafted by a US President" and lauded Title X reform as one of his "landmark pro-life achievements." Although the Bork defeat did not appear in the legacy lists that circulated, the NRLC treated the Senate's Bork nomination vote as equivalent to the 1983 vote on the Hatch-Eagleton Amendment—the only two votes in six years deemed "especially significant" for the cause. Reagan was presented as having suddenly leapt into the fray, pursuing multiple initiatives at once to attack abortion rights.[42]

Vigorously advancing a pro-life agenda in 1987 was a calculated decision, for the White House pushed for action at a point when the President wielded the least amount of influence in Congress. If a measure succeeded, Reagan would be lauded by both right-to-lifers and a broader constituency of social and religious conservatives. If it failed, Democrats, rather than the Republican leadership, would be faulted. Either way, he resisted the narrative of the lame duck President. With the exception of the Bork nomination, Reagan's personal investment in these case studies is unclear. He was happy to offer rhetorical and symbolic support, but White House aides played a large role in determining the substance, timing, and strategy for both the bill and the Title X reforms. In the end, it does not matter whether these actions originated from the President. Simply by acting, by lending his name and his voice to these initiatives, he was acknowledging and rewarding the loyalty of opponents of abortion.

These actions also served to solidify the President's reputation and vision for the Republican Party. As *Lifeletter* argued in January 1987, strong leadership from the White House on abortion could "determine whether the Reagan Revolution continues beyond '88—or all those pro-Reagan Born-Dems go back to the *other* party."[43] Strengthening Reagan's pro-life credentials was a way of unifying and drawing together single-issue right-to-life groups, pro-family groups, New Right groups, and Religious Right groups, for abortion brought together disparate factions in a way that other issues did not. Conservatives wanted to secure their place in mainstream politics, and central to this was embedding the social issues in the Republican Party.

Although it is easy to view pro-lifers as unquestioningly and naively celebrating anything the White House did, the events of 1987 reflected the ongoing political education of the movement. First, in their response to the President's Pro-Life Bill, groups were judicious about their priorities and protective of resources and grassroots energy. Second, some movement leaders consciously chose to treat defeats like victories. However, this praise inadvertently reaffirmed to politician allies that the movement could be placated with gestures, since the execution and implementation were rarely interrogated. In 1987, all sides chose to embrace symbolism over substance and worked together to cultivate a pro-life legacy for the President.

Notes

1. Ronald Reagan, "Remarks by the President in Briefing for Right to Life Leaders," 30 July 1987, Box 1, Pro-Life Leadership Meeting, MBE; Peter Robinson to Ronald Reagan, 29 July 1987, Box 1, Pro-Life (4), MBE; Jean Doyle to Carl Anderson, 5 August 1987, and Jean Doyle to Ronald Reagan, 31 July 1987, both in Box 1, Pro-Life (5), MBE; Carl Anderson, 29 July 1987, Box 2, Pro-Life, GB.
2. Notes from Pro-Life Meeting, 1988, Box 1, Pro-Life Leadership Meeting, MBE; Dee Jepsen to Red Cavaney, 11 February 1983, Box 8 [Pro-Life/ Continued], MBL.
3. McAndrews, *What They Wished For*, 241–5.
4. Doan, *Opposition and Intimidation*, 86–8; Charles Shepard, "Operation Rescue's Mission to Save Itself," *Washington Post*, 24 November 1991; Cuneo, *The Smoke of Satan*, 70–1; Paul Marx to Jack Willke, 19 September 1990, Box 5, Folder 12, Willke, Dr. Jack, PM; Cynthia Gorney, "The Dispassion of John Willke," *Washington Post*, 22 April 1990; Kurtz, "Operation Rescue Aggressively Antiabortion."
5. Wallace Turner, "Hard Times Descend Upon an Anti-abortion PAC," *New York Times*, 9 August 1987; NRLC to NRLC Supporter, 20 April 1987, and Ohio Right to Life Society to Dear Friend, Spring 1987, both in Box 1, Abortion (1), CA; Jack Willke, "Staying Strong with the Basics," *NRL News*, 30 April 1987, 3; Douglas Johnson, "Defunding the International Abortion Lobby," *Crisis*, October 1986, 36, Box 144, Folder 11, Abortion National Right to Life Committee—1982–1991, CLC; Jack Fowler, "White House OK of 'Superbill' Pushed for *Roe* Anniversary," *Lifeletter*, Number 1, 1987, Box 76.1-1, Folder 3, The Ad Hoc Committee in Defense of Life, Inc. (hereafter AHCDL), Hall–Hoag Collection, John Hay Library at Brown University.
6. Brown quoted in "Abortion foes are split on whether to support Kennedy for Supreme Court"; Teresa Ashcraft to Ronald Reagan, 1986, Box 4, Abortion (4), MBE; "Commentary," *March for Life Program*, 22 January 1987, 39, Box 144, Folder 10, March for Life 1983–1989, CLC.
7. Rossinow, *The Reagan Era*, 202. For more on Iran–Contra, see Rossinow, *The Reagan Era*, 181–200, 215–20.
8. *Action Line*, 15 November 1986, 1, PLN; Steven Roberts, "The White House Crisis," *New York Times*, 27 February 1987; Jack Nelson, "Aide's '87 Memo Raised Question of Removing Reagan from Office," *Washington Post*, 15 September 1988.
9. Ellen Hume and Gerald Seib, "Rescue Operation," *Wall Street Journal*, 7 May 1987. For more on Baker as Chief of Staff, see J. Lee Annis, *Howard Baker: Conciliator in an Age of Crisis*, Second edition (Knoxville: Howard H. Baker Jr. Center for Public Policy, 2007), 212–28.

10. Stephen Galebach to John Svahn, 12 February 1985, Box 6, Abortion [Title X Referrals] (3), MBE; Carl Anderson to John Tuck, 20 June 1987, Box 1, Abortion—General (1), CA; Robert Patrick, "President Calls for Bi-Partisan Support of New 'Superbill,'" *Lifeletter*, Number 2, 1987, Fowler, "White House OK of 'Superbill' Pushed for *Roe* Anniversary," both in Box 76.1-1, Folder 3, AHCDL (emphasis in original).
11. Judie Brown, "Pro-life Family Feud: A Solution," Box 3, Folder 30, Brown, Judie 1981–1987, PM.
12. Janet Carroll, "Hyde, Humphrey Introduce 'President's Pro-life Bill,'" *NRL News*, 2 April 1987, 10; Alan Kranowitz to Gary Bauer, 25 February 1988, Box 2, Pro-Life, GB.
13. Alfred Kingon to Donald Regan, 18 February 1987, Box 6, Abortion [Title X Referrals] (2), MBE; Carroll, "Hyde, Humphrey Introduce 'President's Pro-life Bill,'" 5, 10.
14. J.P. McFadden to Anti-Abortion Leaders, 30 July 1987, Box 1, Pro-Life (2), MBE; AHCDL quoted in Beth Spring, "Proposed Prolife Bill Goes for the Jugular," *Christianity Today*, 12 June 1987; Thad Bean, "Superbill Touted by President, Hyde as Co-sponsors Hit 107," *Lifeletter*, Number 6, 1987, Box 76.1-1, Folder 3, AHCDL; Douglas Johnson, "Urgent Legislative Alert," 6 March 1987, Box 10, Prolife Bill Chronology—Summary (5), MBE.
15. "ALL Critique of White House Bill—H.R. 1729," Box 10, Prolife Bill Chronology—Summary (1), MBE; Rice quoted in Jack Fowler, "Superbill Sponsors Hit 93 in House as More Dems Join In," *Lifeletter*, Number 5, 1987, Box 76.1-1, Folder 3, AHCDL.
16. Bean, "Superbill Touted by President, Hyde as Co-sponsors Hit 107," Box 76.1-1, Folder 3, AHCDL (emphasis in original); Albert Veldhuyzen, "An Important First Step to Protect the Unborn," *CWA Newsletter*, June 1987, 2–3, Box 10, Prolife Bill Chronology—Summary (4), MBE; Beverly LaHaye to Mari Masen, 17 June 1987, Box 10, Prolife Bill Chronology—Summary (1), MBE; Connie Marshner to Pro-Family Activists, April 1987, Box 10, Prolife Bill Chronology—Summary (4), MBE; Jim Boulet to Interested Persons, 17 June 1987, Box 10, Prolife Bill Chronology—Summary (1), MBE.
17. Fowler, "Superbill Sponsors Hit 93 in House as More Dems Join In," Fowler, "White House OK of 'Superbill' Pushed for *Roe* Anniversary," and Bean, "Superbill Touted by President, Hyde as Co-sponsors Hit 107," all in Box 76.1-1, Folder 3, AHCDL; Brown, "Pro-life Family Feud," Box 3, Folder 30, Brown, Judie 1981–1987, PM.
18. Johnson, "Urgent Legislative Alert," Box 10, Prolife Bill Chronology—Summary (5), MBE; Fowler, "Superbill Sponsors Hit 93 in House as More Dems Join In," Box 76.1-1, Folder 3, AHCDL (emphasis in original); Jim Boulet to Interested Persons, 17 June 1987, Box 10, Prolife

Bill Chronology—Summary (1), MBE; Brown, "Pro-life Family Feud," Box 3, Folder 30, Brown, Judie 1981–1987, PM.
19. Alan Kranowitz to Gary Bauer, 25 February 1988, and Ronald Reagan to the Congress of the United States, 8 June 1988, all in Box 2, Pro-Life, GB.
20. Critchlow, *Intended Consequences*, 207; https://www.hhs.gov/opa/title-x-family-planning/about-title-x-grants/funding-history/index.html.
21. Judie Brown to Morton Blackwell and Don Moran, 11 February 1982, Box 7, American Life Lobby (3), MBL; Judie Brown to Ronald Reagan, 11 January 1983, FI-004, #119474, WHORM.
22. "ALL Planned Parenthood Booklet," 1982, Box 2, Planned Parenthood (1), DJ; "ALL's Position on Title X," Box 1, [Abortion—Agency for International Development] (3), SG; Nadine Cohodas, "Array of Antiabortion Amendments Planned," *Congressional Quarterly*, 2 November 1985, Box 3 [Abortion] [Hatch Amendment], CA.
23. Maris Vinovksis, *An 'Epidemic' of Adolescent Pregnancy? Some Historical and Policy Considerations* (New York: Oxford University Press, 1988), 23–4, 87; Spencer Rich, "HHS Secretary Fires Abortion Opponent for Insubordination," *Washington Post*, 3 July 1987; J. Willke, "The 14th Anniversary," *NRL News*, 5 February 1987.
24. Willke, "The 14th Anniversary," 3; Douglas Johnson, "White House Swamped with Demands to Cut Federal Funding of Planned Parenthood," *NRL News*, 19 February 1987, 1; Spencer Rich, "HHS Hints Clinics Risk Aid Cutoff," *Washington Post*, 7 February 1987; Alfred Kingon to Donald Regan, 18 February 1987, Box 6, Abortion [Title X Referrals] (2), MBE; Carroll, "Hyde, Humphrey Introduce President's Pro-life Bill," 10.
25. Johnson, "White House Swamped with Demands to Cut Federal Funding of Planned Parenthood," 8; Jo Ann Gasper to Gordon Humphrey, Jesse Helms, Henry Hyde, Jack Kemp, Vin Weber, 26 June 1987, Box 2, Gasper, Jo Ann (2), GB; Cecilie Ditlev-Simonsen, "Fired for Pro-life View, Health Aide Says," *Los Angeles Times*, 8 July 1987; Dave Andrusko, "Bowen Sacks Gasper," *NRL News*, 16 July 1987, 5; *Action Line*, 30 August 1987, 1, Box 79, Folder 6, Abortion Christian Action Council, CLC; Rich, "HHS Secretary Fires Abortion Opponent for Insubordination"; Jack Fowler, "Bowen Fires Gasper for Refusing $ to Pro-abortion Groups," *Lifeletter*, Number 7, 1987, Box 76.1-1, Folder 3, AHCDL; Reagan, "30 July 1987," *The Reagan Diaries*, 521.
26. "Remarks by the President in Briefing for Right-to-Life Leaders," 30 July 1987, Pro-Life Leadership Meeting, MBE; *Action Line*, 30 August 1987, 3, Box 79, Folder 6, Abortion Christian Action Council, CLC; Peter Robinson to Ronald Reagan, 29 July 1987, Box 1, Pro-life (4), MBE; Fred Barnes, "Bringing Up Baby," *New Republic*, 24 August 1987, 10–2.

27. David Savage, "Abortion 'Gag Rule' Likely to Take Effect Soon," *Los Angeles Times*, 20 March 1992; James Rubin, "Appeals Court Rejects Bush Administration's Gag Rule on Abortions," *Associated Press*, 3 November 1992.
28. Humphrey quoted in Stuart Taylor, "Powell Leaves High Court," *New York Times*, 27 June 1987.
29. Dennis Horan, Edward Grant, and Paige Cunningham (eds.), *Abortion and the Constitution: Reversing Roe v. Wade Through the Courts* (Washington, DC: Georgetown University Press, 1987).
30. Douglas Johnson, "Justice Lewis Powell Retires from U.S. Supreme Court," *NRL News*, 2 July 1987, 1, 7; O'Brien, "Federal Judgeships in Retrospect," 345–6.
31. AUL Life Docket, "The Nomination of Robert H. Bork to the U.S. Supreme Court and the Reversing Roe Strategy," 13 July 1987, Box 2, Folder 3, Bork, Robert—Supreme Court nomination, 1987, SBL; James Reston, "Washington; Kennedy and Bork," *New York Times*, 5 July 1987; NRLC Legislative Alert, "Pro-abortion Groups Mount Assault on Supreme Court Nominee Robert Bork," 8 July 1987, Box 2, Folder 3, Bork, Robert—Supreme Court nomination, 1987, SBL; Douglas Johnson, "Baptists, KCs, Cops Urge the Senate to OK Judge Bork, as AFL-CIO and ACLU Oppose," *NRL News*, 10 September 1987, 1.
32. Opposition ranged from the National Association for the Advancement of Colored People, the National Education Association, the AFL-CIO, the Sierra Club, the National Mental Health Association, to the American Civil Liberties Union. O'Brien, "Federal Judgeships in Retrospect," 346.
33. Neil Devins, *Shaping Constitutional Values: Elected Government, the Supreme Court, and the Abortion Debate* (Baltimore: Johns Hopkins University Press, 1996), 105; NRLC Release, "President Fulfills Promise to Appoint 'Constructionist' Justice," 1 July 1987, Box 2, Folder 3, Bork, Robert—Supreme Court nomination, 1987, SBL; Robert Patrick, "'Party of Abortion' Digs into Defeat Bork's Nomination," *Lifeletter*, Number 7, 1987, Box 76.1-1, Folder 3, AHCDL; AUL Life Docket, "The Nomination of Robert H. Bork to the U.S. Supreme Court and the Reversing Roe Strategy," 13 July 1987, Box 2, Folder 3, Bork, Robert—Supreme Court nomination, 1987, SBL.
34. Johnson, "Baptists, KCs, Cops Urge the Senate to OK Judge Bork, As AFL-CIO and ACLU Oppose," 14; Patrick, "'Party of Abortion' Digs into Defeat Bork's Nomination," Box 76.1-1, Folder 3, AHCDL; NRLC Legislative Alert, "Pro-abortion Groups Mount Assault on Supreme Court Nominee Robert Bork," Box 2, Folder 3, Bork, Robert—Supreme Court nomination, 1987, SBL; Kenneth Noble, "Bork Backers Flood Senate with Mail," *New York Times*, 3 September 1987.

35. Larry Lewis to J. Kirk Shrewsbury, 23 October 1987, Box 2, Folder 3, Bork, Robert—Supreme Court nomination, 1987, SBL; "In Pennsylvania, the Mail Was Running 3:1 in Favor of Judge Bork," *Lifelines*, November–December 1987, 5, Box 2, Folder 3, Bork, Robert—Supreme Court nomination, 1987, SBL; Ethan Bronner, *Battle for Justice: How the Bork Nomination Shook America* (New York: W. W. Norton & Company, 1989), 201; Noble, "Bork Backers Flood Senate with Mail"; David O'Steen and Darla St. Martin, "The Lynching of Judge Robert Bork," *NRL News*, 22 January 1988, 5.
36. O'Steen and St. Martin, "The Lynching of Judge Robert Bork," 4; *Action Line*, 30 November 1987, 2, PLN; Bronner, *Battle for Justice*, 160; "The Bork Defeat—What Happened," *Free Speech Advocates*, January 1988, Box 2, Folder 3, Bork, Robert—Supreme Court nomination, 1987, SBL; *NRL News*, 13 August 1987, cover; NRLC Legislative Alert, "Pro-abortion Groups Mount Assault on Supreme Court Nominee Robert Bork," Box 2, Folder 3, Bork, Robert—Supreme Court nomination, 1987, SBL.
37. Norman Vieira and Leonard Gross, *Supreme Court Appointments: Judge Bork and the Politicization of Senate Confirmations* (Carbondale: Southern Illinois University Press, 1998), 35–6; Bronner, *Battle for Justice*, 198; "The Bork Nomination," *The Phyllis Schlafly Report*, August 1987, OA15023, Box 1, Eagle Forum, Linda Arey Files, Ronald Reagan Presidential Library.
38. O'Brien, "Federal Judgeships in Retrospect," 346–8; O'Steen and St. Martin, "The Lynching of Judge Robert Bork," 4, 5.
39. Linda Greenhouse, "Bork's Nomination Is Rejected, 58–42," *New York Times*, 24 October 1987; AUL Life Docket, "Supreme Court Nomination of Judge Anthony M. Kennedy," December 1987, Box 2, Folder 3, Bork, Robert—Supreme Court nomination, 1987, SBL; Brown quoted in "Abortion Foes Are Split on Whether to Support Kennedy for Supreme Court."
40. "In Pennsylvania, the Mail Was Running 3:1 in Favor of Judge Bork," Box 2, Folder 3, Bork, Robert—Supreme Court nomination, 1987, SBL; O'Steen and St. Martin, "The Lynching of Judge Robert Bork," 4, 5.
41. O'Steen and St. Martin, "The Lynching of Judge Robert Bork," 4, 5, 22; *NRL News*, 22 January 1988.
42. Jack Willke to NRLC Sustaining Member, 28 March 1988, and O'Steen, "Facing the Challenge of 1988," both in Box 144, Folder 11, National Right to Life Committee 1982–1991, CLC; NRLC Legislative Office, "US Senate Votes on Abortion January 1983–September 15, 1988," Box 144, Folder 9, Abortion Legislation, 1983–1991, CLC.
43. Fowler, "White House OK of 'Superbill' Pushed for *Roe* Anniversary," Box 76.1-1, Folder 3, AHCDL (emphasis in original).

CHAPTER 7

The Lessons of the Reagan Years

Abstract The chapter charts the impact of the 1980s on the national right-to-life movement, beginning with the 1988 election and the myth-making that burnished Reagan's legacy. It summarizes the fortunes of the various factions within the anti-abortion movement, exploring why some elements were on the margins by the end of the decade. It then analyzes how the lessons of the 1980s shaped the movement's goals, activism, and lobbying in subsequent decades. In 1992, the Supreme Court upheld the fundamental right to legal abortion, but the movement did not abandon democratic engagement and its political focus. Instead, symbolic approaches gained even more significance, as did the state legislatures. The chapter also explores the ways that partisan politics has served to perpetuate the polarized status of abortion in the contemporary United States, and illuminates some of the tensions at the heart of the enduring alliance between the Republican Party and the pro-life movement.

Keywords Right-to-life movement · Presidential elections · Symbolism · Legislation · Abortion politics · Republicans

In March 1988, the NRLC boldly proclaimed that "the pro-life movement has never had a better friend than President Reagan."[1] Almost a year before Reagan left the White House, the largest and most powerful

© The Author(s) 2019
P. Flowers, *The Right-to-Life Movement, the Reagan Administration, and the Politics of Abortion*, Palgrave Studies in the History of Social Movements, https://doi.org/10.1007/978-3-030-01707-1_7

national right-to-life group vigorously promoted a narrative that celebrated his anti-abortion activism and obscured the turmoil and disappointment the movement had experienced during his presidency. Alongside achievements such as the Mexico City Policy, they celebrated actions they had opposed, initiatives about which they had been tepid, and measures that were resoundingly defeated. In their election materials, Reagan was transformed into a President who had confidently and consistently seized the mantle of pro-life leadership. Although most right-to-lifers were genuinely grateful to Reagan, this focus on his legacy in 1988 was also a product of group self-interest—a way to prove that politics and lobbying made a difference so as to energize the base.

One important goal was securing the influence of pro-lifers within the Republican Party. From the start to the finish of Reagan's presidency, moderate Republicans blocked pro-life legislation, tried to defend family planning and international population aid, and were an impediment for anti-abortion nominees. Yet Reagan consistently supported pro-choice Republicans in elections, leading grassroots activists such as Teresa Ashcraft to tell him bluntly, "Please use your office on behalf of preborn babies, not just loyalty to pro-abortion Republican Senators."[2] New Right, Religious Right, and right-to-life leaders feared that moderate Republicans might reassert themselves within the party. The great unknown was whether opposition to legal abortion had sunk deep roots within the Republican Party or whether the pro-life reorientation was shallow and personality driven.

The NRLC was also troubled by the growing ambivalence and pessimism of the grassroots and felt compelled to address the widespread complaint that the Reagan administration "has not done everything it could have to stop the killing."[3] It thus crafted a history of abortion politics in the 1980s in which Reagan had "dramatically exceeded our greatest expectations," "never missed an opportunity to champion the pro-life cause," and refused to be cowed by the "pro-abortion lobby which has so successfully intimidated previous presidents." It presented the 1988 election as "absolutely central to the [the abortion] issue, here in this country and abroad, in our time, and well into the next century." Failure to elect an ally to the White House would be "the worst political disaster that could ever befall us," resulting in setbacks so big they could "completely cripple" the movement. Summaries of Reagan's legacy had pointed headings such as "See what a difference a pro-life administration makes" or "What will happen if a pro-abortion President captures the White House in 1988?"[4] These served to bolster Reagan's reputation and to remind the grassroots that the executive branch was vital for right-to-life victories. Pro-life and socially conservative influence stemmed from being able to deliver highly motivated voters. If abortion did not galvanize the base in 1988, politicians might stop viewing it as a significant electoral issue. The movement needed to remain loyal and engaged, lest it consign itself to political irrelevancy.

One potential problem was the Republican presidential candidate Vice President George H.W. Bush. Several Republican challengers, such as Senator Bob Dole (R-KS), Representative Jack Kemp (R-NH), and the televangelist Pat Robertson, had strong pro-life records. In contrast, Bush's conversion to the cause coincided with being offered the Vice President slot in July 1980, and some viewed him with skepticism. A March 1988 poll of 1400 CAC readers revealed Bush was their last choice among the Republican candidates. A small Texas group innocuously named the Ad Hoc Committee to Elect a Pro-Life President distributed a scathing flyer at the 1988 MfL titled "George Bush—Convert or Con-Man?" with a very negative overview of Bush's history, including actions and statements made while he was Vice President. More strikingly, ALL supported Robertson and refused to endorse Bush. Judie Brown believed that if the pro-life movement and the Religious Right unified behind Robertson or one of the other candidates, Bush would be forced to make policy concessions. She later lamented that in failing to "stand firm for the truth," opponents of abortion "built a stumbling block and fell over it ourselves."[5]

These critics of Bush were the exception, and even MM endorsed the establishment candidate more than two years before the primaries began. Although anti-abortion publications heaped scorn on 1988 Democratic presidential contenders such as Senator Al Gore (D-TN) and Reverend Jesse Jackson because they had changed their stance on *Roe*, they took Bush's transformation seriously. While groups such as CAC addressed Bush's past frankly, the NRLC was more circumspect, simply making broad statements about Bush's endorsement of the Human Life Amendment and his opposition to federal funding for abortion. The NRLC's national stature had a direct influence on how groups such as SBL approached their own election materials. Supporters of Bush often did not draw attention to the fact that his endorsement of the Human Life Amendment was conditional on exceptions for rape, incest, or to save the life of the mother, which absolutists firmly rejected. In carefully crafting a legacy of right-to-life achievement for the outgoing President, they worked to ensure that the grassroots saw Bush as covered in reflected glory and a true believer. Certainly, Bush campaigned as a conservative, courting the New Right and the Religious Right. The NRLC treated Bush like an extension of Reagan and presented Reagan as an overachieving champion rather than a flawed ally.[6]

Major right-to-life groups were not explicitly Republican in orientation, but in 1988 they discussed political success and failure in deeply partisan terms. *NRL News* repeatedly revisited the Bork nomination vote of 1987, concentrating on betrayal by pro-life Democrats and ignoring the actions of pro-choice Republicans. Movement leaders argued that the Bork vote proved that party leadership mattered more than personal belief and that Democrats were completely beholden to the feminist and pro-choice movements. In an NRLPAC flyer for Super Tuesday, Democratic voters were told to put "undecided," "uncommitted," or "no preference" on the ballot, because none of the candidates "deserve your vote." The *NRL News* repeatedly warned that even an ally in the White House would not be enough to end abortion, "so long as defenders of *Roe* control the key levers of power in the U.S. Senate." The core action that anti-abortion Democrats could take was to ensure that "pro-abortion candidates [were] soundly and repeatedly defeated in every election" until the Democrats got "the message."[7] In 1988 almost all Democratic presidential candidates supported *Roe*. The obvious implication was that a pro-life vote was a Republican vote.

Throughout the 1980s, right-to-lifers expended considerable energy in making Reagan and the Republican Party seem like active participants in the fight. They struggled with how to understand the silence and inaction from the White House and the frequent failure of pro-life legislation in Congress. Groups adopted different strategies, in the process revealing much about the consequences for social movements when access to power does not yield obvious results. The anti-abortion movement consisted of complex and often unruly alliances, providing an important glimpse into the many fractures that lie within socially conservative movements.

The Catholic hierarchy, which many had incorrectly viewed as the pro-life movement in the 1970s, spent Reagan's first term attempting to steer right-to-lifers toward a "consistent ethic of life." This vision of abortion politics was ignored by both lay Catholic pro-lifers and the rest of movement, and the hierarchy's perceived pragmatism made them a target for the Left and the Right. Mainstream groups such as the NRLC and AUL had no interest in an expanded definition of life issues, while conservative anti-abortion groups such as ALL and Religious Right groups such as MM roundly rejected the hierarchy's attempts to link opposition to abortion to liberal positions on welfare, defense, and the death penalty. By Reagan's second term, the Catholic hierarchy had almost no role in the nuts-and-bolts of abortion lobbying. In contrast, multi-issue Religious Right groups tended to offer unqualified, effusive praise for Reagan's efforts on abortion, even when actions were primarily symbolic. The Religious Right's interests extended well beyond social issues, and they were generally pleased by Reagan's fiscal conservatism and hawkish Cold War posture. Pro-life groups such as the NRLC engaged with and used Religious Right organizations when they wanted a broad alliance or needed to quickly generate letters and phone calls, but thoroughly rejected the idea that these organizations should shape movement priorities. The 1989 dissolution of MM, which Reverend Jerry Falwell finessed by proclaiming that the "mission is accomplished," seemed to confirm that the pro-life movement was right to keep Religious Right organizations at arm's length.[8] Spiritual belief was often a significant motivating factor for individual activists, but neither the Catholic hierarchy nor conservative evangelical and fundamentalist leaders effectively co-opted movement energies. They were a supplemental, rather than foundational, element of abortion politics.

Of the national right-to-life groups, mainstream organizations such as the NRLC and AUL were the fastest to adjust to the limitations of the Reagan years. By the middle of the 1980s, they were circumspect in their dealings with the White House. They rarely drew public attention to the gap between the President's words and his deeds, nor did they challenge his priorities in Congress. To the grassroots, they presented a narrative that foregrounded a mutually beneficial relationship between the movement and the Republicans in the executive and legislative branches. They used their political access to privately lobby, pushing the administration to offer both symbolic and substantive actions. They were judicious about where they directed their energies, and also attempted to distance themselves from direct clashes with other opponents of abortion. Mainstream groups had the most success in fashioning victories out of sporadic White House interest, and they also worked hardest to craft a pro-life legacy for the President and the Republicans.

In contrast, the loudest, most consistently scathing public criticism of Reagan and the Republicans came from conservatives in pro-life organizations such as ALL, MfL, LAPAC, and HLI. At the start of the decade, this element seemed poised to become a significant factor in federal abortion politics. However, because they abhorred compromise, they were frequently dissatisfied with the White House and Republicans in Congress. They were particularly outraged by the willingness of fellow abortion opponents to engage in negotiations aimed at eroding abortion rights. They rejected the give and take of the political process, and although they still hoped to shape both the right-to-life agenda and Republican policy, they expected to do this through the role of the ideologically pure outsider.

The Reagan years deepened some of the splits within the movement and made it harder for anti-abortionists to effectively lobby politicians. Their experiences at the start of the decade exacerbated pre-existing divisions, in part because activists blamed one another rather than critically assessing their politician allies. For most of the Reagan years, organizations that opposed abortion did not function as a coherent movement, and there were often competing claims about the true pro-life response to an issue or legislative strategy. It was therefore extremely easy for politicians to ignore the movement or to claim that a particular policy represented movement goals. And of course, for supporters of reproductive rights, this further undermined movement claims that they spoke for a sizable proportion of the general population.

The problems inherent in this situation were not immediately apparent. Bush won the 1988 election, appealing to the same coalitions that had elected Reagan. Pro-lifers boasted that they could "take credit for a good portion of his margin of victory."[9] While in office, Bush kept his promises to the movement and pursued an anti-abortion agenda, even as he moved to the political center. He ensured the Mexico City Policy remained in effect and that UNFPA was defunded. He vetoed appropriations bills that included taxpayer funding for abortion and opposed the *Freedom of Choice Act*. The Bush years were also the closest the pro-life movement came to winning their war against *Roe*. On 5 July 1989, the Supreme Court handed down a ruling in *Webster v. Reproductive Health Services*, which pro-lifers interpreted as the start of a new era, claiming that the "post-*Roe* world is now clearly visible and beckoning through the portal." This sense that the end of legal abortion was nigh was heightened when Bush successfully nominated David Souter and

Clarence Thomas to vacancies on the Supreme Court. Together, Reagan and Bush had fundamentally altered the make-up of the court, appointing five new judges to the bench. Yet in the 29 June 1992 decision in *Planned Parenthood v. Casey*, legal abortion was narrowly preserved in a 5-4 decision. O'Connor, Kennedy, and Souter, a triumvirate of Reagan/Bush nominees, authored the plurality opinion, declaring that "liberty finds no refuge in a jurisprudence of doubt" and the weight of precedent meant *Roe* must be upheld.[10] It was a devastating decision for opponents of abortion; Burke Balch, the state legislative director of the NRLC told the *New York Times*, "We've been fighting to overturn Roe v. Wade for 20 years and if necessary we'll fight for 20 more, but for now, we've lost."[11] Pro-lifers rejected both *Roe* and *Casey* as bad law, and the lessons learned during the 1980s had a significant impact on how they approached abortion after 1992.

The Reagan years started a cycle in which some right-to-life organizations and activists celebrated and even initiated symbolic actions. One example was the interest in partial-birth abortions or, more precisely, intact dilation and extraction. The NRLC began pushing for a federal prohibition of the procedure in 1995, and passage of the *Partial-Birth Abortion Ban Act* in 2003 was heralded by the NRLC, AUL, CWA, FotF, and the USCC as a major success—the first federal ban on abortion since *Roe*. Yet for all the celebration, its impact was minimal. Pro-lifers were relatively candid about the intent behind the ban. In 1995, Douglas Johnson of the NRLC explained to a journalist that the core hope was that as the public learned about a specific abortion technique, "they might also learn something about other abortion methods and that this would foster a growing opposition to abortion." For its pragmatism, the NRLC was attacked by groups such as ALL, HLI, and OR, which condemned the focus on partial-birth abortion as political theater. Judie Brown dismissed the ban as a "Republican concept," the "least they could possibly get away with in order to receive the pro-life vote."[12]

The symbolism of the Reagan years has also borne darker fruit. In 1993, only two months into the Democratic presidency of Bill Clinton, Dr. David Gunn, an abortion provider and long-standing target of OR, was shot dead by a pro-lifer outside a clinic in Pensacola, Florida. Gunn was the first of 11 people, four of whom were doctors, assassinated by right-to-lifers during the presidencies of Clinton and fellow Democrat Barack Obama. Pro-life murderers view killing abortion doctors as "justifiable homicide," taking one life to save thousands of fetal lives.[13]

There is a fringe element in the movement that defends anti-abortion terrorists, but the Religious Right, the Catholic hierarchy, and mainstream right-to-life groups strongly disavow them. As David O'Steen of the NRLC explained after a fatal clinic bombing in 1998, the fundamental right-to-life goal is to "restore respect for human life. Violence opposes that goal." Although anti-abortion murderers operate on the extreme margins of the movement, they clearly share its partisan imperatives. It is striking that this type of violence occurs only when a Democrat is President. While this book charts the political frustrations experienced by the movement when their ally is in the White House, opponents of abortion draw significant strength and comfort from having the nation's leader on their side. It is no coincidence that the worst examples of pro-life violence occur when the movement experiences a withdrawal of this support and prestige, demonstrating the power of the strategies pioneered by Reagan.

Another important part of the pro-life movement's political education in the 1980s was an expanded understanding of what victory looked like and where it might be achieved. In 1988, they thought the Senate, combined with the presidency, needed to be the focus. After *Webster* and *Casey*, the national right-to-life movement did not abandon the judicial strategy or its interest in the democratic process. However, it did reorient, directing an increasing amount of energy toward the states. Interpreting the Supreme Court's "undue burden" framework as a challenge, states passed legislation that placed gestational limits on abortion and mandated abortion counseling, ultrasounds, waiting periods, and parental consent requirements for minors. This strategy has recently accelerated; since the 2010 midterm elections and the conservative landslide at the state level, thousands of new abortion provisions have been introduced. Between July 2011 and July 2016, 334 abortion restrictions became law, and this period accounts for 30% of all the restrictions passed since 1973. The landscape of abortion provision has been dramatically reshaped.[14]

National groups such as AUL and the NRLC are at the forefront of this shift, using their expertise and experience in federal lobbying and litigation to drive sophisticated multi-state campaigns. AUL produces an annual *Defending Life* playbook and wrote much of the model legislation adopted since 2010. It has been particularly successful in reframing the pregnant woman as a victim of abortion and convincing legislators that abortion providers require heightened levels of regulation and medical control.¹⁵ While AUL has worked to limit abortion provision on the ground, the NRLC has been at the forefront of new efforts to restrict abortion rights, using the notion of fetal pain to justify a ban on the procedure after 20 weeks (a cutoff that experts suggest is not based on medical science). Between 2010 and 2017, 16 states passed a version of the *Pain-Capable Unborn Child Protection Act*. This legislation was also introduced in the 113th, 114th, and 115th Congresses, passing three times in the House of Representatives.¹⁶ The cumulative effect of this state and national legislative activity is to ensure that even as abortion remains legal, access is increasingly fraught, and pro-choice supporters are engaged in a constant cycle of lobbying and lawsuits to prevent further erosion of reproductive rights.

It can seem as though the pro-life movement is currently in the ascendance, but many of the problems that plagued the movement in the 1980s persist today, as illustrated by two contemporary approaches. The *Pain-Capable Unborn Child Protection Act* and the *Heartbeat Protection Act* both originated as state bills and attempt to restrict access to abortion after a certain point in pregnancy: 20 weeks in the first instance, six to eight weeks in the second. The *Pain-Capable Unborn Child Protection Act* is supported by the NRLC and AUL, which believe it will stand up to judicial review and will help shift the Supreme Court away from the notion of viability. It also capitalizes on public discomfit about abortions performed late in pregnancy. However, not all in the movement back pursuing yet more incrementalist legislation, and a rival model emerged in Ohio in 2011. The *Heartbeat Protection Act* was drafted by grassroots activist Janet Porter, founder of Faith2Action, a Religious Right and family values organization that works against legal abortion and homosexual rights. The NRLC has consistently dismissed the *Heartbeat Protection Act*, describing it as a "pointless and futile strategy."¹⁷

The introduction of both bills in Congress in 2017 initially seemed like a major challenge to the supremacy of the NRLC and AUL, but to date the rival models have produced nothing but public squabbling and performative votes. Porter argued that with an ally in the White House and Republican majorities in both houses of Congress, the movement should try to ban as many abortions as possible (although a similar political climate existed for four years under Republican President George W. Bush). The NRLC still refused to prioritize the *Heartbeat Protection Act* and was consequently attacked by other opponents of abortion. Troy Newman of OR lamented, "There has been no greater betrayal of innocent blood since Judas betrayed our Lord." Representative Steve King (R-IA), who introduced the legislation in Congress, called on grassroots activists to challenge the NRLC's "hypocrisy."[18] To date, neither bill has been successful. On 29 January 2018, Senate Majority Leader Mitch McConnell (R-KY) forced a procedural vote on the *Pain-Capable Unborn Child Protection Act*, even though he did not have the votes to break a Democrat-led filibuster. It was defeated—an outcome expected by all commentators based on Senate numbers and because the same thing occurred in 2015. It was clearly a vote aimed at pacifying pro-life and Religious Right voters in time for the midterm elections.

The polarization between the two parties on abortion can make the enduring anti-abortion alliance with the Republicans seem unremarkable, for how can there be meaningful competition between the "party of life" and the "party of death." But of course, this relationship is predicated on a series of calculations and choices. Most Americans do not view abortion as a key voting issue, but opponents of abortion are more likely than pro-choice Americans to only vote for a candidate who shares their views. Since the 1990s, right-to-life and Religious Right voters have wielded special influence in Republican primaries and, in a system with non-compulsory voting, they offer a dedicated and highly motivated voting bloc. However, there are other ways that national groups could approach elections. Rather than focusing on the Republican candidate most likely to win, they could encourage the grassroots to vote only for candidates with the strongest pro-life track record. They could hold elected officials accountable and encourage the grassroots to vote against Congressional incumbents who have not delivered. They could even urge the grassroots to stay home on Election Day. In short, they could reject what Judie Brown of ALL described as "Ronald Reagan's 11th commandment—never speak ill of ... Republicans." They could also work to make abortion a bipartisan issue again through groups such as Democrats for Life. After all, despite three decades of highly partisan abortion politics, approximately one-third of Democrats identify as pro-life. Instead, since the 1980s, mainstream right-to-life groups have framed political contests as though there is no choice but to actively support Republicans. What is particularly striking about the NRLC is how frequently it supports establishment Republicans and how willing it is to do battle with state pro-life groups with different political priorities.[19]

It has been over 20 years since the Republican Party last seriously addressed its stance on abortion. In 1992, two pro-choice Republican organizations testified before the platform committee that the pro-life plank was "a millstone around our pro-choice candidates' necks." In 1993, Richard Bond, the outgoing Republican National Committee chair, blamed pro-lifers for Bush's defeat and described the plank as "zealotry masquerading as principle." In 1996, the Republican presidential candidate Senator Bob Dole (R-KS) went on record asking the platform committee to include a "declaration of tolerance" acknowledging the "diversity of views" within the party on legal abortion. His call for the party to be a "big tent" was supported by Republican National Committee Chairman Lee Atwater (former advisor to Reagan and Bush). This was a dramatic about-face from Dole, who had a long history as a right-to-life Senator and was instrumental in inserting the original abortion plank in 1976. Pro-life and Religious Right groups warned that if Republicans modified the plank the grassroots would stay home on Election Day. The plank was not changed and Dole was resoundingly defeated. While some Republicans spent the Clinton years questioning the influence of social and religious conservatives within the party, the candidacy of George W. Bush in 2000 ultimately reaffirmed the importance of conservative Christian (specifically, evangelical Protestant and Catholic) voters in Republican political strategy.[20]

Abortion now essentially functions as a litmus test for Republicans with federal ambitions. Candidates must embrace a right-to-life position even if their actual track record is murky, as was the case with George H.W. Bush, Mitt Romney, and Donald Trump. The movement accepts this performance of pro-life fealty every four to eight years as a demonstration of political good faith—the right and proper acknowledgment of their perceived influence on the base. Polling in 2017 indicated that 65% of Republicans believe abortion should be illegal in all or most cases.[21] In Congress, the partisan realignments outlined in Chapter 2 mean Republican elected officials are almost universally pro-life. In the 115th Congress, only two Senate Republicans and two House Republicans voted against the *Pain-Capable Unborn Child Protection Act*. Yet, as demonstrated by the Senate vote on the bill, the Republican leadership is still willing to perform its commitment to the cause without any expectation of delivering votes or results.

There are several explanations for this paradox. One is cynicism. For decades, Republicans have maintained pro-life loyalty on the cheap and there have been no electoral repercussions for failure. Given that over one-quarter of Republicans still identify as pro-choice, there is the strong possibility that too much right-to-life action will alienate voters.[22] Certainly, current public opinion polls show broad support for *Roe*, with a July 2017 PEW poll finding that 57% of Americans thought abortion should be legal in all or most circumstances.[23] Another factor is that even Republican politicians who identify as pro-life generally do not share all the movement's beliefs. Very few elected officials are absolutists. Exceptions—particularly those for rape and incest—frequently cause ugly conflict among opponents of abortion. Since a vocal element of the right-to-life movement rejects all exceptions, this means that even Republican pro-life action can provoke condemnation from some anti-abortionists.[24]

Many have questioned right-to-life and Religious Right support for the ideologically flexible Trump, particularly given his 1999 identification as "very pro-choice."[25] This misses the point of the lessons of the Reagan years. Right-to-lifers do not need Trump to be a true believer so long as he talks and occasionally walks like an ally. His bellicose and vivid rhetoric excites them. Jeanne Mancini, president of MfL, noted that during the campaign, "he went farther than any other candidate has ever gone in talking about [Supreme Court] justices and … late-term abortion." His running mate Indiana governor Mike Pence has impeccable right-to-life credentials. Even Trump's status as an outsider to the Republican Party and Washington, DC works in his favor, for decades of working with the establishment has not brought right-to-lifers any closer to outlawing abortion.

Trump has mirrored many of the performative and policy elements of Reagan's pro-life politics. He sent key members of his cabinet to address the MfL in 2017, addressed it himself via live video feed in 2018, and proclaimed 22 January 2018 to be National Sanctity of Human Life Day. Trump nominated Neil Gorsuch to the Supreme Court, seemingly keeping his campaign "promise" to nominate "only pro-life justices." He reinstated the Mexico City Policy, approved the defunding of UNFPA, and reintroduced the Reagan era "gag rule" to try to prevent PP from accessing federal family planning funds. Trump has also gone beyond the Reagan template, dramatically expanding the scope of the Mexico City Policy, directly calling for the Senate to pass the *Pain-Capable Unborn Child Protection Act*, making multiple interventions into Congressional debates about abortion, birth control, and health insurance, and physically attending and keynoting a pro-life gala held by the Susan B. Anthony List. In Trump's first 18 months in office, he has offered anti-abortionists symbolism and substance.[26]

The significance of abortion in contemporary American politics has been a constant since Reagan's 1980 presidential campaign, and the intertwined relationship between the right-to-life movement and the Republican Party often seems inevitable. In practice, as this book outlines, this alliance has always required considerable work and compromise, most of it by pro-lifers. Most anti-abortion groups have remained enthusiastically loyal to Republicans even though they have not achieved their core goal of completely ending legal abortion. Many national and state pro-life groups have prioritized secondary and even tertiary goals in the hopes of getting their politician allies to expend capital on their cause. Organizations that reject this tactical compromise operate on the fringes of the movement but have not ceded their right to speak on behalf of the cause, and thus the divisions between groups sometimes derail legislative and judicial approaches. Ronald Reagan spoke regularly of the "terrible national tragedy of abortion" and many elected Republican officials have since echoed this language, yet few make policy choices that follow their words.[27] Right-to-life politicians and activists often claim they are lone voices in the wilderness, standing up to the status quo and speaking an uncomfortable truth at great personal, social, and political cost. In practice, pragmatism and performance have become the defining features of most elements of conservative national abortion politics.

Notes

1. O'Steen, "Facing the Challenge of 1988," Box 144, Folder 11, National Right to Life Committee—1982–1991, CLC.
2. Teresa Ashcraft to Ronald Reagan, 1986, Box 4, Abortion (4), MBE.
3. Andrusko, "The Extraordinary Difference a Pro-life President Makes."
4. O'Steen, "Facing the Challenge of 1988," Box 144, Folder 11, National Right to Life Committee—1982–1991, CLC; Jack Wilke, "NRLC's Determined to Have Pro-life Successor to Reagan," *NRL News*, 22 January 1988, 3; Jack Wilke to NRLC Sustaining Member, 13 June 1988 and Jack Willke to NRLC Sustaining Member, 28 March 1988, both in Box 144, Folder 11, National Right to Life Committee—1982–1991, CLC; "Thank You President Reagan and Vice President Bush," Box 11, President's Accomplishments Pro-Life, MBE.
5. For discussion of Bush and abortion, see Amy Jones, "George Bush and the Religious Right," in Martin Medhurst (ed.), *The Rhetorical Presidency of George H.W. Bush* (College Station: Texas A&M University

Press, 2006), 149–70. *Action Line*, 1 April 1988, 1, Box 96, Folder 7, Abortion—Major Articles, 1985–88, CLC; "George Bush—Convert or Con-Man?" and "This Little Guy Wants You to Vote Pro-life ...," flyers, both in Box 76.1-2, Folders 5 and 6, Ad Hoc Committee to Elect a Pro-Life President, Hall–Hoag Collection, John Hay Library at Brown University; Brown, *It Is I Who Have Chosen You*, 112.
6. Dave Andrusko, "Profiles of Two Leading Pro-abortion Democratic Candidates for President," *NRL News*, 24 March 1988, 1; "Thank You President Reagan and Vice President Bush," flyer, Box 11, President's Accomplishments Pro-Life, MBE; NRLC, "George Bush and Dan Quayle Fact Sheet on Abortion," and NRLPAC, "For Life's Sake—Vote George Bush," flyer, both in Box 2, Folder 6, Bush–Dukakis Election—Comparisons, 1988, SBL; J. Shrewsbury to Sandra Faucher, 29 August 1988, Adrian Rogers to Fellow Pastor, 23 September 1988, and "The Abortion Issue: Where Do the Candidates Stand?" draft flyer, all in Box 2, Folder 6, Bush–Dukakis Election—Comparisons, 1988, SB; "The Reagan/Bush Record on Abortion, 1981–1988," *NRL News*, 20 October 1988, 9.
7. NRLPAC, "If You Want to Vote Against Abortion Tuesday March 8 ..." flyer, Box 144, Folder 11, National Right to Life Committee—1982–1991, CLC; David O'Steen and Darla St. Martin, "The Road to Reversing *Roe v. Wade*," *NRL News*, 22 January 1987, 10; Darla St. Martin, "The Power to End Abortion," *NRL News*, 22 January 1988, 7.
8. Peter Steinfels, "Moral Majority to Dissolve," *New York Times*, 12 June 1989.
9. *Action Line*, 15 November 1988, 4, PLN.
10. NRLC, "The Presidential Record on Life: President George H.W. Bush 1989–1993," https://www.nrlc.org/uploads/records/bush41record0608.pdf; James Bopp and Richard Coleson, "*Webster* Opens Door to Post-*Roe v. Wade* World," *NRL News*, 13 July 1989, 1; *Planned Parenthood of Southeastern Pennsylvania. v. Casey*, 505 US 833 (1992).
11. Tamar Lewin, "Long Battles Over Abortion Are Seen," *New York Times*, 30 June 1992.
12. For more on the *Partial-Birth Abortion Ban Act*, see Sara Dubow, *Ourselves Unborn: A History of the Fetus in Modern America* (Oxford: Oxford University Press, 2011), 153–83; and Schoen, *After Roe*, 199–244. Johnson quoted in Alissa Rubin, *National Review*, 4 March 1996, 28; Brown quoted in David Courtwright, *No Right Turn: Conservative Politics in a Liberal America* (Cambridge: Harvard University Press, 2010), 255.
13. Liam Stack, "A Brief History of Deadly Attacks on Abortion Providers," *New York Times*, 29 November 2015; Mason, *Killing for Life*, 46–71;

O'Steen quoted in Art Toalston, "Fatal Abortion Clinic Bombing Condemned by Pro-life Leaders," *Baptist Press*, 30 January 1998. For more on anti-abortion terrorism, see Haugeberg, *Women Against Abortion*, 100–36; Risen and Thomas, *Wrath of Angels*, 339–72; and Schoen, *After Roe*, 155–98.
14. https://www.guttmacher.org/infographic/2016/334-abortion-restrictions-enacted-states-2011-july-2016-account-30-all-abortion.
15. Olga Kazhan, "Planning the End of Abortion," *The Atlantic*, 16 July 2015.
16. "Pain-Capable Unborn Child Protection Act," factsheet, NRLC, 9 January 2017, https://www.nrlc.org/uploads/stateleg/PCUCPAfactsheet.pdf.
17. "Statement of Carol Tobias on Senate Introduction of Pain-Capable Unborn Child Protection Act," 7 November 2013, https://www.nrlc.org/communications/releases/2013/tobiasstatement110713/; Erik Eckholm, "Anti-abortion Groups Are Split on Legal Tactics," *New York Times*, 4 December 2011; Molly Redden, "The Strict Abortion Ban That Abortion Foes Fear," *Mother Jones*, 2 February 2015.
18. Porter quoted in Claire Chretien, "Congress to Hold Hearing Today on Banning Abortions of Babies with Beating Hearts," *Life Site*, 1 November 2017; Newman quoted in Janet Porter, "National Right to Life Betrays Babies—Blocks Congressional Vote on Pro-life Heartbeat Bill," *Christian News Wire*, 18 January 2018; King quoted in Claire Chretien, "U.S. Congressman: Pro-life 'Turf Battle' Preventing Vote on Bill to Ban Nearly All Abortions," *Life Site*, 12 January 2018.
19. http://news.gallup.com/poll/183449/abortion-edges-important-voting-issue-americans.aspx; Brown, *It Is I Who Have Chosen You*, 162; http://news.gallup.com/poll/147941/republicans-unified-democrats-abortion.aspx; Kirsten Anderson, "Controversy as New Group Challenges Georgia Right to Life for National Right to Life Affiliation," *Life Site*, 27 March 2014.
20. Young, *Feminists and Party Politics*, 130; Carol Long, "Republicans Urged to Abandon Babies," *NRL News*, 9 February 1993, 6; John King, "Dole Wants GOP Platform to Include 'Declaration of Tolerance,'" *Associated Press*, 7 June 1996; Robert Shogan, "Abortion Foes Shred Dole's Tolerance Clause," *Los Angeles Times*, 6 August 1996; Critchlow, *The Conservative Ascendancy*, 261.
21. PEW Research Centre, "Public Opinion on Abortion," factsheet, 7 July 2017, http://www.pewforum.org/fact-sheet/public-opinion-on-abortion/.
22. http://news.gallup.com/poll/147941/republicans-unified-democrats-abortion.aspx.
23. PEW Research Centre, "Public Opinion on Abortion," factsheet.

24. Daniel Newhauser and Lauren Fox, "GOP Leaders Pull Abortion Bill After Revolt by Women, Moderates," *The Atlantic*, 21 January 2015; Ben Johnson, "NRLC Letter Sparks Debate among Pro-life Leaders on How to Treat No-Exceptions Lawmakers," *Life Site*, 3 September 2013.
25. In 2011, Trump told the Conservative Political Action Conference that his views had changed and he was now pro-life.
26. Philip Bumb, "Donald Trump Took 5 Different Positions on Abortion in 3 Days," *Washington Post*, 3 April 2016; Mancini quoted in Emma Green, "Will the Pro-Life Movement Split with Trump on Issues Other Than Abortion?" *The Atlantic*, 27 January 2017; Bradford Richardson, "Pro-life Movement Praises Neil Gorsuch, Supreme Court Pick," *Washington Times*, 1 February 2017; "President Trump Addresses the 45th March for Life," 19 January 2018, https://www.whitehouse.gov/articles/president-trump-addresses-45th-march-life/; "President Donald J. Trump Is Standing Up for the Sanctity of Life," factsheet, 19 January 2018, https://www.whitehouse.gov/briefings-statements/president-donald-j-trump-standing-sanctity-life/; Bradley Mattes, "President Trump to Pro-life Movement: 'I Have Kept My Promise,'" *Life Site*, 24 May 2018. For a discussion of the Religious Right's support for Trump, see Neil Young, "Catholics and Evangelicals: Does Donald Trump Mean the End of the Religious Right?" in M. Gayte, B. Chelini-Pont, and M. Rozell (eds.), *Catholics and US Politics After the 2016 Elections: Understanding the Swing Vote* (Cham: Palgrave Macmillan, 2018), 63–81.
27. Ronald Reagan, "Remarks to Participants in the 1985 March for Life Rally," 22 January 1985, http://www.presidency.ucsb.edu/ws/index.php?pid=38733&st=March+for+Life&st1.

Index

0–9
1964 election, 25, 50
1972 election, 28
1976 election, 25, 26, 29, 65, 147
1980 election, 16, 25, 27–29, 31, 32, 42, 43, 46, 49, 50, 52, 54–56, 64, 72, 120, 149
1982 midterm election, 53, 76, 79, 80
1984 election, 25, 28–31, 72, 90, 92, 97, 101, 102, 116, 127
1986 midterm election, 116–118, 126
1988 election, 31, 56, 117, 121, 123, 130, 131, 138–140, 142
1992 election, 31, 125, 146
1996 election, 147
2000 election, 147
2010 midterm election, 144
2018 midterm election, 146

A
abolitionism, 7, 24, 54, 69, 120
Abortion and the Conscience of the Nation, 7, 32, 72, 114, 116
Abortion and the Constitution, 125
absolutism, 20, 64, 66, 70, 119, 139, 142, 145, 148
Action Line. *See* Christian Action Council (CAC)
Ad Hoc Committee in Defense of Life (AHCDL), 18, 27, 48, 51, 52, 55, 56, 70, 71, 79, 104, 116, 118–121, 127, 131
Ad Hoc Committee to Elect a Pro-Life President, 139
African American pro-lifers, 24
Agency for International Development (AID), 90–94, 96, 98, 99, 102–105
AIDS, 117, 128
A.L.L. About Issues. *See* American Life League (ALL)
American Bar Association, 68
American Citizens Concerned for Life (ACCL), 18, 20, 27, 32, 46, 70, 78, 122
American Conservative Union, 128

American Life League (ALL), 2, 19, 20, 24, 27, 30, 32, 49, 66, 67, 69, 70, 72, 74, 92, 95, 100, 119, 121, 129, 139, 141–143, 146
Americans United for Life (AUL), 17, 20, 42, 46, 70, 73, 91, 122, 125–127, 129, 141, 143–145
Anderson, Carl, 95, 97, 114, 118, 124
Anderson, John, 27
Ashcraft, Teresa, 116, 138
Atwater, Lee, 29, 79, 147

B
Badger, Doug, 55
Baker, Howard, 27, 29, 69, 75–77, 80, 117
Baker, James, 48, 50, 76, 98
Balch, Burke, 143
Bauer, Gary, 28, 77, 124
Benedick, Richard, 99, 100
Bernardin, Joseph, 72
Biden, Joe, 126, 128
Black Americans for Life (BAL), 24
Blackwell, Morton, 79, 80
Bond, Richard, 147
Borcherdt, Wendy, 43
Bork, Robert, 5, 68, 114, 126–130, 140
Bowen, Otis, 123, 124
Brink, David, 68
Brown, Harold O.J., 20, 47
Brown, Judie, 19, 23, 49, 69, 70, 75, 92, 98, 100, 119–121, 139, 143, 146
Brown, Paul, 1, 19, 24, 49, 64, 70, 74, 81, 98, 116
Buchanan, Patrick, 52, 104
Buckley, James, 65, 99–101
Buckley, William, 72
Bush, George H.W., 27, 50, 124, 139, 140, 142, 147
Bush, George W., 105, 145, 147
busing, 25, 67, 80, 128

C
Carter, Jimmy, 26, 27, 29, 46, 95
Casey, Dan, 128
Catholic Church, 6, 17, 20, 23, 26, 28, 30, 33, 48, 64, 66, 68, 70–73, 80, 81, 99, 120, 140, 141, 144
  conservative Catholics, 19, 20, 23, 71, 81, 92, 97
Cavanaugh-O'Keefe, John, 22, 92, 94, 102
Central Intelligence Agency (CIA), 97
Chafee, John, 29, 124
China, 90, 93–97, 103, 104, 106
Christian Action Council (CAC), 20, 31, 47, 55, 70, 71, 74–76, 98, 114, 120, 124, 127, 139
Christian Broadcasting Network, 23
Christian Voice (CV), 22, 127
Church Amendment, 26, 67
City of Akron v. Akron Reproductive Health, Inc, 55
civil rights, 25, 126, 128
clinic rescues, 8, 22, 23, 115
clinic violence, 8, 143
Clinton, Bill, 105, 125, 143, 147
Cold War, 95–97, 104, 141
Concerned Women for America (CWA), 22, 120, 121, 127, 143
conservatism, 2–6, 9, 10, 21, 24, 25, 29, 42, 44, 47, 48, 50, 53, 75, 77, 80, 94, 95, 97, 101, 117, 123, 126, 131, 139, 140, 147
Conservative Caucus (CC), 70
Conservative Political Action Conference, 75
consistent ethic of life, 72, 120, 140

constitutional originalism, 68, 126, 127, 129
constitutional strategy, 4, 8, 16, 26, 29–31, 42, 43, 57, 64–66, 68, 69, 76, 81, 82, 114, 116, 119, 125
contraceptives, 18, 24, 29, 66, 71, 92, 97, 121, 122, 148
Council for National Policy (CNP), 47
court-stripping legislation, 67, 68
Craven, Erma, 24
Craven, Marie, 49
Crum, Gary, 32
Culhane, Anne, 49
culture wars, 5, 34, 130
Curran, Gary, 95, 98

D
Defending Life, 144
Democratic Party, 16, 25, 26, 28, 29, 31, 46, 50, 79, 80, 90, 105, 117, 125, 128–131, 139, 140, 143, 146
  1976 Democratic National Convention, 30
  1976 Democratic Party Platform, 26
  1980 Democratic National Convention, 30
  1980 Democratic Party Platform, 30
  1984 Democratic National Convention, 30
  1984 Democratic Party Platform, 30
  New Deal coalition, 28
  pro-life Democrats, 18, 24, 26, 29–31, 49, 80, 119, 127, 129, 131, 140, 146
Democrats for Life, 146
Denton, Jeremiah, 55
Department of Health and Human Services (HHS), 32, 122, 123
Dobson, James, 23
Doe v. Bolton, 16
Dolan, Terry, 21, 51
Dole, Bob, 26, 139, 147
Dole, Elizabeth, 33
Douglas, William, 42
Doyle, Jean, 17, 96, 99, 114
D'Souza, Dinesh, 124
Dukakis, Michael, 31

E
Eagle Forum (EF), 46, 53, 128
Eagleton, Thomas, 80
East, John, 55
Economic Recovery Act, 76
Engel, Randy, 19, 91, 92, 95, 98
Equal Rights Amendment (ERA), 21, 26, 27, 43, 44, 46, 47, 49–51, 53, 66
exceptions, 20, 66, 68, 119, 139, 148

F
Faith2Action, 145
Falwell, Jerry, 22–24, 50, 51, 53, 141
family planning, 5, 8, 19, 27, 32, 82, 90, 92, 98, 99, 101, 106, 114, 118, 121, 122, 124, 130, 138, 148
Family Protection Act, 53
family values, 6, 19, 21, 43, 45, 47, 49, 51, 53, 66, 99, 118, 122, 131, 145
Faucher, Sandra, 30, 31
Ferraro, Geraldine, 30
Fielding, Fred, 48
Fiore, Charles, 19, 70, 76
Focus on the Family (FotF), 22, 23, 120, 143
Ford, Gerald, 25, 26, 29, 42, 65, 126
Foreign Assistance Act, 90

Foreign Assistance Authorization Act, 103
Frech, Frances, 65
Freedom of Choice Act, 142

G
gag rule, 124, 148
Galebach, Stephen, 96, 118
Gandhi, Indira, 93
Gasper, Jo Ann, 32, 122–124
Gemma, Peter, 49, 51, 53
gender gap, 30, 44, 56
Gephardt, Dick, 31
Gerster, Carolyn, 17, 20, 27, 43, 45–47, 49, 51, 54
gestation limits, 145
Ginsburg, Douglas, 129
global gag rule. *See* Mexico City Policy
Goldwater, Barry, 25, 29, 44, 50
Gore, Al, 31, 139
Gorsuch, Neil, 148
Grassley, Charles, 55
Gray, Nellie, 1, 9, 17, 18, 27, 44, 49, 51, 54, 73, 116
Gribbin, William, 80
Griscom, Tom, 124
Griswold v. Connecticut, 16, 71
Gunn, David, 143

H
Handbook on Abortion, 17
Hatch-Eagleton Amendment, 29, 69, 80, 81, 116, 120, 125, 130
Hatch, Orrin, 68–71, 73, 74, 76, 80
Hatfield, Mark, 74
Heartbeat Protection Act, 145
Heflin, Howell, 127
Helms Amendment, 26, 67, 90, 92, 94
Helms, Jesse, 26, 47, 67–71, 73, 74, 76, 78–81, 90, 118
Heritage Foundation (HF), 75

Higgins, George, 28
Hohl, Anna, 79
homosexuality, 6, 21, 46, 145
Horan, Dennis, 18
Humane Vitae, 71
Human Life Amendment, 8, 16, 26, 27, 31, 42, 43, 53, 64–67, 76, 81, 82, 99, 114, 119, 139
    personhood, 65–69
    states' rights, 65, 69, 74, 80
Human Life Bill, 29, 64, 67, 69–71, 73, 76–78, 81, 118
Human Life Federalism Amendment, 29, 64, 68–71, 73, 74, 76–78, 80, 81, 120
Human Life International (HLI), 19, 20, 22, 70, 72, 91, 92, 115, 142, 143
Human Life Review, 18, 32, 72, 95
human rights, 95
Humphrey, Gordon, 125
Hyde Amendment, 26, 30, 67, 69, 102, 114, 118, 121, 139
    Washington, DC, 1, 114
Hyde, Henry, 47, 55, 119, 121

I
incrementalism, 18, 20, 42, 64, 70, 141–143, 145
Inouye, Daniel, 103
Internal Revenue Service, 21, 25
International Planned Parenthood Federation (IPPF), 91–94, 102
International Women's Year Conference (IWYC), 46, 47
Iowa Right to Life Committee, 78
Iran–Contra affair, 117, 128

J
Jackson, Jesse, 24, 31, 139
James, Kay, 24

Jefferson, Mildred, 17, 20, 24
John Paul II, 120
Johnson, Douglas, 17, 75, 116, 119, 143
Johnson, Lyndon, 50
judicial strategy, 8, 16, 18, 30, 42, 43, 48, 53–55, 82, 125, 130, 143, 144, 148

K
Kasten, Bob, 103
Kemp, Jack, 103, 118, 123, 139
Kemp–Kasten Amendment, 103–106
Kennedy, Anthony, 2, 129, 130, 143
Kennedy, Edward, 27, 126, 128
King, Steve, 146
Kirkpatrick, Jeane, 92, 95, 96
Koop, C. Everett, 20, 21, 32
Kowansky, Adelaide, 49
Krol, John, 48

L
Lampe, Joseph, 78
Library Court (LC), 75
Life Amendment Political Action Committee (LAPAC), 18–20, 27, 28, 49, 64, 70, 74, 116, 142
Lifeletter. See Ad Hoc Committee in Defense of Life (AHCDL)
Lutherans for Life, 20

M
Mall, Roger, 78
Mancini, Jeanne, 148
March for Life (MfL), 1, 17, 18, 27, 32, 33, 44, 70, 73, 116, 139, 142, 148
Markman, Stephen, 74
Marshner, Connie, 75

Marx, Paul, 19, 23, 72, 91, 92, 98, 100, 115
McConnell, Mitch, 146
McCormack, Ellen, 26–28
McFadden, Jim, 18, 48
McHugh, James, 95
McPherson, M. Peter, 98, 103–105
Mecklenburg, Marjory, 17, 18, 20, 32, 122
Meese, Edwin, 8, 33, 45, 48, 76, 129
Mexico City Policy, 5, 8, 95, 96, 98, 101, 102, 104–106, 114, 116, 138, 142, 148
Minnesota Citizens Concerned for Life (MCCL), 68, 69
Mondale, Walter, 30
Moral Majority (MM), 22, 23, 25, 47, 50, 53, 70, 71, 76, 77, 79, 98, 120, 121, 127, 139, 141

N
National Association of Evangelicals, 20
National Committee for a Human Life Amendment (NCHLA), 20, 120
National Conference of Catholic Bishops (NCCB), 17, 20, 72, 80, 120
National Conservative Political Action Committee, 128
National Organization for Women (NOW), 26, 29, 42, 128, 130
National Pro-Family Coalition (NPFC), 22, 75
National Pro-Life Political Action Committee (NPLPAC), 18, 20, 27, 49, 51, 53, 56, 70, 71, 76
National Right to Life Committee (NRLC), 17–20, 23, 24, 27, 28, 30, 32, 33, 42, 45–47, 51–54, 56, 65, 66, 70, 73, 75, 76, 79, 81, 93, 95, 96, 100, 102–105,

114–116, 118–120, 122, 123, 127–130, 137–141, 143–146
National Right to Life News. *See* National Right to Life Committee (NRLC)
National Right to Life Political Action Committee (NRLPAC), 18, 30, 140
National Sanctity of Human Life Day, 32, 148
National Security Council, 98, 100
National Women's Political Caucus, 26
natural family planning, 19, 99
Neary, Denise, 129
neo-liberalism, 9, 76, 77, 80, 94, 97, 141
Newman, Troy, 145
New Right, 7, 16, 19, 21, 25, 28, 29, 42, 44, 47, 48, 50–53, 55, 64, 70, 73, 75, 81, 98, 117, 128, 131, 138, 140
Nickles, Don, 47
Nixon, Richard, 25, 28
Nofziger, Lyn, 43, 50
Northern strategy, 28, 131
nuclear freeze, 72

O
Obama, Barack, 105, 143
The O'Connor Report, 53
O'Connor, Sandra Day, 4, 42, 44–56, 64, 81, 125, 127–129, 143
one-child policy, 90, 93–96, 103, 104, 106
O'Neill, Tip, 42
Operation Rescue (OR), 23, 115, 143, 145
O'Steen, David, 68, 144

P
Packwood, Bob, 29, 79
Pain-Capable Unborn Child Protection Act, 145–148

Partial-Birth Abortion Ban Act, 143
Pathfinder Fund (PF), 91
Pence, Mike, 148
Pennsylvania Pro-Life Federation (PPLF), 127, 129
Phillips, Howard, 21, 48, 51
Phillips, Kevin, 28
The Phyllis Schlafly Report. *See* Eagle Forum (EF)
Planned Parenthood Federation of America (PP), 24, 91, 102, 122, 123, 130, 148
Planned Parenthood v. Casey, 143, 144
population, 5, 8, 19, 27, 32, 82, 90–94, 96–106, 122, 138
Porter, Janet, 145
Porter, John, 124
Powell, Lewis, 125, 126, 129
Presbyterians Pro-Life, 20
President's Pro-Life Bill, 5, 114, 118–121, 130, 131
pro-choice movement, 8, 16, 55, 93, 103, 127, 128, 140, 142, 145
Pro-Life Action League (PLAL), 20, 22, 70
Pro-Life Action Network, 23
Protestant pro-lifers, 17, 18, 20, 21, 23, 47, 66, 78, 120
pro-woman frame, 94
Public Health Service Act, 121, 122
public opinion on abortion, 25, 28, 29, 76, 147, 148

Q
Quarracino, Antonio, 92

R
Radich, Rita, 30
Ray, Robert, 105

Reagan, Ronald, 1, 2, 4, 5, 7–10, 16,
  17, 19, 22, 25–33, 42–56, 64,
  66, 72, 74–77, 79, 81, 90–92,
  94–96, 98, 100–103, 105, 106,
  113–125, 127, 129–131, 137,
  138, 140–144, 146–149
Regan, Don, 104, 120
Rehnquist, William, 44, 125, 126
Religious Right, 6, 7, 16, 19, 21–23,
  25–29, 33, 42, 44, 47, 48, 50,
  51, 53, 64, 70, 72, 76, 81,
  117, 118, 120, 127, 128, 131,
  138–141, 144–148
Religious Roundtable (RR), 22, 70, 71
Republican Party, 2, 4, 7, 8, 10, 16,
  21, 24–29, 31, 34, 42, 44, 46,
  48, 50, 54–56, 64, 72, 75–77,
  79–82, 90, 91, 101, 102, 105,
  114, 116–118, 120, 123–125,
  129–131, 138–141, 143,
  145–149
1976 Republican Party Platform,
  26, 147
1980 Republican National
  Convention, 27
1980 Republican Party Platform,
  27, 32, 42, 43, 45, 46, 49, 52
pro-choice Republicans, 27, 29, 31,
  77, 79, 81, 82, 105, 117, 124,
  125, 128, 129, 138, 140, 146,
  147
Republican National Committee,
  147
1984 Republican National
  Convention, 101
1984 Republican Party Platform, 29
1988 Republican National
  Convention, 31
1992 Republican National
  Convention, 31
1992 Republican Party Platform,
  147
1996 Republican Party Platform, 147
Rice, Charles, 68, 119
Right to Life Party, 26, 27
right to privacy, 16, 54, 94, 126, 128
Robertson, Pat, 23, 139
Robison, James, 51
Roe v. Wade, 2, 7, 8, 16–18, 20, 21,
  24–26, 30–32, 42, 47, 50, 54,
  55, 65, 67, 68, 75, 82, 95, 106,
  118, 125, 126, 128–130, 139,
  140, 142, 143, 148
Romney, Mitt, 147
Roosevelt, Franklin D., 28
Rusher, William, 73
Rust v. Sullivan, 124

S
Salas, Rafael, 102
Sanger, Margaret, 24
Scalia, Antonin, 125, 129
Schaeffer, Francis, 21
Scheidler, Joseph, 22
Schlafly, Phyllis, 43, 44, 46, 49, 51,
  53, 66, 128
school prayer, 67, 80
  School Prayer Amendment, 78
Schweiker, Richard, 32
second-wave feminism, 3, 6, 16, 21,
  26, 27, 29, 30, 42, 44, 46, 47,
  55, 56, 66, 128, 140
secular humanism, 6, 22
Shultz, George, 92, 103
The Silent Scream, 32
Siljander, Mark, 46, 47
Smeal, Eleanor, 42, 128
Smith, Chris, 103
Smith, William French, 48
Souter, David, 142
Southern Baptist Convention (SBC),
  20, 127
Southern Baptists for Life (SBL), 21,
  127, 139
Southern strategy, 25, 28

Soviet Union, 96, 117
Specter, Arlen, 29, 127, 128
squeal rule, 122
Starr, Kenneth, 51, 52
State Department, 97–100
State of the Union, 32
state regulation of abortion, 144
Stevens, John Paul, 43
Stewart, Potter, 43
Supplemental Appropriations Act, 103
Supreme Court, 2, 4, 5, 8, 16, 30, 31, 42–44, 48, 50, 52, 54, 64, 65, 68, 114, 118, 124–128, 130, 142, 144, 145, 148
Susan B. Anthony List, 148
Symms, Steven, 47

T
Terry, Randall, 23, 115
Therapeutic Abortion Act, 25
Thomas, Cal, 76
Thomas, Clarence, 143
Thornburgh v. American College of Obstetricians and Gynecologists, 55
Thurmond, Strom, 129
Title X, 5, 114, 118, 120–124, 130, 148
Trueman, Patrick, 91
Trump, Donald, 10, 105, 145, 147, 148

U
Uhlmann, Michael, 48, 72
UN Fund for Population Activities (UNFPA), 91–96, 98, 102–105, 114, 142, 148
UN International Conference on Population
 Budapest, 96
 Mexico City, 90, 97, 99, 100, 102, 103, 106
UN Population Award, 93
US Catholic Conference (USCC), 18, 20, 72, 73, 78, 80, 120, 143

US Coalition for Life (USCL), 19, 20, 65, 91
US Constitution, 64, 95
 14th Amendment, 16, 66–68
 25th Amendment, 117
 constitutional originalism, 68, 126, 127, 129

V
Vatican, 99, 100, 120
Vatican II, 71
viability, 145
Viguerie, Richard, 21, 49, 51, 53, 75

W
Watergate, 18, 117, 126
Webster v. Reproductive Health Services, 142, 144
Weicker, Lowell, 29
Weyrich, Paul, 21, 25, 51, 75
Whatever Happened to the Human Race?, 21
Williams, George Hunston, 20
Willke, Barbara, 17
Willke, Jack, 17, 28, 45–47, 49, 51, 54, 81, 93, 100, 102, 105, 115
women pro-lifers, 17
Woods, Michael, 105

X
Xinzhong, Qian, 93

Y
Yard, Molly, 128
Young, Curtis, 71, 74

Z
Ziyang, Zhao, 96